Maybe We'll Make It

The publication of this book was made
possible by the generous support of the
BRAD AND MICHELE MOORE
ROOTS MUSIC ENDOWMENT.

For Ezra

Contents

Maybe We'll Make It

Prologue

I stared through the sheer Swiss-dot curtains that hung in the window of my childhood bedroom. I watched the bloodred Midwest sun as it set past the crooked tree line at the edge of our property. I knew staring at the sun was bad for my eyes; still, I couldn't help but watch the ball of fire as it sank beyond the horizon. I felt pulled to it even though I knew looking at it was dangerous.

My west-facing window had a perfect view of McCloud Road, a dusty gravel path that snaked back and forth until it fed, like a tributary of a river, into the two-lane highway. The road led nowhere but I walked it often, kicking gravel, with the hope that one day it might take me somewhere else.

As a little girl, I was plagued by rebellion. My straight blond hair grew long and unruly, into jagged corkscrew curls that turned light auburn. Elusive dreams beckoned me. My lust for life had me chasing after intangible things from the very start. I moved recklessly, running full speed ahead to what, I did not know. But I was always driven to do whatever I set my mind to, even if it meant burning some bridges along the way.

I felt compelled to run away from home, which I attempted more than once. I longed for my own life far away and a family of my own.

I would close my eyes, take a big breath, and make a promise and a wish on the dead tufts of dandelion heads. The seeds would parachute through the still summer air, propagating in the Bermuda grass of the yard. I would lie on my back, arms folded behind my head, and search for cherub angels guarding the gates of heaven beyond the clouds. I would scour the sky for a holy face, talking as though someone were always listening, and then strain to hear the whisper of God in my ear.

The first movie I remember watching was *The Wizard of Oz*. I was three years old and my parents had just bought their first VCR. From that moment on, I imagined I was Dorothy, with her cute little dog and her fairy godmother and her fortune-tellers. I envied her smooth chestnut hair, her blue gingham dress, and those mystical red slippers. I walked on a stack of drying hay bales singing "Over the Rainbow" and searched for a scarecrow who might come to life and point me in the wrong direction. I wanted to click my heels and be somewhere else. I waited patiently, listening for the sound of the wind to change, and when the moment was right, I would lasso a tornado and ride it straight out of that desolate, worn-down ghost town.

CHAPTER 1

The Unpaved Road

I was born on April 15, 1983, at 8:58 P.M. at the Franciscan Hospital in Rock Island, Illinois. My birth was not an easy one; my mother was petite and had very narrow hips. I was only seven pounds, twelve ounces, but I got stuck in the birth canal. It was then that my nose was broken for the first time. After a grueling, twenty-eight-hour labor, I fell into the arms of my parents, Duane and Candace Price, a farmer and a teacher, respectively. I was mostly healthy, so the doctors placed me in an incubator and called it a day.

After a couple of days, my parents took me home to Aledo, Illinois. They lived down a gravel road off Highway 94, just five miles north of town. Aledo was home to some 3,600 people, a country church, and some farm animals. The closest town was Hamlet. A wooden sign that still stands there today reads, WELCOME TO HAMLET—POPULATION 42.

My father, Duane, was the third of five children. He worked the family farm with his father, Paul, his mother, Mary, his uncles, three brothers, one sister, and many cousins. They were successful for many years, growing corn and soybeans. None of them pursued higher education because of an unspoken understanding that they would grow up and inherit the family farm. The farm thrived for decades.

My mother, who went by Candy, grew up the third of five children, poor but well loved. My grandfather, Howard Duane Maule, was a chiropractor. In our small town, people thought chiropractic medicine was basically witchcraft, so he didn't have a lot of customers at first. My grandmother, Patricia Louise Fischer, was a homemaker, and though she was very petite, standing only five feet tall, her heart was bigger than the whole damn town. My mother wore hand-me-downs from her older sister and rarely had any new toys or fancy belongings. When they didn't have enough money for a Christmas tree one year, they awoke one morning to find six Douglas fir trees in their yard, a sweet offering from some caring folks in town.

My folks were high school sweethearts. Candy was head cheerleader. My father played baseball and was the star running back of the football team. They both ran with a pretty rowdy crowd. After my mother graduated from high school, she attended Western Illinois University. She taught physical education and later became a third-grade teacher. Everybody liked her, and she was known for being great with children. She was like a celebrity in our small town. When we were at the grocery store or a local restaurant, young people often came up to say hello. "Your mom changed my life," they told me. She had compassion to go around and always gave a piece of herself to others.

My father was sharp-witted and incredibly handsome, like a cross between Harrison Ford and Bruce Willis. He could also intimidate any boy I brought home with one quick glance. An ex-boyfriend once noted, "Your dad's not very big, but I bet he could whoop just about anybody's ass. I wouldn't cross him." Duane always had a great sense of humor with those who knew him well, but, to this day, he is a man of few words. When he does speak, you're gonna wanna listen, because it's always worth hearing.

My parents were married in the summer of 1977 at the Lutheran church just up the street from my mother's parents' house. It was a small but tasteful wedding that reflected the times. My mama's bleach-blond hair was perfectly feathered. She wore light-blue eye shadow with her simple lace wedding gown. Daddy sported a white bell-bottom tuxedo and a teal cummerbund and bow tie.

As newlyweds they lived in a tiny, one-room shack in a town called Joy for about a year while they saved up money for a down payment on a big yellow farmhouse that sat five miles north of Aledo. The home was perched atop a large hill on a beautiful five-acre plot. It had been built in the late 1970s, and it had shag carpets and a large natural-stone fireplace in the family room; there was a *Brady Bunch* vibe to it. It was surrounded by thick woods and open fields, and the countryside was my refuge as a child. I found solace among the flowers and trees. When that didn't work, I curled up with a good book and got lost. I loved *Where the Red Fern Grows*, *Charlotte's Web*, and *Little Women*. I had a large collection of books and often stayed up late reading with a flashlight beneath the covers.

The family business thrived for decades until the farming crisis of the mid-'80s. In response to Russia's invasion of Afghanistan in 1979, President Carter stopped all grain exports to Russia, and the price of corn, soybeans, and wheat plummeted. The embargo devastated small and family-owned farms (and may have cost Carter a second term), and even though President Reagan ended the embargo, the recovery took decades; most farms never recovered at all. It is still a sore subject in my family that hardly anyone will talk about.

More trouble followed in 1985, when the bank refused to let them farm their way out of a small debt. The banks had loaned many small family farmers money to invest in their own grain bins. It was meant to save farmers money in the long run by making it easier for them to dry their own corn, but it was an expensive undertaking. The same year brought a crippling drought that yielded the sparsest harvest in ages. Everything crumbled. In 1986, the bank got further involved in the decision-making part of my family's business. A young, arrogant banker created an elaborate Ponzi scheme that swept the farm out from under my family. The loss was devastating. No one was ever the same after that. Decades later, karma caught up with that corrupt banker, and he did time for some other crimes. I believe in praying for my enemies, but the news was like bittersweet retribution.

Some of my earliest memories are from my paternal grandparents' farmhouse, and I remember the rest of it from photos. It was a modest, white, two-story home with a green metal roof, tall ceilings, hardwood floors, lush shag carpet, and classic vintage wallpaper. The couches in the main living room were patterned in colonial scenes and covered in clear plastic. It was a simple, no-frills farmhouse, but it seemed massive to me when I was small. Aunts and uncles and cousins were always popping by to work and to be fed. The Dutch oven in the kitchen was always on the burner, and the comforting smell of slow-cooked pork shoulder wafted through the rooms. With that many people constantly gathering in the home, I realize the size was an optical illusion. It's not that the house was big, but the love inside it was.

My grandparents had two giant dogs, a chocolate lab and a yellow lab. I remember the day they packed everything up and left. The family gathered at the farm to say goodbye to that way of life and the land. The dogs went to live with the neighbors; my grandmother Mary was pretty heartbroken that they couldn't bring the pets with them. Nonetheless, she packed up their things with her head held high. I never saw her cry. She was stoic like that.

My grandparents moved into a tiny ranch-style home on the edge of town. From their kitchen window you could see perfect rows of corn in fields that belonged to someone else. I sometimes caught Grandpa Paul gazing out that window with a faraway look in his eyes. Combines rolled by and the crops grew and were harvested, year in, year out. He sat quietly at the kitchen table with a dip of snuff in his mouth and watched the seasons change.

Grandpa Paul and Grandma Mary took all sorts of odd jobs; even though they were almost old enough to retire, they had little saved. The grain bin disaster left them with nothing. My father took a job as a guard at the East Moline Correctional Center and worked weekends as a mechanic. Most of my uncles went to work construction. No one on my daddy's side of the family had a college education, but they were good with their hands and were hard workers. Three months after my father lost the farm, my mom was laid off from her teaching job.

My parents did whatever they had to do to keep our house. They sold their boat, one of the cars, the snowmobile, all the tractors and farm equipment. They reluctantly spent that winter standing in the unemployment line. It bothered my parents; they prided themselves on being self-sufficient and hardworking. My mom went back to school to get her elementary teacher certification and began to teach full-time. She gave birth to my sister Britni in 1986. My sister Kylie followed in 1990. We spent a lot of time with my mother's parents while our parents worked. My grandmother Patricia cooked almost every meal for us during the week and spoiled us rotten with cookies and treats after she picked us up from school.

My dad worked second shift for many years at the prison. My sisters and I slept in my parents' bed a lot of nights with my mother when he was gone. I remember listening to the coyotes howling out in the distance, crying because I worried they would eat him up when he arrived home in the middle of the night. The house stood alone at the top of a hill, and the northern wind whipped and howled along with the coyotes. Sometimes the wind seemed to speak in a voice that brought stories from distant places. The windows were old and drafty, and a wood-burning stove in the basement only did so much to heat the house. One evening, the door to the stove was accidentally left open and the insulation in the ceiling of the basement caught fire. Luckily, the smoke detector went off and the fire was put out before we all turned to ash in our beds. During those cold nights, my sisters and I piled seven or eight blankets on my bed and slept together to keep warm. We were like baby kittens, all cuddled up, talking and giggling and telling stories until we drifted off.

My parents bought me a record player for my room, and I loved playing albums and running around the room, singing and dancing to the music. I remember dropping the needle on my own to listen to the Muppets and Cabbage Patch Kids on repeat. My mom also taught me some songs to sing on my own—I must have been about three years old. I had a whole routine worked up for "Let Me Entertain You." From a very young age, I felt a lot of joy when I performed.

My mother wanted me to have all the opportunities she grew up without, so she put me in dance and tumbling lessons when I was a toddler. I studied tap, jazz, ballet, and gymnastics. I loved singing songs and writing my own plays. I was always putting on a show for anyone who would watch. I liked to choreograph my own routines and taught them to my sisters and friends, later forcing my parents to pay admission to see our "show." Of course, there were aspects of the dance world that now make me uncomfortable. I was dancing to "Five Foot Two" while wearing skimpy outfits, blue eye shadow, and cherry-red lipstick at six years old. Still, it was a good outlet for my emotions, and I had a lot of emotions.

When I was seven, my parents bought my sisters and me a piano. I had begged to take lessons, and I finally got my wish. I had been writing songs and poems from the time I could read, from about first grade, and I sung them a cappella into my cassette player. With piano, I could finally accompany myself.

In fourth grade, I auditioned for show choir around Christmastime. I practiced singing "Silent Night" in my grandmother's living room. My mom and my grandmother Patricia came running into the room and asked, "Was that you singing?"

I told them it was.

"We didn't know you could sing like that!"

"Like what?" I asked.

"Like that! Like a grown-up. Where did that voice come from?"

They demanded I serenade them over and over again. They fawned over me, insisting I sounded like a full-grown woman when I sang, despite being only nine years old.

I had always enjoyed singing, but now that I knew other people thought I was good, it was even more fun. I made the show choir that year, and the theme was country music. Suzy Bogguss was a hometown hero and had made it big in Nashville. Her songs played on the radio, and we included a couple of them in the school program. My first solo was Patsy Cline's "Walkin' after Midnight," and though it was just a small part, I felt pretty accomplished.

Every week I traveled to Iowa to work with a voice teacher named Sue Clark. Mrs. Clark had a reputation for being a hard-ass and was hands down the best instructor in the area. She was very strict and didn't waste any time whipping me into shape. She taught classical-style singing, proper breathing techniques, and pronunciation. I was a first soprano and had a very wide range. We worked a lot on Italian numbers and vibrato. I owe a lot to Sue. She gave me a strong backbone and built my confidence.

While some instructors were building up my confidence, others were beginning to tear it down. During career day, I wrote that I dreamed of being a Broadway performer when I grew up. The guidance counselor, Mrs. Erdmann, pulled me aside and demanded I choose a different career. She insisted, "Dancing and singing is not a real job. It is simply not practical." The other students smirked and rolled their eyes when I shared my aspirations with the class. It absolutely crushed me.

School was often hard. Kids can be cruel, and I was picked on for being a scrawny little bookworm. One day a boy pushed me off the second floor of a timber form on the playground. I smashed my face on the way down. Blood poured from my already less-than-perfect nose and onto the green grass beneath my feet. I didn't shed a single tear until I got to the nurse's office and she handed me a mirror. My nose was broken for the second time. I hated my face. I hated myself, and I didn't feel worthy, because I knew I was ugly and unpopular.

Britni and Kylie and I did everything together and were best friends growing up, but as the oldest, I was the ringleader and bossy mother figure to both of them. We enjoyed building forts and getting lost in the expansive woods that surrounded our property. I loved to imagine I was Laura Ingalls Wilder in *Little House on the Prairie*. The three of us found plenty of mischief to keep us busy, and we marveled at the magic of nature. Our summers were wild and free. We searched the fields for arrowheads and other Native American artifacts. We swam in the pool until we collapsed from exhaustion. The chlorine turned our blond hair green and we washed it with lemonade to neutralize it. I ran around the countryside barefoot, wearing nothing but a swimsuit or a calico dress.

My daddy often took us fishing over at his friend Rick's pond. I was good at fishing and learned to bait my own hook and take the fish off and release it. We used rancid-smelling stink bait to catch catfish, and once, when I was seven, I had the biggest catch of the day. I watched my dad and Rick clean the giant catfish and cut its head off, but only after I said a prayer and we had a proper ceremony for its death.

It was common to come home and see a pheasant or quail in the kitchen sink. We owned two bird dogs, Lacy and Cheyenne, and my father went hunting with them often and brought home dinner. He and his friends cleaned deer and hung them from the rafters in the garage and then sent them through the meat grinder. I liked watching *Bambi*, and I would cry and plead with him to stop hunting, but in time I realized it was our way of life. I eventually helped him grind the meat, package it, and label it. I figured it was better to get the blood on my hands and help provide for my family than to let someone else do the dirty work.

My sisters and I rode our bikes around the gravel roads, sought adventure, gathered wildflowers, and hung out at our aunt and uncle's house, half a mile up the road. My aunt Lisa rescued horses from slaughter, and I helped her with them every so often. She let me adopt a horse of my own to help raise in their pasture. I named him Indiana Jones. He was black and had a white stripe down his face. When he first came to their home, he was malnourished and scrawny, but they nursed him back to health, and after just a few short months, he looked like a new dime.

Indiana was wild and was never properly broken in, but he took an immediate liking to me. I had no fear and a fair amount of riding experience, but nothing could have prepared me for the ride Indiana took me on. At first, I just rode him around inside the pasture. I was amazed by how calm he was with me. He never bucked or pulled. I even stood on the back of his saddle and attempted a few amateur stunts, pretending I was a trick rider in some famous rodeo.

One afternoon, my family went on a ride outside the pasture. We rode up and down the gravel-covered McCloud Road in the summer sun, and Indiana was perfectly behaved. I felt as though I alone had broken him, and that I was a real cowgirl. We were headed back to the trailer when all of a sudden Indiana's ears perked up, and he took off like he'd been hit with a bolt of lightning. I hunkered down and clutched the reins for dear life as he made for the barn in a dead sprint. Indiana jumped over ditches and rocks, rushed under trees. I was sure it was my time to die.

My dad came galloping up on a giant horse appropriately named Big Red, like John Wayne in some old western movie. "Pull back on the reins! Jump off! Margo, jump off!"

I hollered back, "Hell no!"

As I rounded the corner past my aunt and uncle's double-wide trailer, I slipped out of the saddle and rolled under a barbed-wire fence. Miraculously, I came out unscathed. I had no broken bones and not one scratch, but I broke out in hives and burst into tears. My mother was more shaken than me, but my father was hell-bent on my getting back on a horse. I was scared to death at the thought of it. But even more than that, I didn't like the thought of not being brave. I wiped away my tears, brushed the dirt from my clothes, and climbed back on to a different, more experienced horse named Shasta. From that moment on, I had a new level of respect for those strong, wildly unpredictable animals, but I also had less fear about my own mortality. I wondered how many times Calamity Jane had cheated death. And although I couldn't quite prove it, I believed I could be Annie Oakley's distant relative.

Much as I loved the space and proximity to nature, growing up in a town as small as Aledo was a recipe for trouble. Poverty and boredom plagued

Mercer County, and drugs like alcohol and meth ate up the rural Midwest. Alcohol abuse affected me personally as a child growing up. To protect relationships with people I love, I don't want to name names, or give specific stories, but I know I was scarred by the heavy use of it around me. I drank my first beer at the age of twelve. I knew I was too young to be drinking, but everywhere I looked, that's how people were both celebrating and coping.

All the popular kids drank and partied on the weekends. I figured if I wanted them to like me, I should party too. Even though I despised the taste of alcohol, I immediately loved the way it blocked out all the noise around me, how it anesthetized me from everything—bad grades in math, problems at home, even my internal, self-hating dialogue—all numbed, muted, for a brief, spectacular moment.

On weekends, my friends and I went to the local theater that showed the same movie on repeat four times in a row. In the early days, we got buzzed on candy and Mountain Dew and made out with boys. The Mountain Dew was quickly swapped for booze—a much more sophisticated choice, and finding it was never a problem. There always seemed to be some sleazy sucker willing to illegally buy us the alcohol of our choosing. It was common to procure a keg of beer, find an empty field, and start a raging party. My teenage years were spent driving on the outskirts of town. Our weekends were suddenly centered on getting wasted and avoiding the local police.

It was also around this time that my anxieties began to manifest in the form of an eating disorder. I starved myself and hid my food in napkins at the dinner table, discretely disposing of them later. I weighed myself multiple times a day, took diet pills, and worked out incessantly. If I felt I had overeaten, I would make a trip to the bathroom and simply throw it all up.

It was all a thinly veiled attempt to fit in. Only I didn't. I stood out like a sore thumb. All through middle school, I had braces and glasses, I was gangly and flat-chested. My strawberry-blond curls were untamable and frizzy. I was insecure as hell and never felt like I would look like the women in the 1990s issues of *Seventeen* magazine that I read. The covers had headlines like "How to Be a Guy Magnet," "10 Secrets to Perfect Skin," "Sexy Hair Secrets," and "Are You a Good Flirt?" The pressure to be some kind of perfect sex object was inescapable.

I wanted to be free from my toxic thoughts and growing list of bad habits. I began to journal and write poems. I was gifted a diary for my birthday, and I loved being able to be introspective and then lock away all of my terrible thoughts. My privacy quickly vanished when I found that my little sisters had picked the lock and read every word. They threatened to blackmail me until my war tactics forced them to take an oath of sibling silence—sworn to for life by a sacred pinky promise.

Around this time I became dead set on buying my own guitar. For my eighth-grade graduation, my parents threw a party, and all of my relatives and people from church came and brought me cards full of money. It added up to seven or eight hundred bucks; I thought I was filthy rich.

My mom's eccentric brother, my uncle Kevin, took me up to a used-instrument store in the Quad Cities. Initially, I wanted an electric guitar, but they convinced me it was best to learn on an acoustic. I picked up all the expensive ones. I had dreamed of a Martin or a Gibson or a Fender. But, in the end, I got a cheap Japanese model, a Samick. It was small bodied, with medium-brown wood and a high-gloss finish. I brought it home and immediately took it up to my room and started struggling through the G, C, and D chords. It was not easy, but it was fun. I cut down the long, brightly colored, glitter-coated fingernails on my left hand. I pushed down on the strings. It hurt and it sounded terrible.

A junior named James Puckett passed me a book of guitar chords, and that was all I needed to get going. He showed me how to look at the lines in the book with the six strings on the guitar and how to match the finger dots for the chords. I sat around for hours, alone in my room, practicing. I was determined to work up my hand strength so it sounded smooth and round when I strummed, instead of like a brassy fart.

The real drinking started the summer before high school. My friend

Jacquie was one of five children, and her parents, Gina and Jerry, were very lenient, both too busy working to care. We stayed at her house the most because we could pretty much get away with murder. Her house was where I first watched horror movies, where I smoked my first cigarette (a Virginia Slim I stole from Gina's purse), and where I French-kissed my first boyfriend. Their home was a large two-story on a big lot at the edge of town, near the high school. The massive backyard butted up to a beautiful little winding creek and the largest cemetery in town. We often camped down there between the tombstones and the massive oak trees. It was easy to sneak out of Jacquie's place, and just as easy to sneak boys in.

We broke into her parents' liquor cabinet once and stole a giant bottle of vodka. That night I learned how to quickly take shots without tasting the alcohol. After I'd had about fourteen shots of vodka, Gina and Jerry just laughed at me. Gina said, "Yep, she's a Price!" My family was known for being legendary partyers who could hold their booze. I didn't exactly take it as a compliment but accepted it as a part of my rowdy bloodline.

My parents sensed that I was experimenting and running wild, and they tried hard to keep me on a short leash. They weren't about to let their firstborn child get a DUI—or worse, get knocked up. My mom snooped through my belongings and eavesdropped on my phone conversations, finding everything from Marlboro Lights to fifths of vodka to NoDoz pills. The town was small, so gossip about my partying and sneaking out almost always got back to them. I was grounded a lot, but I became increasingly secretive and learned how to better cover my tracks.

My friends and I sometimes camped at the bottom of my parents' property and snuck out bottles of hooch, Zima, wine coolers, or hard liquor for our backwoods rendezvous. On one such night, my parents woke up to the sound of the four-wheelers the boys had driven over. It must have been about two or three in the morning. My daddy jumped into his truck and chased them off, speeding down the gravel road after them until they escaped into a field. My reputation for being the bad girl was definitely growing. If I could only be good, like my sisters, maybe I would amount to something someday.

I started going out with my first serious boyfriend, Billy, when I was about fourteen. My parents put him through quite the screening before he could take me out on a proper date. When he came over to my house to watch a movie, my mother made sure she was within earshot the entire time. Whenever it got too quiet, she busted into the room and pretended to vacuum and clean around us. My daddy barely spoke to him, but then again, he was a man of few words who barely spoke to anybody.

Our families went to the same Lutheran church, and Billy and I often served as acolytes together, which involved getting to church early, wearing white gowns, and walking down the aisle to light the candles at the beginning of service. We also helped serve grape juice and wine and the cardboard-like wafers during the weekly Communion. Whenever we found a moment alone, we snuck off to fool around in the church elevator or in the basement. It felt especially forbidden, feeling each other up and making out in those white robes. Billy was a really sweet guy, with a great sense of humor, and he wasn't hard on the eyes either, with his jet-black hair, emerald eyes, killer smile, and a perfect dimple smack-dab in the middle of his cheek.

He was also a Virgo and a troublemaker who drank, experimented with drugs, and got in trouble with the police for vandalism several times. My folks didn't like him, let alone trust him. They only tolerated him because they knew the more they objected to our relationship, the more I would want to date him. They were right.

I lost my virginity to Billy when I was fourteen years old, in the back seat of a Chrysler minivan. I immediately regretted it, but like the drinking, it felt like what I was supposed to do. I was the last of my friends to lose my virginity. I'm lucky I didn't get pregnant before graduation. It was like the opposite of the Virgin Mary's immaculate conception, but an equally spectacular miracle.

The summer after my junior year, my friend Morgan and I decided to take our younger sisters out for a classic regional hazing ritual. I was sixteen, and Morgan was fifteen, with long, dark hair and stunning features. She had big, brown doe eyes and high cheekbones, and I always thought she looked like a young Loretta Lynn. Our younger sisters, Britni and Erica, were both thirteen. We thought it was kinder that we haze them ourselves rather than allow strangers to do it—a sort of better-the-devil-you-know situation.

As tradition had it, the seniors took the freshmen out to a place called Albino Cemetery, way outside of town. There was a giant stone cross that stood in the center of all the graves. The freshmen had to shimmy under the wrought iron fence, climb up on to the stone pillar, and kiss the cross. Some seniors left the freshmen there to walk back to town, or even pushed them into a predug grave, but we weren't going to go that far.

I left the car running and we all got out, army-crawled under the fence, and started trying to read the tombstones under the moonlit sky. We climbed up, kissed the cross, and started running back to the car. I was driving my four-door silver Saturn, which I had proudly bought with money I saved working for three long summers. I'd only had my driver's license for about three or four months and was not a very experienced driver. As I got back behind the wheel, I saw bright lights coming from behind the farmhouse next to the cemetery.

A middle-aged man on an ATV was speeding straight toward us. He was wearing a flannel shirt and a trucker cap over his stringy hair.

A chill shot up my spine. "What do we do?"

"Just go at him, he's bound to move!" Morgan frantically suggested.

I took a deep breath, revved the engine, and started driving down the gravel road. I thought he would stop or get out of the way, but we were about to collide. I slammed on my brakes. He hit his at the same time. We stopped, face to face as he jumped off the ATV and approached. He slammed his hands on the hood of my car and screamed something unintelligible. He had a wild look on his face, and I figured he was drunk or maybe high on meth. Now that he was close, I noticed he had one brown eye, one blue eye, and terrible teeth.

Britni and Erica screamed bloody murder as the man walked around the side of the car and began pulling on the door handles, trying to get in. I thought for sure he was going to rape or kill us, but the doors were locked.

When he realized he couldn't get in, he got even more angry and started to scream even louder. He kicked at the doors and clawed at the handles like a rabid dog trying to catch a rabbit. "This is private property, hear?! We don't like strangers trespassing on *our* land. Now open the fucking door!"

We were terrified. I reversed the car a few feet and tried to drive around him and his ATV, but he jumped in front of me. Finally, I put my foot on the gas and gunned it past him. He hollered out loud as we passed him; I am ninety percent sure I ran over his toe. We drove past the cemetery and the gray farmhouse at the back of the property. A dim, yellow light glowed from inside when the front door opened. An old, bald man in overalls and a woman with long, white hair came out of the house to shake their fists at us.

The three of them jumped into a beat-up truck and chased us down the road. We were all terrified, tears streaming down our faces, afraid of what they would do to us if they caught us. I drove as fast as I could, fishtailed all over the gravel, and nearly drove us into a ditch. We could see the headlights behind us for several miles, but finally I shook them and we made our way back to town.

When we arrived, we pulled into a gas station to assess the damage that had possibly been done to my car. Thankfully, there was just some grass and mud stuck up in the wheels from where I had run off the road in sheer panic. We all held hands and said a prayer, thanked God for getting us out of the situation alive, and made a vow not to tell our parents. All we knew was that we had dodged a bullet, and we had one hell of a story to tell come next Monday at school.

CHAPTER 2

Rearview Mirror

Graduation couldn't come fast enough. The walls of my town were closing in on me. Despite my parent's wishes, I spent my free time raising hell with Billy and my friends, and it seemed there was more trouble to get into than ever before. We increasingly took buzzed joyrides around town. We are lucky we didn't kill ourselves. We went through a *Big Lebowski* phase and drank Kahlúa White Russians. I almost always got sick, but it tasted like a milkshake and was easier to get down than beer. I vividly remember going to a party at this guy's place in a trailer park—he must have been at least twenty. He was trying to be edgy by showing raunchy porno films on his grainy TV. I didn't feel very comfortable, but my friends and I stayed and drank a lot, trying to prove we were mature and tough. I puked my guts out on the porch of his trailer, thinking, *Why am I wasting my time doing this right now?*

Drinking was so common, so pedestrian, everyone in my circle of friends was experimenting with one substance or another. I'd grown up with the impression that cannabis was bad—it was an illegal drug that would lead you down a path to addiction and failure—but alcohol was okay. My parents drank it, my teachers drank it. Hell, even the preacher drank it out of tiny glass thimbles for Communion at church. Jesus couldn't be wrong.

My friends and I skipped school whenever we could. I told my parents I had to be at school early for a study group, and instead we got stoned in someone's car while we drove forty-five minutes to a Denny's. By the time we got there we were starving and ate our weight in pancakes. We forged notes from our mothers for made-up orthodontist appointments. Sometimes we got away with it and spent the afternoons at the mall. Other times we got caught and punished with in-school suspension. My behavior made my parents uneasy, but there was little they could do to change it.

Lots of friends were doing harder drugs. My friend Vincent was a funny guy, well-liked by everybody. He and Billy were very close friends, and before we had our licenses, Vincent would drive the two of us around in the back of his big, black Buick. We cruised the back roads, smoking cigarettes and listening to Nirvana. On multiple occasions, Vincent completely blew through the stop signs at the crossroads. It scared the shit out of me because sometimes the corn was so high you couldn't see who was coming. It made sense later, when I found out how often he was dosing LSD. Two weeks before graduation, he shot himself in the head. Billy was in shock. The tragedy completely shook our small student body. We all felt guilty that no one had seen the warning signs. His mother was a teacher at our high school. Seeing her grieve for her firstborn son was devastatingly hard to watch. After his wake, Billy and I drove the back roads, holding hands in silence as we listened to "Pineola" by Lucinda Williams on repeat.

Along with Lucinda Williams's *Car Wheels on a Gravel Road*, I connected to Fiona Apple's *Tidal* and Jewel's *Pieces of You*. All through high school, I played those albums repeatedly until the CDs were so worn and scratched they wouldn't spin anymore. They exuded honest, singular styles of songwriting backed by real instruments. Lucinda was unflinching, a goddamn modern-day poet. Fiona's music was dangerous.

She didn't seem to feel the need to people please or to walk around smiling all the time when she didn't mean it. It was refreshing to hear someone talk openly about their battle with depression and going to therapy rather than pretending to be some cookie-cutter pop princess. Jewel also talked about her struggles openly and had been homeless for several years during her rise to fame. She had crooked teeth and a nose that looked like mine. These singers were real, and most of all, they were unique. They were a breath of fresh air compared to all the sugary pop music that dominated the radio at the time. I knew I never stood a chance in that world. I had no aspirations of becoming some kind of Mickey Mouse toothpaste commercial. I wanted to do something poetic, something with an edge.

The corn grew taller each year, with its pesticide poison, and so did I. I had learned many cover songs but had aspirations to compose more of my own. I was playing guitar during any free time I could find and had also started smoking grass more frequently. Those two things seemed to go hand in hand. Jacquie and I went on bake cruises in her boxy, white Grand LeMans that had a red velvet interior; we dubbed it the White Rat. To avoid the local police, we took it down all the back roads on the outskirts of town and smoked weed out of soda cans. We crushed in the top of a can to make a bowl and poked tiny holes in it with the back of my earring to let the smoke escape. We played our burned CD mixes at an unreasonable volume and screamed the lyrics to Tracy Chapman's "Fast Car" until our lungs bled. I sometimes sat in the back seat with my guitar, crudely strumming Tom Petty and the Heartbreakers songs while everybody sang along.

My parents had always told me I had to get a college degree to amount to anything, and it was always understood that I would go to a university after I graduated. There was no other option. Hoping to get a small scholarship, I auditioned for the cheerleading team at Northern Illinois University. I made the varsity squad, but my heart wasn't really in it.

I worked hard every summer teaching dance and gymnastics, lifeguarding, and giving swimming lessons. I liked having my own money.

I saw that it gave me control, and that was appealing to me. More than money, though, I wanted to be able to afford freedom from a conventional life. I couldn't imagine working an office job. I was driven and wanted to be successful, and I tried to figure out how I could achieve that without becoming a corporate pawn.

That fall, I somewhat reluctantly moved in to a coed dorm at Northern Illinois. My roommate, Lindsay, was from the Chicago suburbs, and every other word out of her mouth was "dude" or "fuck." She had an eyebrow ring, smoked Marlboro Lights, and had a bad attitude. I liked her from the start. We became fast friends, and the two of us played our favorite songs for each other and sang harmony together at the top of our lungs.

We were quickly introduced to every other degenerate on our floor. Our room was directly across from the men's restroom, and we frequently woke up to a puddle of piss or puke outside our door. I still wasn't able to tolerate the taste of beer, and in the beginning we had enough money to spend on liquor, mixers, wine coolers, and Boone's Farm. But champagne taste on a beer budget can't last forever, and soon everyone on our floor pooled their money for PBR and Busch Light.

I bought a fake ID, with a photo of a girl who looked nothing like me, but it worked down at the local bar. We went out on Wednesdays, quarter beer night, for tiny draft beers in plastic cups. The owners had to know that nearly fifty percent of their clientele was eighteen to twenty years old, but they turned a blind eye because it was good for business. During my first semester I was cheering for the varsity squad, attending most of my classes, and pulling decent grades. With college cheerleading came more pressure to be thin. My eating disorder was still lingering, along with continued bouts of binge drinking. Vodka was my drink of choice, and I challenged anyone I met to a shot contest. It was as if I needed to prove I could keep up with the boys. I often threw up before I went to bed, hoping to rid myself of the extra alcohol calories.

One Tuesday night after cheerleading practice, I went over to my boyfriend John's dorm. Everyone was already way ahead of me. They started pouring me shots of Skol vodka in a coffee-mug-shaped shot glass. I'd taken about fifteen shots before we realized the tiny glass was a double—I'd had roughly thirty shots of vodka. What happened next is blurry; what I know was told to me afterward. I completely blacked out for about five hours. I awoke in John's bed and got up to go to the bathroom. When I came back, I entered the room across the hall from his. A couple I barely knew was sleeping inside, and I took off my pants and got into bed with them and passed out cold, thinking it was John's room. They woke up and tried to shake me awake. I was unresponsive. They got the RA, and when she couldn't wake me, they called an ambulance.

The paramedics came in and broke smelling salts under my nose, and still I was unresponsive. They picked me up, carried me out to the ambulance, and revived me during the ride to the hospital. I woke up cussing like a truck driver. They were sure I had alcohol poisoning after drinking so much, and they informed me I had to have my stomach pumped. Even though I was incredibly messed up, I knew, being just eighteen, I was about to be in serious trouble.

At the hospital I was asked whom to contact. I didn't have my cell phone on me, and the only number I remembered was my parents'. I refused to let the hospital pump my stomach, so they gave me a couple of glasses of water and sent me away with a $2,000 hospital bill. I was intoxicated for two days straight and felt like I had been run over by a car. A couple of days later came orders from the school to go to a rehab program for underage students. When I returned home for the weekend, I could see the disappointment in my mother's eyes. She had every right to be worried about me after the stunt I had pulled. She also commented on my weight gain and suggested I go on the Atkins diet, which was the fad in those days. She suggested we find a tutor to get my grades up. Her words stung because they were true. I looked haggard and bloated, and my grades were slipping because I was frequently hungover and skipping class. I knew I had to quit drinking. It was the first time I'd been bitten by the poison, but it wouldn't be the last.

I was so self-conscious about gaining the freshman fifteen, I went back to starving myself and throwing up after meals. I quit drinking, but I didn't exactly get sober. I traded vices and switched to smoking tons of weed, hash, opium, and whatever other drug I could get my hands on. I tried it all, but the only thing that stuck was herb. My grades improved as soon as I quit drinking. My GPA rose from 2.7 to 3.4. I changed majors from communications to theater and dance, and I minored in Spanish.

I still didn't know what exactly my calling was, but I felt it was on the stage. I studied modern dance and ballet and worked hard to improve my technique. I loved Martha Graham, Bob Fosse, Mikhail Baryshnikov, and the Nicholas brothers. The way they conveyed emotions through movement was thrilling to study.

While dancing started as a mostly healthy habit, it once again developed into an obsession with my body appearance and weight, to a level that I knew wasn't healthy. Ballet culture glorified thin bodies, and lots of girls and guys in the program struggled with eating disorders. It was rumored that the director of the ballet department rigged the scales to measure us all several pounds heavier. Many of the girls, including me, lived on a steady regimen of diet pills and cigarettes, while others binged and purged, using vomiting and laxatives.

Still, I was dedicated to the idea of being a professional dancer. I daydreamed about performing on Broadway or becoming an actress and doing theater work. In the back of my mind I knew I wouldn't be able to do any of that in the small suburb of DeKalb. I longed to move to New York or Los Angeles.

At the beginning of my sophomore year of college, I took psilocybin mushrooms for the first time. It turned my world inside out in the best possible way. I bought a couple of ounces of mushrooms from my ex-boyfriend Billy to sell for some extra cash. We were on good terms again and decided to take them together platonically. Per Billy's instructions, I consumed an entire eighth myself and downed some orange juice to intensify things. We walked around outside and the world came alive, visually and sonically. Colors flew at me and my whole being was tapped into a deep vibration I had never felt before. I experienced a great sense of peace and a connection to all living things.

Music had never felt more symbolic. We listened to the Jimi Hendrix Experience, and I watched the patterns of the curtains mutating before my eyes. It's really hard to describe what that first intense trip was like, but it felt like a conversation with God. It stripped away parts of my ego and revealed to me what I already knew in my heart. We are not our bodies, we are souls, temporarily imprisoned inside of this human experience. My value was not in my beauty or the lack thereof. The mushroom trip shined a light on my insecurities and made me face my fears about the future. We are all going to grow old and die one day, so why sacrifice your life to do something that doesn't thrill you? There was renewed hope in my dreams. In that moment, I had found the secret to understanding the universe and what my role was in it: I would drop out of school and become a musician.

A couple of clubs in town had open mic nights, and I began signing up once a week to play covers and a few originals. I started writing songs during my free time. I was consumed with becoming a better songwriter and performer. I started spending more time with musicians and artists. I did not audition for cheerleading for my sophomore year. I wanted to be someone else. I stopped wearing makeup and shaving my armpits and my legs. I dyed my hair dark brown. I was a part of the counterculture now.

I made plans to quit school and move as soon as the academic year was over in May. My parents were scared for me to be more than a couple of hours away from them. They suggested I visit Nashville if I wanted to become a musician. It was still eight hours south, but it seemed more reasonable than their firstborn going off to New York or Los Angeles. I had an older cousin named Star who lived in Nashville, and my great-uncle Bob lived there too. He was well connected, and my mom thought he could help me out. I visited Star during my spring break in March, and she showed me around the city. It was different from what I expected. I didn't relate to any of the pop country that was coming out of there at the time, but I found a strong songwriting community and a healthy underground scene for indie bands. The weather was so nice, and I could go hiking and canoeing and fishing at the state parks. Nashville stole my heart in that four-day stay. It was settled. I would leave the Midwest and head south for Music City, USA.

CHAPTER 3

Fifty-Seven Dollars

I counted seventeen red-tailed hawks perched in the trees along the interstate as I stared out the window of the car, and I took it as a good omen. The date was May 29, 2003, and we had packed up my belongings in my daddy's pickup truck and rolled into town looking like the Beverly Hillbillies. We had some old furniture tied down in a flatbed trailer, including a twin bed, a rolltop desk that had been my grandmother's, and two bright-orange, ratty couches I had inherited from my parents. My folks had planned to trash them, but I loved that every time I sat on them, I felt like I was transported back to 1977. Everything I had was worn, but I valued the sentimental.

Besides, Star had plenty of nice belongings for our new place. She and I moved into an apartment with vaulted ceilings in Antioch, Tennessee, just twenty minutes outside of Nashville. Star wasn't the best influence, but she had a colorful personality and there was never a dull moment with her around. She was just two years my senior but much more experienced at living on her own. We had grown up together and she could talk me into trying just about anything. Star had been arrested for cocaine possession when she was only seventeen and had a felony on her record. I shouldn't have been surprised when she offered me some during my first week in town, while we were out dancing with her friends at a club called Envy.

"You want a bump?" She flashed her kohl-rimmed eyes down at the bag of white powder in her hand. Uppers weren't really my thing, but I agreed anyway. We went into the bathroom with a few other girls, and she pulled out a tiny silver spoon with a snake head on the handle. I took a whiff and immediately regretted it. The left side of my face felt like it was burning.

"What is this?" I asked, panicking.

Star and her friends started laughing. "It's meth! Ha ha ha, you just did meth!" Star was beside herself.

"Jesus Christ, why didn't you tell me?" I was scared and angry. I stormed out of the bathroom, went outside, and paced in the street. She could be so two-faced sometimes, it terrified me. That night was not the last time she tricked me into taking a drug I thought was something else.

Nashville and city life were all so new to me, I felt like I was going one hundred miles per hour when I first arrived. I didn't have much money to burn at the bar or at fancy restaurants, but anytime I found myself out and about, someone usually offered to buy me drinks. Although I still had a fake ID, I only drank occasionally back in those days. I was still distancing myself from alcohol because of the incident at Northern Illinois. Nonetheless, I liked to spend my evenings taking in the night-life. I found myself spending lots of time at random little coffee shops, dives bars, and clubs. I enjoyed spectating and occasionally performing at writers' nights, poetry readings, and karaoke bars. The people I met were almost always friendly. The southern charm and warm hospitality were intoxicating, and I was really leaning in to my new life.

I had only been in Nashville a couple of months when I totaled my second car. Star and I had been out dancing all night during the summer solstice, and I drove myself home around five A.M. I looked down for one second to follow directions on a comedically large paper map of the city when the box truck in front of me stopped abruptly at a yellow light. I slammed on my brakes, but it was no use. I ran into the back of the truck and crushed the front of my car.

So there I was. I had no car and no real friends in town yet. I had fifty-seven dollars left to my name and hadn't found a job, although I'd tried. I didn't want to ask my parents for money, so I knew I needed to find employment soon.

Star had run off to spend a couple of weeks in Hilton Head, South Carolina, with an older man named Giovanni. Giovanni wore Gucci tracksuits and thick gold chains. He let everyone know he was loaded— I mean filthy rich—and involved with the Mafia. Star asked if I wanted to come, but I was intimidated by him and the crew of yes-men he kept close by. More than that, I knew I needed to get my life together. There was barely any food in the fridge, and I was living off of hummus, stale bread, cereal, and soy milk. I spent two weeks alone playing records, writing songs, and reading books on astral travel.

I had been given a copy of *The Essential Bob Dylan* and became obsessed with "Maggie's Farm." I sat around smoking tiny crumbs of weed from a metal one-hitter and listening to the song on repeat. I was completely obsessed with Dylan's lyrics, delivery, and attitude. He was mystical. How he channeled the words and the sound that he did was a secret I yearned to unlock. The way he sang wasn't perfect, but it was honest.

Listening to Bob led me to artists like the Band, Skip James, Victoria Spivey, Leonard Cohen, Karen Dalton, John Prine, and Kris Kristofferson. Joni Mitchell turned my world upside down. Her playing, her voice, and especially her lyrical prowess were unique and incredibly refined. *This is how you write a song*, I thought as I listened to "Blue" on repeat. "A Case of You" had to be one of the most perfect songs ever written. She didn't revisit the same old clichés; she dug deep and mined some of the best compositions I had ever heard.

I was enjoying the time and the space to myself, and despite being broke, the solitude was glorious. I penned several songs that week. None of them were great, but I was learning. It beat going to a lecture hall to listen to uninspired professors, that was for sure.

A couple of weeks later, Star returned from her trip and my privacy was gone. With my parents' help and an insurance policy, I got a new-to-me used car. I landed a job selling cheap clothes at Wet Seal in the Antioch Mall. The pay was minimum wage, and I wasn't good at budgeting, so money was always tight.

When Star was five years old the doctors had discovered a hole in her heart. She had to have open-heart surgery, which left a jagged scar that ran down the middle of her rib cage. The incident had convinced her that she was the reincarnation of Cleopatra. She had a large collection of Egyptian-style artifacts that she cherished as if they were straight out of an ancient tomb. She loved incense and precious stones. She dressed lavishly and bought designer clothes, shoes, and bags. She drove a much nicer car than me, and the inside dash was decorated in glitter and adorned with voodoo dolls. Our apartment was decorated with Bob Marley posters and houseplants—lots of succulents and philodendrons. Star listened to a lot of reggae and rap, and I had no complaints about that.

Star was a Gemini with multitudes of personalities. She always said, "If you *pretend* you are somebody, people will think you *are* somebody." I followed her lead and began to dress more outlandishly when we went out to dance clubs and wild parties. She had a lot of eccentric friends who were different from most of the people I had met in the Midwest; she knew mystics and tarot readers, drug dealers and Reiki healers, drag queens, rappers, producers, and engineers. One evening she took me backstage at a Wailers concert, and we smoked a couple of spliffs with the band. It was the first time I'd been put on a guest list, and I had never experienced such an open atmosphere. It didn't hurt that she was casually dating the drummer, Zebulon.

I wasn't great at holding a job, and after a few short months of working retail at the Antioch Mall, I was over it. I pulled a no call, no show one morning and they canned me. Luckily, Star got me a job making continental breakfast at the Hotel Preston she managed out on Briley Parkway. It was terrible for my night-owl schedule. I had to get there at four in the morning to make biscuits and gravy, waffles, and powdered eggs. Many mornings I arrived irritable and sleep deprived. I wasn't much of a cook and had never worked in the service industry before. The job was also minimum wage, and there were no tips. I didn't last more than a couple of months before my irresponsibility got me fired again.

Star was understandably frustrated with me but had one more connection for a job. She swore she would disown me if I screwed it up. It was at a Men's Wearhouse in the Cool Springs Galleria, selling cheap suits. I hated it more than any other job I'd had thus far. It required that I dress in business casual, and the other employees were cold to me. I never sold a single suit. I walked out one afternoon on my lunch break, before I could even collect my first paycheck.

Weeks passed and I remained unemployed. I tried busking down on Broadway with my guitar, a tip jug, and a handful of wildflowers for adornment. Busking seemed like a rite of passage for anyone who aspired to be a songwriter, and I loved watching the tourists pass by. I studied the other street performers to see what did and didn't make money. Well-known songs that were recognizable to the folks passing by were more likely to work, but I didn't know many covers that seemed to impress the straw-cowboy-hat-and-fanny-pack-wearing crowds who walked the strip, drunk on light beer. Still, I remember feeling accomplished when I counted the money I had made. Forty-five bucks for about five hours of work. I shoved the crinkled paper money into the pocket of my blue jeans, packed up my guitar, and went home feeling proud of my little hustle.

I picked up a copy of the pocket-sized local paper called *All the Rage* and began looking for open mics to play. I dreamed of one day being able to get a proper gig at one of the real venues in town. I made a vow to myself that I would work to go from playing dive bars to the holy grail of stages, the Ryman Auditorium. I made a list of all the places I wanted to play in between: Winners, Losers, Springwater, Mercy Lounge, Exit/In. I accepted that I was on the bottom of the food chain, but the only way to go was up.

I began frequenting a little hotel bar called Hall of Fame Lounge inside the Best Western off Music Row. It was easy to get on the list to play there. It felt cozy. There was wood paneling on the walls and tacky Cracker Barrel–like decorations—antique signs, photos of no-name old-timers, bad taxidermy. I was told Townes Van Zandt used to play there before he died, and that was enough to pull me in. I made friends with a couple of the middle-aged writers who hung out there. Most of the folks at the Hall of Fame were older, but that was fine with me. I almost preferred the company of old folks to that of my peers.

I didn't have many original songs but quickly found that the ones I did have didn't really cut it. I studied the writers who got strong reactions from the crowd. What made their songs good? Stories? Melody? Themes? Humor? Sadness? All of it. I knew I had a lot to learn. I came back week after week and signed my name on the clipboard, waited for my turn to sit on the stool and sing my songs.

My mom was convinced that I already should have made it and that my songs were already good. She believed in me even when I did not. Candy arranged for me to go over to my uncle Bobby Fischer's house and play him some of my tunes. He was well connected in the business, knew a lot of the right people, and had lived in Nashville for over thirty years. Many notable musicians cut his songs, from George Jones to Charley Pride, Tanya Tucker to Reba McEntire. My mom was sure Bob could help me get my career on the right path.

I visited his house in Green Hills one afternoon to get his opinion and see if he could plug me in to the music industry pipeline. He was in his late sixties at the time and had a kind soul. His wife, my great-aunt Helen, gave me a warm hug and poured me a cup of coffee. It was good to see family. I followed Uncle Bobby to his den and we sat in chairs across from each other.

"Well, let's hear what you got."

"Um . . . okay. Let me think what I should play you." Even though he was family, I was nervous as I tuned my guitar.

I don't remember what I played for him, but I only had a handful of songs in my catalog at the time. When I finished my whispery folk number, he sat there in silence. I shifted uncomfortably in my chair and waited for some feedback. He looked me dead in the eye and said, "Here's what you need to do. You need to go home and throw away your television, get rid of your computer and your phone and your radio. Just sit there and write and keep writing for a long time. Focus on it. Don't do anything else with your free time, just learn to write."

I was heartbroken, but deep down I knew he was right. I nodded and tried not to cry. I knew I was still learning, but I'd thought there would be some kind of compliment sandwiched with the criticism—like "You've got a great voice, kid!" or "That one metaphor was pretty clever." Nothing. Just brutal honesty and the cold, hard truth. I was not ready yet.

I left with my head hanging down and returned to my apartment. *What am I doing here anyway?* I thought. *Who do I think I am? I'm not special. I'm not a poet. I can't write songs.* The icing on the cake was that I still needed to find paid work.

The rest of the summer was an endless string of dead-end jobs, spliff smoking, and slacking off. Star and I went out to Percy Priest Lake to do some innocent cliff diving and ended up making an unlikely friend. Walking out onto the edge of the man-made lake, we had lit up a joint. We had just sat down when a park ranger drove up behind us in a golf cart. A scrappy-looking dog rode shotgun in the passenger seat, and another mutt rode in the back. The park ranger looked to be in his midsixties. He had scraggly gray hair and ice-blue eyes, wore camouflage shorts, and had a beer belly. He sported a ragged US Marine Corps hat covered in fishing lures and vintage pins. What he wore best was the wild look in his eyes.

"Well, what's goin' on over here?" he asked sternly.

"Just enjoying the view!" Star said.

I snuffed the joint out on the rock and fanned away the lingering smoke. My heart raced. We were busted for sure.

"Well, don't waste it! Smells like good stuff! Bring it over here," the ranger said, smiling.

I laughed nervously and relit the joint. I enjoyed getting stoned with older folks. I passed it to him, and he took a huge hit, started coughing like crazy.

"Woah!" he said between coughs. "That is fire! Where'd you get this weed?"

"I'd tell ya, but I'd have to kill ya." I winked.

He cackled like a loon and shook my hand. He had a firm grip and a kind smile. "The name's Ozzy." It was pronounced oh-zee. "I run this here park and I live in that trailer back there." He pointed up into the clearing of the woods, where I spotted a double-wide surrounded by junk and a couple of motorcycles. "Now, y'all weren't thinking about jumping off these here cliffs, were ya?" He gave us a sly grin.

"Oh no, Mr. Ozzy. We were just gonna smoke this and watch the sunset," Star lied.

"Well, I got hired by the state to see that no one jumps off these cliffs. It's extremely dangerous—people have died!" His eyes widened. "Right below where you're standing, there's a submerged, rusted-out car underneath this rock overhang. A man just drove his vehicle off the edge one night and they never pulled it out. Couple of kids got impaled on it. So don't even think about it, ya hear?"

"Thanks for the heads-up," Star said and passed the joint.

"This pot is really, really good. Think I could buy some off y'all? I got some ditch weed and a pipe up in my trailer. Why don't y'all come up and smoke more?" Ozzy suggested.

His invite seemed innocent enough, but I was still cautious. I noticed he carried a gun on his hip, and I didn't know if we should trust him.

"Got anything to drink?" Star asked. I poked her in the back. By then I knew she was always looking for bad trouble and could be straight-up reckless, controlling, and manipulating. She liked to order me around, and sometimes I found it easier to go along with whatever she wanted—to avoid confrontation.

"Sure I do, if you like Miller Lite! Hop on. I'll drive ya both up." We got in the golf cart and rode up to his little trailer-park abode.

Ozzy's place was trashed, and I could tell right away he was a bachelor. The clearing was littered with beer cans, plastic lawn chairs, and American flags. Everything inside the trailer was covered in animal hair; he owned several dogs and cats. On the walls were black-and-white photos of days gone by, marine corps flair, and war memorabilia. It wasn't much to look at, but he gave us the grand tour. I liked how proud he was of his canned-ham trailer. It was his honky chateau, his cooked castle, his own little Shangri-la.

"I served in Vietnam, was in the marines," he told us. "Greatest thing I ever done." He cracked a can of beer and took a big swig. "The government set me up here to retire in peace and keep an eye on the park. There have been some gays that come up here to screw in broad daylight on these picnic tables—right in front of families and children. I gotta keep the riffraff out and make sure no dumb kids decide to jump into these no-swimming areas. Other than that, I just sit out by the firepit with my dogs and enjoy the nature."

He handed us both a lukewarm Miller Lite. We followed him outside to a firepit in front of the trailer. Ozzy was rough around the edges; he wore his life in his wrinkled face and *King of the Hill* beer gut. His eyes had a mischievous spark but also an unexpected softness; they caught me off guard. I suspected he had a Stone Age mentality simply from the way he said "some gays," but he was a character to converse with and really did seem to have a good heart.

We sat there until way past dark listening to his stories and bickering now and then when we didn't see eye to eye on a subject. When it was time to leave, Ozzy seemed sad. I doubted he had many visitors. "Are y'all gonna come back and bring me some of that grass you smoked me up with? I got a lot of pain these days. It would really help me out."

I agreed to come back and sell him a dime bag or two. Ozzy saw us off and opened the gate to let us out of the park. He watched us, like a grandparent, as we pulled off onto the main road. I saw his silhouette waving long after we drove off. It wouldn't be the last I saw of that old mountain man.

CHAPTER 4

Strays

The idea of waiting tables had never appealed to me, but it was the easiest way to make money fast. I had never worked at a restaurant before, but I was desperate for a way to make rent. I was more than willing to try working a job I despised if it got me where I wanted to go. I applied at several fine-dining establishments and some classic, down-home diners. I finally got hired at the TGI Fridays up the street from my apartment. I got a pair of nonslip kitchen shoes, black slacks, a black collared shirt, and a small, black apron. I was making cash in no time. The food was terrible, the customers were rude, and the tips were meager. But my boss, Liz, loved Bob Dylan as much as I did. We got on well.

Most of the employees were into substance abuse of one kind or another. The bartender, Joshua, had peroxide-blond hair, and his arm, which bore a sleeve of Sublime tattoos, was littered with needle marks. I smiled at the customers and was polite even if they treated me like dirt. They always wanted extra ranch. They loved fried food, frozen margaritas, and Long Island iced teas. I went home smelling like grease and painted in ketchup, but it was a job and I needed it badly.

I was still living with Star, but I became more introverted as I focused on writing songs, like Uncle Bob had advised. I locked myself in my room for hours, noodling on my guitar, trying to find the right words, rummage up new chords, and write a song that would get a reaction out of the hippies and the boomers at the Hall of Fame Lounge. Star and I began to drift apart, and I started to think about moving out. I needed a space free of distractions, and I definitely wasn't getting that while living with her. I had reached the end of my tattered rope.

Our falling-out came after we went to party at a local karaoke bar, Larry's, up the street from our apartment. It was a seedy sort of place with lots of neon signs and a few ripped-up leather barstools, mostly occupied by hard-livin' locals. Star and I were both drinking Coronas we'd ordered from a waitress wearing enough hair spray to start a fire. At first everything was on the up-and-up. I belted "If It Makes You Happy" by Sheryl Crow at the top of my lungs and had the townies in the palm of my hand. As I made my way back to the bar, sipping my beer, a drunk girl bumped into me and I chipped my tooth on the bottle, cutting my lip in the process. Warm blood trickled down my chin.

"Watch it!" the girl warned over her shoulder. I gave her no reply and ducked into the bathroom to clean myself up.

"I don't wanna be here anymore. Let's go soon, please?" I said to Star when I returned from the bathroom.

I walked outside into the dirty parking lot. I sat down on the ground, felt the jagged edge of my tooth with my fingertip. I cursed the beer and the lady who ran into me, lit up a cigarette, and waited for Star to emerge. She finally came out, trailed by a group of guys who had been following us around and trying to buy us drinks all night.

"They're coming back to our place to smoke a blunt! Let's party!" Star declared, her eyes bugging. There was no arguing with her; once she got an idea in her head, she was gonna do it no matter what anybody else said. Plus, she was driving. We got in the car with a couple of the guys, and the others trailed us in a separate car. I wondered what she was doing, inviting these strange men up to our apartment with us when they all seemed suspect and wasted.

When we arrived home, she was in overdrive. Really putting on the charm for these newfound friends. "Don't act so bored, Margo. We have a peach blunt to smoke."

"I'm just tired and uncomfortable . . . that's all," I said quietly.

"Well, wake up and get comfortable! It's only your own fault if you're having a bad time. I'm going to make some tea. Want some?"

"Sure."

Star disappeared into the kitchen while I hung out with the unwanted company on the small patio balcony. They seemed nice enough, but most of them were sloppy drunk. It was well past three A.M., and I knew nothing good ever happened after three A.M.

Star emerged from the kitchen carrying a silver tray with small cups of tea. As she passed them out, she said, "This will make everyone feel better and more awake for your drive home." The guys took several sips, even though they didn't really seem like tea-drinking types. Star lit up the blunt and passed it around. When everyone finished, she began to cackle hysterically.

"What's so funny?" one of the guys asked.

"I hope you like mushrooms!" She smiled. "We're about to take a trip on the philosopher's stone!"

"What the hell?" the man said. "How you gonna do that without askin' us?"

I was irate. The last thing I wanted to do was go down the rabbit hole with a bunch of people I barely knew. I had a headache from the blunt and the beer. I ran my tongue over the jagged edge of my chipped tooth and excused myself to go to the bathroom.

I headed straight for my room and locked the door. I stared up at the ceiling. A shadow appeared under the crack of the door, followed by a firm knock. It was one of the men.

"Hey, girl, you lonely? Why did you leave the party? You should come out and chill with us."

I pretended to be asleep. I could see the figure pacing beneath the crack but eventually he disappeared. I shivered and ran into my bathroom. The shrooms were starting to kick in and I felt twisted. It was not a good trip. Music blared, bleeding through the walls of the main room long into the night. I couldn't sleep. My mind was racing. I tossed and turned, thinking about why Star had dosed me without my consent. I made up my mind that night that I had to get out of there and get my own place.

A couple of weeks later, a dear friend from college, Madeline, came down for a weekend to visit. She liked it so much, she decided to move to Tennessee. She was carefree and easygoing. Madeline was fair skinned, with strawberry-colored hair that she kept in a pixie cut. Most everyone who saw us together assumed we were a lesbian couple because of her tomboyish style. She was really bubbly and energetic and talked fast with a Chicago accent. I knew Star would be upset when I told her I was moving out, but I wasn't on the lease. I gave her a month's notice and did my best to avoid her until I left. I began packing immediately.

Madeline and I moved in to an apartment a few units over in the same complex. We decorated it like the bohemians we were, hanging a seventies-style beaded wood curtain at the entrance to our new place. We plugged in a lava lamp and adorned the walls with paisley tapestries and a poster of Salvador Dali's *The Persistence of Memory*. We scraped together some cash and scored some secondhand furniture, including a black futon for guests to sleep on.

In my bedroom, above the bed, I proudly hung my '66 Bob Dylan poster. In it, he looked especially androgynous with his dark sunglasses and angular cheekbones. My desk was littered with necessary clutter: tattered notebooks, a coffee mug with pens and pencils, a Virgin of Guadalupe candle, matchbooks, incense, a little white-and-blue horse-head ashtray that had been my great-grandfather Fischer's. My guitar sat on display right next to my desk for easy access, and on the opposite wall was a small bookshelf that was home to my favorite novels and poetry books.

I had a small but refined library—Sylvia Plath's *The Bell Jar*, T. S. Eliot's *The Waste Land*, Arthur Rimbaud's *A Season in Hell*, Audre

Lorde's *Sister Outsider*. I was falling in love with poets and writers I had
never read before. On the wall above my desk was a collage I had made
with pictures of musicians, artists, activists, and bohemians: for inspiration, I had decoupaged together portraits of Janis Joplin, Frida Kahlo,
Leonard Cohen, Vincent van Gogh, Johnny Cash, Ronnie Spector,
John and Yoko, Angela Davis, Patti Smith, Joan Baez, Linda Ronstadt,
Elizabeth Cotten, Howlin' Wolf, and many others. My bedroom was my
humble sanctuary, a shrine to my idols, and a great place to write. But
most of all, in the tradition of Virginia Woolf, it was a room all my own.

On a wooden antique dresser I kept some framed photos of my family, mostly pictures of my sisters and me from childhood. The three of
us talked on the phone often and wrote each other letters and emails.
I missed them both and felt guilty I wasn't there to watch them grow up,
to guide them through their tumultuous teenage years.

Madeline and I went down to the shelter and got a couple of cats.
Mine was a scrappy-looking calico that had dark markings around her
eyes like mod eyeliner. I named her Blondie. The cats took to terrorizing
the house immediately. They were indoor cats on account of us living
on the third floor and there was nowhere for them to go outside. Those
cats were always running around on the furniture and climbing up the
curtains and the walls, but I was glad to have their company.

I was still holding on to my job at TGI Fridays, but I showed up later
and later for my shifts and often called in with no excuse at all. Everyone
there was flaky and hated the job. The only reason I didn't get fired was
because Liz liked me. For months I fantasized about quitting, but I did
my best to plaster on a fake smile and refill the sweet tea when asked.
You'll catch more flies with honey than vinegar.

Although Madeline held down a steady job at the Sprint phone store,
she was always looking for a party. Back in college, before my alcohol-
poisoning incident, we drank together frequently and did mushrooms
and opium. She was the first person to introduce me to cocaine. She
loved to smoke weed and cigarettes. Spliffs were our main shared vice.

Madeline was supportive of my songwriting and tagged along with me to open mic nights down at the Hall of Fame Lounge. I had been hanging out with older folks, but she made friends with some people closer to our own age. One of them was named Delaney; he was socially awkward but seemed harmless enough.

Through him, I met a group of Belmont University students who rented a house on Caruthers Avenue. It was a small, inconspicuous brick home, but the inside was dirty and dark, and it felt like a drug den. The place belonged to some guys named Rick and Donavan, but there was always a random, burned-out hippie passed out on the couch who didn't "technically" live there. The Caruthers house was always full of aspiring musicians, audio-engineering students, hipsters, hedonists, hangers-on, and an overabundance of guitar players. You could also get your hands on any number of substances. Madeline and I went over there one night to buy a bag of grass.

It was around nine thirty on a cold night in early February when we showed up. Most everyone there seemed lit up on psychedelics. The house was packed, and every seat was occupied with the usual suspects: stoners, guitar pickers, and a couple of acid casualties. There must have been about twenty people crammed into the living room, laughing their asses off and jamming to the theme song from *Fraggle Rock*. It was a real scene.

A quiet boy with dark hair sat in a busted-up recliner, playing along on a bass guitar. He didn't appear to share in the jovial mood of the song like everyone else. He was tall and incredibly thin, with a shaggy Beatles haircut that made him resemble George Harrison the most. I noticed his strong-looking hands as he ran them up the fretboard, but what caught my attention the most were his piercingly sad blue eyes framed with tired, dark circles. He looked like he had a lot on his mind.

When the music ended, Rick got up from the couch and introduced us to everyone. When we got to the man playing the bass, he stood up and walked toward me. His eyes nervously met mine as he reached his hand out to greet me.

"Hi, my name's Margo," I said shyly.

"Jeremy. Nice to meet you." He gave me a firm handshake.

I sat down and nervously rolled a joint. Madeline and I got up to use the bathroom.

I immediately started talking about Jeremy. "Did you see that guy in the chair by the door? He's so handsome."

"Ha ha, no, I didn't notice him. I was checking out the tall blond in the corner." She looked closely at herself in the mirror, running hands though her auburn hair and spiking it up a bit.

"Well, I guess I can see how you could look right past him—he seems quiet. But I swear, I'm gonna marry him." I washed my hands in the dirty sink and put on some lip gloss.

We stayed a few more hours, singing songs and making friends. I left without getting Jeremy's last name or phone number. We never said much more than hello, but I felt drawn to him and hoped I would see him again.

I was technically still involved with someone else at the time. His name was Joe and he was half Swedish and half Mexican. He spoke three languages and was majoring in biology at Augustana College back in Rock Island, Illinois. Joe had studied abroad in Thailand for several years and had learned Muay Thai kickboxing. He had good taste in music, and he burned me mix CDs with a lot of music from the 1960s and '70s. His favorite band was the Grateful Dead and he owned bootlegs of every single live show they'd ever played. He also sold grass, which was how I first met him.

When I made the decision to move to Nashville, we agreed to stay together even though he didn't like the South. I got the feeling he didn't think I had what it took to make it in the music business, and that stung. To make things more complicated, he had decided to study abroad again, this time in South America. He had hardly called or written to me in the two months he'd been gone, and he blamed his absence on his lack of phone cards and internet service. I'd recently heard through a mutual friend that he had cheated on me with a sorority girl named Barbie. He adamantly denied it, but I didn't trust him. It all hurt.

Weeks went by and I returned to the Caruthers house, hoping that dark-haired, sad-eyed boy would be there, but he never was. I was beginning to think I would never see him again. Then one night Madeline wanted to throw a party. She invited Delaney and his new roommate, along with several other random new acquaintances, including my boss, Liz, and her girlfriend, Angel.

"Ugh, not Delaney!" I said. "He's *so* annoying. I'm not in the mood to hang out with him, and I'm sure his roommate's as insufferable as he is. I'm going out to shoot some pool with Star up the street."

I put on a pair of bell-bottoms and a T-shirt and let my hair down from a messy bun. Just as I was about to head out, the doorbell rang. It was Delaney. Next to him was Jeremy.

"Oh, hi!" I said. "You must be Delaney's new roommate. I'm Margo." I wondered if he remembered me.

"Jeremy. I believe we met at Rick's place once." He did remember.

"Oh, yeah, that's right. So nice to see you again."

"I thought you were leaving," Madeline said, grinning.

"Star just called and said they were, um, closed or something," I lied.

I led them into the kitchen and we made awkward conversation with the group. Later, I got out a guitar and nervously started to play. Everyone was busy tying one on or making out, except for Jeremy and Delaney, who listened contentedly as I strummed and sang.

"That's really pretty," Jeremy said when I finished. "I like your voice. Did you write that yourself?"

"Yeah, still working on that middle part." I passed him the guitar. "Do you want to play something?"

He began fingerpicking quickly and singing something that sounded like a mix of the Beatles and Elliott Smith. Our friends were drunk and really loud by this point. I hushed them and leaned closer to him to hear.

"I love that melody," I said when he finished. "You play so well."

"Thanks." He blushed and put the guitar aside. "Do you want to come outside with me while I have a smoke?" We walked out onto my balcony. He cupped his hands around mine and lit my cigarette.

Feeling some chemistry, I immediately told him that I was "sort of" seeing someone.

He confided that he was going through a difficult divorce. "That's why I came to Nashville, not to play music but to get away from a woman." He laughed. "We've been separated for a year, but she won't sign the papers. It's a mess." He assured me the relationship had been over for some time.

The night rolled on and we ran out of booze. Eventually, most of the girls went over to Liz's house to procure a bottle of liquor. Madeline put on *American Pie* and the rest of us sat down on the couch to nightcap with a joint.

Jeremy and Delaney had both drunk too much to drive, so they agreed to crash at our place. Delaney slept in the living room and Jeremy claimed the small sofa in my bedroom.

"Do you mind if I play some music while we sleep?" I asked.

"Not at all." He lay back on the couch.

I put on Jeff Buckley's *Grace* and walked to my bed. As I passed him, he grabbed my arm. "Do you think your boyfriend would care if I gave you a kiss?"

I shrugged. "Probably not. We've barely spoken in months."

He pulled me on top of him. We made out for quite a while and then ripped our clothes off like hungry animals. We slept together that night, *Grace* playing softly as we fell asleep in each other's arms.

Jeremy called me a couple of days later and asked if I wanted to go see a band called Moon Taxi at Windows on the Cumberland. I had butter-flies; I was sure it was a date. The show was on February 13, 2004, close enough to Valentine's Day to add both romance and pressure. Jeremy was pretty quiet as we observed the band from the balcony. We had a beer and listened for about an hour. Afterward, we drove to his place to trade songs again.

He and Delaney lived on the second floor of a rundown complex. The apartment was small and could have used a deep clean, but it was decorated neatly enough for a place lived in by two guys in their early twenties. It had brown shag carpet and linoleum floors. There were some crooked paintings on the wall that looked like they'd been picked up from Goodwill, a record player, a great record collection, and lots of books and papers stacked in piles around the room.

He didn't have a cell phone, which I admired. Nearly everyone I knew had a cell phone. He had a landline and an answering machine that he used to record song demos on. He wasn't into watching sports or playing video games, which impressed me even more. We hung out that night, talking for hours, spinning records, and smoking inside the house. He told me he was adopted, and he'd had a strict upbringing. His adoptive parents were traditional, avid Baptists. His father, Tommy Joe, was an ex-cop, a banker, and a proud marine corps veteran who had served in Vietnam. His mother, Sandra, was a real-life saint and stay-at-home mom who was very involved with the church. They didn't necessarily approve of Jeremy's dreams of being a writer and a musician, but they loved him all the same and sent him care packages often.

Jeremy had never met his birth mom, but he knew she'd used drugs when she was pregnant with him because he'd been born addicted to crack. Because of that, he had a stroke during the labor. When he was just a baby, Sandra noticed he was not using the right side of his body. His left arm stayed curled up by his side, and he didn't reach out with it to grab anything. She took him to see a specialist, who told her he had cerebral palsy and would be an invalid. "There is no chance he will have a normal life. He won't be able to talk or walk, and you may as well put him in an institution for children with special needs," the doctor told her. Sandy had strong faith and didn't want to believe the news. She composed herself, marched out of that doctor's office, and took Jeremy back home to Tom and Jeff, Jeremy's older brother, whom they had adopted a couple of years earlier.

She got a second opinion and immediately began working with Jeremy on her own, doing lots of stretching and exercises to strengthen his arms and legs. Jeremy had to wear a leg brace on his left leg—it looked similar to the ones Forrest Gump wore—but Sandy worked with him daily until he was strong enough to walk without it. His parents got him a guitar and a keyboard, instruments that helped to stretch his tendons and build coordination. He was homeschooled until he was fourteen, and then he attended a private Christian high school. At eighteen, he pawned a vintage Gibson guitar given to him by his grandfather and left home to find himself with a couple thousand dollars in his pocket.

On a whim he moved to Colorado. He lived there in a tent for six months on Vasquez Road in Winter Park. He found work at the Rocky Mountain Roastery as a barista and saved up enough money to rent an apartment. Then he went to New York and explored the East Coast for a couple of years. When Jeremy fell on hard times, he slept in a park for weeks in Boston, selling poems and drawings for whatever change he could get. At one point, he lived in an abandoned Greyhound bus in the woods outside of Gardner, Massachusetts, with his friends Jake and Sarah. And he married an auburn-haired woman named April. They'd first met in Newnan, Georgia, where she was waitressing at a Waffle House.

Jeremy told me that April had been abused by her father and her brother. She also struggled with a drug addiction that she hid from Jeremy. Jeremy's parents hadn't approved of them dating and living together, so they'd convinced Jeremy to marry her after he'd only known her for a few months. A couple of years into their difficult marriage, they separated and began living in different states. During that time, April got pregnant and told Jeremy the baby was his. Once the due date came closer, he did the math and realized there was no way the baby could be his child. He told her he wanted a divorce, but she didn't take the news well. April became suicidal and violent, and at one point she tried to run him over with a car.

"She seems like a real fixer-upper," I told him with a nervous laugh. He seemed ashamed the marriage hadn't lasted. He had come to Nashville to run away from his ex-wife and wasn't looking to get into another serious relationship. He was still going through the divorce process. I told him I understood, but I was a little crushed. *Maybe he'll change his mind*, I thought.

When Joe finally called from South America, I told him it was over for good this time. He swore up and down that he hadn't cheated on me, but it didn't matter, because I didn't love him anymore. He didn't believe in me, and I could feel that. He never encouraged my writing or my songs or my decision to move to Nashville. All the more reason to move on and make a clean break.

I waited all week for Jeremy to call, but he never did. I called his landline several times and left messages, but he never answered or called back. I wasn't used to being rejected, and it caught me off guard. I eventually ran into him at the Caruthers house and cornered him.

"I'm just not looking for a relationship right now," he said plainly. "I think you're a really sweet girl, but I just want to be friends. I'm sorry."

I was devastated, but continued to hang out with him as friends because I enjoyed his company so much. We frequently went to get coffee, or I went over to his place and we sat and played guitar together. We swapped records, books, ideas, and philosophies. He was working as a line cook at Baja Burrito and brought me paper bags full of tiny foil-wrapped fish tacos with cabbage.

I had quit my job at TGI Fridays and was working as a waitress at the Flying Saucer Draught Emporium downtown. It was a pretty degrading place to work, as all the girls who worked there had to wear Catholic school girl uniforms, but I was raking in the dough—two to three hundred a night, sometimes more. At times I wondered if Jeremy might be hanging out with me only because I was always getting him stoned and buying him meals and drinks, but I didn't care. I just wanted him to like me.

We were also sleeping together occasionally, so I thought he must have some feelings for me. Still, he was careful to never introduce me to anyone as his girlfriend. I was always just his "friend." I was staying over at his place at least twice a week and even had an extra toothbrush in his bathroom. I took that as a sign that we were, in some way, dating.

During that time, Jeremy was really struggling with blood sugar issues. He didn't have diabetes, but out of nowhere he would get disoriented and nearly faint. I hated to see him having health problems, but I liked taking care of him. He was incredibly thin, and I often wondered if he was hiding a darker problem. Mostly, he just wasn't eating healthy; his car was always littered with bags from Arby's and Mrs. Winner's Chicken, as well as empty packs of Camels.

We spent a lot of time holed up in his bedroom watching music documentaries. My obsession with Bob Dylan was growing, and Jeremy was a full-blown Dylan aficionado. He had a copy of *Dont Look Back* on VHS. His bed was just a single mattress on the floor with no box spring, where we sat and watched the video on repeat. I was enamored of the film and began chain-smoking immediately after watching it. We were both puffing on Camel Lights in those days. We burned one down to our fingertips and put it out in an antique ashtray that sat in the center of the floor, then immediately lit up another. I wanted to be his Joan, and I wanted him to be my Bob, but I also wanted to be Bob, and he definitely didn't want me to be his Joan. He didn't want to settle down again, and I had the itch to tour and travel the world. Even more, I was longing to make an album.

At one point, Jeremy was really hard up for money. He had an eight-track recorder, a Roland Digital 880, and though I had no idea how to use it, I needed a way to make demos and he was short on rent. I bought it along with a microphone for about two hundred and fifty bucks.

I took it home and put it on my desk. I immediately started laying down all my demos, beginning with a song I had written called "Urban Sprawl." I would put down the guitar, then a vocal, and then layer a harmony and some simple percussion on top. I tried to put some reverb on it, but it sounded like I was singing from the bottom of a well. I pressed every button on the damn machine but I couldn't get the effect off. Finally I called Jeremy on the phone. He sounded frustrated but tried to talk me through it. When the troubleshooting didn't work, he agreed to come over and show me how to work the machine again. With ease, he put just the right amount of delay on the vocal. He mixed my guitar and harmony lines together, and everything sounded balanced. Jeremy dreamed of having his own studio and engineering and producing. It was only an eight-track machine, but he definitely had a better ear for recording songs than I did at that point.

"Would you put another guitar part on this? Like a lead or something?" I asked him. "It seems kind of empty with just me alone."

"Yeah, I can do that." He picked up a guitar and pressed the button on the fourth track until it turned from green to red. He laid down some pretty fingerpicking and a lead in the space I had left blank.

"That sounds incredible!" I gushed.

Jeremy had also written a new song called "Dear Doctor." It had all these different time signatures and cool parts to it, like a Beach Boys song or something. Five years my senior, he had ideas that were often more realized than mine in the early days.

"You should record a demo of it on here," I said. "Even though this is at my house now, you can come use it whenever you want. I don't mind at all."

"Well," he said, "I was going to go to the Villager Tavern and get some drinks with some friends. I'm not sure if I have time."

"I'll buy us some beers and bring them back here and we can record more. I'll sing harmony on your new song if you want. Come on, stay and hang out!" I pleaded.

"Ah, okay. Villager can wait, I suppose."

Whenever I offered to "buy us some beers" I meant that I would provide the money and he would purchase them, because I was still underage. We jumped in his messy, white Honda Accord. His car was hands down the dirtiest car I had ever seen. He brushed the trash off the passenger seat so I could sit down.

Even though we weren't technically dating, he often reached over and held my hand when we drove places together, softly running his thumb along the top of my hand in a figure eight motion. I thought, *This proves that he really does like me.*

We got back to my apartment and recorded one of the strangest songs I had ever heard. It had a folky kind of vibe to it, but with all the different parts and interludes it also felt like a lost Brian Wilson song off of *Smile*. We added shakers made of pill bottles, bells, whistles, and lots of background vocals. When we finished, it sounded like a serenade of the patients in a cheery mental institution.

Jeremy stayed over that night and many others. We became inseparable, building a bond and a real friendship around music. Neither of us fit in with the Belmont students, no matter how hard we tried. We were feral and uncultivated, but I loved how we could be alone together.

I spent my twenty-first birthday with Jeremy, Madeline, and her boyfriend. We went to the local Irish pub and played darts. I was a little bummed that no one offered to pick up the tab, and also that Jeremy showed me no mercy and kicked my ass in darts, but I had a great night nonetheless.

Even though working at the Flying Saucer wasn't my dream job, I was really starting to get the hang of being a great waitress, and I was bringing in a lot of dough. When I worked a double shift, I went in at nine in the morning and stayed until four the next morning. There were a lot of businesspeople who came in for lunch and happy hour beers. There were lonely, artsy, introverted employees from the Frist Art Museum who liked to drink a pint, scribble in their notebooks, and hand roll their tobacco. Mondays were two-dollar pint nights, which attracted Vanderbilt students who lived off Mommy and Daddy's money. They'd order ten beers and barely tip.

The Flying Saucer was sometimes referred to as a high-class Hooters, and some men treated us as if we were call girls. The regulars were wealthy older men who liked to smoke cigars and ogle women forced to wear Catholic school girl outfits. As I took their orders, they'd often put their hand on the small of my back or on my shoulder. I squirmed away, arching my back to be just out of their reach. I dealt with all sorts of comments. "Your legs look great in that skirt, honey." "Nice ass!" If I ever objected to being objectified, they would say, "Aw, don't get mad, sweetie. I'm just trying to give you a compliment!" Once, we had to call the police because we found a man sitting outside masturbating in broad daylight. Some men left their phone numbers and random pickup lines jotted down on napkins and coasters. Sometimes they left their hotel room keys. Sometimes men were respectful and left nothing but a great tip. But a lot of the time, at the end of a long shift, the humiliation burned.

I made lots of close girlfriends there. We sat at the bar together at the end of the night, telling jokes, shooting the shit. I would take off my Mary Jane high-heeled shoes, light up a smoke, pour myself a pint, and count out my money, dreaming of better things to come. I longed for the day when I wouldn't have to waitress anymore, when I might be able to spend my nights singing for the people in the bar rather than serving them drinks.

The restaurant atmosphere started to accelerate my alcohol use again. We were all rewarded with a shift beer after work, and that usually meant having several. My eating disorder had taken something of a back seat after my macro dose of mushrooms, but I was always conscious of my weight, because being attractive was an unspoken rule of the job.

My drug use was as adventurous as ever, and I continued my search for enlightenment in capricious substances, hoping to expand my third eye. One weekend, when Jeremy and I had my place to ourselves, we decided to experiment with salvia. *Salvia divinorum* is a member of the sage family and native to Mexico. I read that the Indigenous Mazatec people used it during religious ceremonies, and some claim the plant is the actual incarnation of the Virgin Mary. Some have visions of a sacred woman during their trip. The side effects are similar to those of acid, but salvia is a natural hallucinogen. It was legal in Tennessee at the time that we bought it, but it is now illegal. The package came with instructions on how to smoke it to get the best results:

1. Load a proper hit.
2. Inhale it fully for sixty seconds.
3. Get higher than you've ever been in your life.

We both smoked it at exactly the same time so we could experience it together. It was supposed to be intense for twenty minutes but could last up to an hour. We inhaled and then sat in total silence for what felt like eternity. I saw an intense light, as though I might have been close to crossing over. I also had the strange and overwhelming feeling that I couldn't go left. The way forward, both physically and metaphorically, was to the right. I thought about the direction in which my life was going. I felt a gravitational pull to do something, but I didn't know what.

When I finally snapped out of it, I realized that Jeremy had been sitting quietly next to me the entire time. His experience was completely different. He said that there were stitches dividing the middle of my living room, splitting everything down the center. The way he described it was really gory and frightening. He explained that the TV, the coffee table, the photo hanging on the wall, even my cat, Blondie, had stitches. The more I imagined it in my own brain, the funnier it became. I started to laugh hysterically, and so did Jeremy. We went out onto my tiny balcony and sat down on the ground and twisted up a joint. The sky seemed to be melting away, along with my troubles and my sense of time. Jeremy and I sat talking nonsense to each other, watching the sun sink behind the buildings and the trees, searching for the face of the Virgin Mary in the rolling hills of Antioch, Tennessee.

CHAPTER 5

Lay Around with the Dogs

After that night, I didn't hear from Jeremy for a couple of days. I did my usual routine of calling his landline and leaving voicemails on his answering machine. I even drove by his apartment a couple of times to see if his car was in the lot. It was, so I got the hint that he was ignoring me. He finally called a week or so later and asked if I wanted to go out to dinner. I was ecstatic. I got dressed up and drove to the restaurant to meet him.

He was quiet, moody, and definitely not conversational. The waiter brought our food to the table. Jeremy said he wanted to talk.

"I don't think we should see each other anymore. I mean, I really like you, but I'm just not ready to be in a relationship."

I stared down at my plate. "Seriously? You met me for dinner to tell me this?" I was angry and confused.

"I wanted to tell you in person. I just want to be friends. Nothing personal. I'm sorry."

We finished our meal in silence. When the bill came, I demanded, "You pay it for once."

"I don't have enough cash to cover it." He sheepishly pulled a crumpled ten-dollar bill out of his pocket. "I just paid rent today. I'm so sorry, Margo."

"What the hell, man? You ask me out to dinner, dump me, and then ask me to pay for the meal?"

"Well, we weren't *technically* dating. I told you I wasn't ready to be your boyfriend."

He was right. He had warned me. I knew he was going through a rough divorce, but I was in love with him regardless. I threw a pile of cash down on the table and stormed out without saying a word. He followed me out to my car and tried to stop me so we could end things amicably, but I didn't want to be amicable, I wanted to be madly in love.

I peeled out of the parking lot with tears running down my cheeks. I didn't look at him, but I could sense him standing in the middle of the parking lot, watching me drive away.

I spent the next few months writing sad-ass songs and working like a dog. I picked up as many shifts as I could and spent time with the other girls who worked at the Saucer. I became really close with a couple of the other waitresses. We went to see shows together and had weekly dinner parties. I did everything I could to keep my mind off Jeremy.

I eventually started dating Hank, a bartender and musician who worked at the Saucer. He was a really talented guitar player, and he wrote great songs too, but like me, he didn't have many connections in town. He played in a band and got some bar gigs here and there. Hank lived with my friend Stephanie and two other guys in a rundown house over by the DMV on the outskirts of Nashville. He lived recklessly, and trouble found him even when he wasn't looking for it.

Hank wasn't much to look at. He wore thick, rose-colored glasses and looked almost a decade older than he actually was. He wore wifebeater tank tops and leather sandals, and he had skinny legs, strong arms, and a belly that reflected the fact that he always had a beer in his hand. But he was a bona fide Nashville cat who could pick the fire out of the guitar and mandolin. He was talented, funny, and well versed in Appalachian

folk music, bluegrass, and '60s psychedelia. All of that was more important to me than good looks.

I started hanging out at his place a lot, and there was always a group
of people over there playing music in the basement or around the firepit outside. They covered a lot of songs by the Band and were heavily
influenced by Bill Monroe and the Louvin Brothers. Hank had diverse
tastes. He also turned me on to Toots and the Maytals and the Meters
and showed me my first chords on the mandolin. We spent a lot of our
time jamming with his hillbilly friends.

My time with Hank is a blur. It was filled with bad luck and worse
decisions. He truly brought out the worst in me, but I always felt bad
for him because I knew he was madly in love with me and I didn't feel
the same way about him. I was simply killing time and the pain of missing Jeremy. Even though I was spending most of my nights sleeping in
Hank's bed, my heart was somewhere else.

One evening I was driving down Murfreesboro Road on my way to
Hank's house when a woman turned blindly into my lane. I slammed on
my brakes and tried to swerve, but I T-boned her. I totaled my third car
in five years, but for once it wasn't my fault. The police showed up and
we exchanged insurance. I ended up getting another used car and a good
amount of money in the settlement.

One night at Hank's place we were all drinking and laughing on the
splintered porch, carrying on, shooting empties with a rifle. Hank's other
roommate, Max, suggested we shotgun beers, because we apparently
weren't drinking fast enough. He pulled out a long kitchen knife to cut
open the cans. When he was done, he threw the knife into the deck so
that it was sticking into the wood straight up and down. We guzzled the
beer and crushed the cans, and as I turned around to walk back inside,
I felt a warm sensation in my foot. I was roaming around shoeless and
it was pitch black outside except for a small bit of light coming through
the sliding glass door from the kitchen. I looked down and realized I
had stepped on the knife and cut the webbing between my toes.

I walked inside to assess the damage. It was terrible. Blood was spraying everywhere. The cut was massive, and I'd drunk so much, my blood wouldn't clot. As if handling firearms while intoxicated wasn't dangerous enough. My subconscious mind could almost hear my mother yelling at me as I started to faint. Hank picked me up and carried me into the bathroom. He put me in the bathtub and rinsed off my foot beneath the faucet.

"Honey, it's bad. You need stitches. I'm gonna drive you to the ER." He looked like he was going to pass out too.

"Like hell you are! I don't have insurance. You know how much an ER bill is? I don't have the money to pay for that. Just wrap it up. Get me some superglue and some duct tape. I'll be fine." I was good at arguing my point.

In hindsight, I wish I had gone, but I don't much care for people telling me what to do, plus I was broke.

Hank wrapped my foot up tightly in a dish towel. We bound it in duct tape. He cracked open another beer and handed it to me.

"You're little but you're one tough son of a bitch!" He laughed as he watched me hobble out of the bathroom and back to the party. I kept going for several hours before passing out cold.

The next day was rough. I was in terrible pain. I got some gauze, cleaned the wound, and dressed it properly. I called in sick to the restaurant for the day because I couldn't walk. It was really bad. One of the cooks at the Saucer offered me some pain pills. The Tylenol and weed weren't cutting it. Hank drove up to get them and came back with a little blue Xanax bar. I had never seen such a pill in my life. It had four sections to it, but no one told me that I should just take a piece of it, so I foolishly downed the whole bar.

I didn't wake up for three days. Madeline was in and out, working and hanging with her boyfriend per usual, so Hank stayed with me at my apartment. I was dead to the world. When I finally woke up, Hank took me to get some food. Then he drove me to the doctor. I was not healthy. My foot was in bad shape, but too much time had gone by to stitch it. They gave me an antibiotic so it wouldn't get infected. They also informed me that I had a kidney infection, and they hooked me up to an IV. "Best cut back on the booze and the sex," the nurse said under her breath as she started the saline drip.

Running around with Hank and his band of merry pranksters was fun, but my mind kept exposing my heart. I found myself thinking about Jeremy constantly.

Hank tried to cheer me up by taking me to get a new puppy. I didn't really think I was in any position to get a dog, but he said that these weren't just any dogs, they were beautiful, blue-eyed Australian shepherd mixes, and they were the smartest dogs ever. "Let's just go see some puppies. You don't have to leave with one," he said with a toothpick hanging out of his teeth. "I mean, what's the worst that can happen?"

When I got there I promised myself I wasn't leaving with a pup, but when a tiny, speckled-gray pup ran up to me with one blue eye and one brown eye, I knew it was over. He had white paws and a long tail and was the cutest dog I'd ever seen.

"Oh my, what a cool-looking pup! What kind of dog was the father?" I asked.

"Honey, I don't know," the woman said. "He's just a mutt and we need to get rid of him. If you want him, he's yours for free."

I blurted out, "I'll take him! He's perfect." I picked him up and he licked my face. He was just six weeks old. We climbed up into Hank's beat-up pickup truck, and the pup rode in my lap, howling the whole way home and looking out the back window at the farm and the brothers and sisters he had left behind.

"What are you gonna name him?" Hank asked.

"I'm not sure . . . gonna have to think on it."

"Leroy. You should name him Leroy," he suggested.

"That's a good name, but I don't think he looks like a Leroy. I'm not gonna decide now. The name will come."

A few days passed, and my foot healed enough for me to go back to work. While I recovered, the pup had been by my side nonstop. I dreaded the thought of leaving him alone in my apartment all day, so sometimes I took him to work with me. My boss loved dogs, and the customers loved him too. The puppy slowly warmed up to me and we became best friends. He slept curled up at the nape of my neck and followed me everywhere.

I took him for a ride in my car one day and popped in a Creedence Clearwater Revival CD. The beginning riff of "Suzie Q" came on and the pup suddenly perked up. He balanced on the seat and the armrest, stood up to look out the window, and smelled the breeze. He looked so happy with his little tongue hanging out. The music seemed to calm him.

I scratched him behind his ears and on top of his head. "Your name's Creedence," I declared as I turned up the song.

Taking care of him was definitely an adjustment. I had to get up and let him out early in the morning. I took him on walks, and it was great to get out and be moving more. Creedence was a high-energy dog who should have been herding sheep. As he got older, I started leaving him at home more during my work shifts. I often came home to find he'd torn my favorite shoes to pieces. But it was a small price to pay to have some companionship. Creedence pulled me out of my slump without me even realizing it. We went hiking all the time together, and I slowly began spending more time outside with him and less time day drinking with Hank.

Several months had passed and I hadn't even crossed paths with Jeremy. Then one night I stopped in at an all-night diner and music venue called Cafe Coco for a bite to eat. I went in with a rowdy group of friends from the restaurant after our shift and saw Jeremy sitting at a table alone, drinking coffee and writing in his notebook. He looked more downhearted than ever. He glanced up at me, and we made eye contact for a brief moment. I didn't stop to talk or say hello—I just walked right by him. I didn't know if he wanted me to bother him or not, and besides, I was just starting to get over him.

Days passed and my mind wandered as I waited tables. I thought I saw his face every time a handsome man with dark hair came through the door. One day my phone rang. It was Jeremy. He wanted to hang out.

"Ah, sure, why not?" I said. "I've been writing some new songs. I kind of have this little gig opportunity in Murfreesboro this Thursday night. You could play a few songs too, if you wanna join me." It was barely a gig, more of a prearranged open mic, a thirty-minute set at a smoky bar in a college town just outside of Nashville. I was excited nonetheless. I had been writing a lot; some of the songs were about Jeremy. As I invited him, I wasn't even sure I wanted him to hear them.

"Yeah, that sounds like fun. I'll go. I'll play, or I can just listen. It's whatever," he said. "I'll see you then."

On Thursday evening I must have spent three hours nervously getting ready, changing several times before finally getting in my car to drive to the bar, which was called Liquid Smoke. It was a cigar bar, and in the early evening when the sun was still up, you could see tobacco smoke billowing in the room like cumulonimbuses. A giant, neon-blue fish tank was built into the wall of the women's bathroom. It was a quirky little place.

We both arrived early so we could catch up and talk before the set. We talked nonstop until the music started. When they called our names, Jeremy got up first and fingerpicked a few new songs. It was so nice to hear him play. It was obvious he had been playing a lot, and his newer songs were great. He was shy onstage and didn't talk much between songs, but he seemed genuinely happy up there. In those days he was usually so withdrawn and sullen, but onstage his half grin was magnetic.

When he was done, I got up and played my new songs, including one called "Burn for Thee." It was in A minor and very moody—and it was definitely about Jeremy.

> When he tied my hands above my head
> To the posts of my bed, I didn't cry
> I only cried when you left
> Me for dead
> I know that you never meant
> I know you never meant to do me no harm
> No and you never did

But love it is a funny thing
No I never did believe that you'd leave
Leave me alone here with him
But you did

I got me a rope
I tied you to the chair
I'm gonna make you watch me
As I cut off my hair

And I got me a match
And some kerosene
I'm gonna make you burn for me
Like I burned for thee

Now I lay around with the dogs
I can't find a place where I wanna be
And I can't sleep while you're gone
From me

I played that song and a few more, and they passed the tip jug around for every new performer. We made thirty-three dollars.

"I like your new songs. They're good . . . different than your old stuff," Jeremy mused as he lit up a smoke. We sat at the bar and talked until the bartender rang the bell for last call. Jeremy invited me to drive over to his house, but I had to get home to Creedence. I gave him a hug, got in my car, and drove back to my apartment.

Things went on like that for several months. We'd meet up to get coffee and talk about music, or sometimes we'd play a round of darts at Villager. I hung out with him at his friend Nate Nussey's home studio. The two were starting to record songs together, and I wanted to watch the process. Nate was also helping to build several music studios in downtown Nashville.

"Six-Eight Nate" was an engineering and musical genius. He could play every instrument you handed him, including drums, piano, bass, saxophone, xylophone, mandolin, and both electric and acoustic guitar. And like a virtuoso, at that. He had a custom Everly Brothers–edition Gibson acoustic guitar that I adored. It had star inlays on the neck and a double pick guard. Nate was so kind, he always let me borrow and play his prized acoustic for my small-town gigs. He was financially well off and much more responsible than Jeremy and me. He was always looking after us.

It was much more fun to hang out with the two of them than Madeline, who was spending more and more time with her burnout boyfriend. She'd fallen head over heels for him, and I didn't quite see the appeal. He was a gas station attendant at the Tiger Mart up on West End Avenue and had a couple of faded neck tattoos. I tried hard not to judge the book by its cover, but something in his eyes told me he was untrustworthy. Soon, I realized they were smoking and snorting meth. Madeline had grown moody, pale, and skinny as a rail. I could barely recognize my spunky, energetic friend.

One day I came home to a handwritten note in my apartment.

Margo,
I'm embarrassed to tell you this but we got scabies. We are going to the laundromat to wash all of our bedsheets and clothes in hot water. We need to fumigate this place so we'll be at Kyle's apartment for several days so they can kill them. You might want to go to the doctor and see if you have them too. So sorry dude. See you in a few days.
Peace,
Madeline

The letter was a hard pill to swallow. Madeline had quit paying utilities because she spent most of her time at Kyle's, and she was three weeks late on the last month's rent and showed no sign that she was planning to pay it. I didn't want to ask Jeremy if I could stay with him, and I definitely didn't want to tell him about the scabies, so I hit up Ozzy out at Percy Priest Lake to see if I could camp on his property with Creedence while they fumigated the house.

He said I could and asked me to bring him some of that "fire weed you're always smokin'." I packed up my camping gear and drove out to set up my site. I needed somewhere for Creedence to stay while I was at work. When I got out there, Ozzy fell in love with him.

"Where did you get this pup? My god, it's the best dog I've ever seen! Sit," he said. Creedence sat. "Smart as a whip too, huh?"

"Yes, he is! Love of my life," I said. "There might be one or two of them left! I think there was a red merle out there still. He was the runt."

"Really? The runts make the best dogs. See if he's still out there. I could use another compadre out here to add to my gang of misfits."

"Will do," I promised. "Where should I set up my site?"

"Wherever your little heart desires. Prolly up behind my camper and in between the porta potties would be safe. I got a couple of my old Vietnam buddies coming out to have a fire with me tonight. Maybe you can get out your guitar and strum us a few," he said with a wink.

"Yeah, maybe I will." I smiled and thanked him for letting me stay there.

"Anytime, child. Anytime."

The sun went down on the lake and his friends arrived one by one on Harley-Davidsons and in rusted-out trucks. They were a rowdy bunch. Most of them were veterans of the Vietnam War turned bikers, rabble-rousers, and cowboys. They wore scraggly ponytails or trucker hats, Wrangler jeans, leather vests, cowboy boots, and oversized belt buckles. Ozzy cooked up some pork and beans over the fire, using bark from a nearby tree as his kindling. I serenaded the group of miscreants with my guitar as dusk fell over the glistening, man-made lake. These old-timers were rough around the edges, but they were harmless. Over the years, Ozzy would become like a grandpa or an uncle to me—but one whom I got stoned with. None of the men were ever disrespectful to me; they were all too old to do much besides drink their faded memories away. I enjoyed hearing their war stories and their musings on the good old days.

After he'd had a few too many, Ozzy revealed to me that he had cancer. "Agent Orange, that's what got me. I was exposed to too much of it in 'Nam. Doc says I got a few more good years left, though."

I sat there in silence, not really knowing what to say. "I'm sorry to hear that, Ozzy. I had no idea . . ." My voice trailed off.

"Well, there's no sense in bein' sorry, and there's certainly no sense in cryin' about it." He wiped away a few tears. "I'm just gonna enjoy my days of fishing and hanging out with my critters. What good would worry do? I'm old anyway. I've lived a hell-raisin' life!" He exhaled cigarette smoke and looked up at the stars.

"Yeah, you're right about that." I sighed. It hurt to see a man who had served our country living below the poverty line in a rat-infested trailer, eating food out of a can, and not getting the proper care he needed at the end of his life. I sat out there with him and stared up at the sky, wondering why things sometimes turn out the way they do.

Creedence and I crawled into our tent and fell asleep under the canopy of stars and the sound of a barred owl calling from a tree.

I awoke the next morning in time to make it to the lunch shift at the Saucer, which started at ten thirty. I took a whore's bath in the bathroom sink at the restaurant. My boss was surprised to see me so early, as I was almost always late. I also had Creedence with me, and I explained that my apartment was being fumigated. They were understanding and allowed him to hang out in the managers' office.

This routine went on for several more days, after which I finally returned to my place. Madeline was there with her deadbeat boyfriend, watching television and looking like a haggard mess. I went to my room and avoided them. I was still salty about the scabies.

That weekend I went back home to visit my parents, and when I returned to the apartment, the hot smell of garbage permeated the house as soon as I opened the door. Madeline had disappeared. The cat's litter box was overflowing with shit. The electricity bill hadn't been paid, so the AC was off. This was August in the South, and the apartment was like a sauna. The refrigerator was full of rotten food, including a pile of deer steaks and sausages my dad had given me. Madeline had also run off with a couple of pieces of my jewelry, including a ring my father had given to my mother in high school. It had a blue morning-star stone with three tiny diamonds on the side. I rarely took it off, but for some reason I had slipped it off and left it on the bathroom counter right before I left. Other items were missing, but that was the only one that was important to me.

"That rat bastard!" I said out loud to nobody.

I tried to clean up the mess in the fridge, but my stomach felt weak and I couldn't get far without running to the bathroom to throw up. When I told Jeremy about it, he immediately came over to help me dispose of the mess. He put on a pair of cleaning gloves, disposed of the bloody deer steaks, and cleaned out all the other rotten food. We breathed through our mouths and laughed together. I cried a little thinking about paying all the rent myself for the remainder of my lease. I would make it work, but I'd be stretched thin.

A few months later, I packed up my belongings and put them in storage. I didn't have much except for my single bed, a desk, my records, and my two gaudy orange couches. I locked up my storage unit, but I had no plans for where to go. Jeremy and I were still in the friend zone, so I couldn't ask to shack up with him, and I wasn't about to ask Star if I could move back in with her. I gave my cat, Blondie, to my neighbor Raymond, who was really excited to have some companionship. It was just me and Creedence now.

I packed a suitcase, my guitar, and my camping gear and headed out to Percy Priest Lake to seek shelter with Ozzy. I knew he wouldn't turn me away.

When Creedence and I arrived, we were greeted by Ozzy, his friend Rick, and Ozzy's four dogs. I had delivered to him the red merle runt from the same litter as Creedence, and Ozzy had named him Tippa Canoe because he had a white tip on his tail. The pups were excited to see each other. I was so grateful to have a place to stay, but I didn't know how long I could last without a proper bathroom and shower. It took some getting used to, but soon I embraced it like the dirty, freeloading hippie I was. No bills to pay, no sounds of the city seeping through my window, just the freedom of being young and untethered to bills, room-mates, or rent. I showered a few times a week at my girlfriends' houses and saved my tips for an eventual deposit on a new place.

Occasionally, I ventured over to Nate's house to listen to him and Jer-emy record songs for what would eventually be an album called *Hidden in Plain Sight*, which they released under the band name Blind Driver in 2005. When I was leaving one night, Jeremy followed me outside to walk me to my car.

As the screen door shut, he reached for my hand. We stood in the dark as the June bugs bounced around a yellow lightbulb on the front porch. He leaned down and looked me in the eyes. "I want us to be together, Margo. I feel like I messed up. You know that Dylan song that says, 'If you find someone who gives you all of her love, take it to your heart, don't let it stray'? It came on while I was driving earlier and it made me think about you. I want to give it another shot."

I was taken aback. "Well, I'm gonna have to think about it. You know, I really did like you. I don't want to get hurt again."

His blue eyes focused on me intensely. "You won't. I promise. I really think we are good for each other."

He kissed me on the forehead. Creedence and I drove back to my campsite at Percy Priest Lake. My heart was on cloud nine and I knew I wanted to take Jeremy back. I just had to let him sweat for a minute.

Jeremy had moved out of the apartment he shared with Delaney in Berry Hill and into a small, derelict duplex behind a record store called Grimey's on Alloway Street and Eighth Avenue. Grimey's was attached to a music venue called the Basement. The apartment was quaint—two small rooms and one bathroom. One bathroom shared between four people wasn't ideal, but it was better than no bathroom at all.

Jeremy shared the space with his friends from Massachusetts, Jake and Sarah. Jake looked a bit like a burned-out Jim Morrison. He and Sarah both had long, dark hair and smoked furiously. Sarah was shy and sweet, and I felt a kinship with her immediately. Jake was intense and complicated, and a brilliant musician in his own right. He moved to Nashville in late 2004, following Jeremy, with the plan to start a band. Their close relationship and musical bond intimidated me. The three of them had lived together on a Greyhound bus years ago. Jake and Sarah were both young but had been together for almost seven years. I envied their devotion to each other; they were inseparable. I longed for a history like that with Jeremy. And I wanted to be in their band, but I was a girl, and I was pretty sure that wasn't the vibe Jake was looking for.

I began staying in their little apartment with Jeremy instead of out at the lake. It was cleaner, but not by much. Jeremy's room had a single mattress on the floor, his record player, a J-45 Gibson guitar, and an old wooden desk with ragged notebooks and paper scraps. The duplex was dark and musty. Everyone chain-smoked inside, and the smell hit you like a ton of bricks when you walked in. There was also a spinet piano that was overflowing with ash and cigarette butts and covered in dust, even though we played it often. But the best part was, I didn't pay rent. Jeremy wasn't wild about the fact that I had a dog, and Creedence could be trouble. He was still a pup and he loved to chew things. One day we woke up to find him gnawing on the edge of a rare Beatles album, but he was so cute, we couldn't stay mad at him for long.

Jeremy and Jake wrote songs and rehearsed constantly. Nate often played with them as well. I was trying to get my foot in the door in any way I could and eventually talked my way into becoming their drummer. We formed a short-lived band we dubbed River Bottom. We never even played a proper show, but we had a lot of rehearsals fueled by coffee, cream, and nicotine.

Jeremy and Jake had been best friends and musicians with a shared vision for years. But after months of recording the same songs over and over, Jeremy knew Jake was never going to follow through on finishing or putting out any music. Jake was eccentric and neurotic.

He grew increasingly paranoid and extremely reclusive. It took its toll on everybody. He often demeaned Jeremy and picked apart his playing, his clothing, and his health problems, and he even poked fun at him for being adopted. One day during band practice I told him to lay off. He was defensive and taken aback because no one ever called him out. Words were exchanged and it got heated. We packed up our things and left, and that was the end of River Bottom. I felt like I had been pegged the Yoko in the situation, but I didn't care; I loved Yoko. And besides, I wasn't trying to be Yoko. I wanted to be John Lennon.

Even though Jake never recorded a proper solo album, and his bands Money Penny and Dead at 27 fell by the wayside, his influence on both Jeremy and me can't be overstated. He had such a great ear for melody, and his songs seemed to come from worlds outside himself. To quote his words, "Tell me, friend, where did you go? You threw away that rock and roll." It was a hard split for Jeremy.

"So what? The band is over," I told him. "You've got to do what's best for you." Eventually he did. Jeremy and I went back to focusing on our solo work.

I wanted to play at the Basement's New Faces Night so badly, but I couldn't get a gig to save my life. Jeremy got a show there before I did. I watched him play and felt both proud and jealous at the same time.

We were both determined to make proper albums, and that became our new focus. We weren't really writing together in those days, but we encouraged each other to write often and to work at our craft. We went to little coffee shops all over Nashville to scribble in our notebooks, drawing, making collages. Every spare moment was spent creating.

In 2005, we moved out of Jake and Sarah's apartment and got a place of our own on Wyoming Avenue. Our new home was similar to the dump we had occupied on Alloway, but it was *our* dump. We paid $500 a month plus utilities to rent a two-room brick duplex built on a slab. It was in a nice neighborhood in West Nashville called Sylvan Park, but we had the worst home on the street by far.

We immediately converted one of the bedrooms into a music room and recorded a couple of EPs there. Jeremy's was titled *Vermillion*, and the cover was a black-and-white photo of him sitting at a piano holding a red lightbulb over his head. My first compilation was called *No Halo*. It was just me and an acoustic guitar—very simple, plain, and folky. My cover artwork was homemade as well. I stood at a Kinko's copy machine for hours printing the album art onto pieces of card stock and folding them into the CD cases myself. We recorded both albums on the eight-track machine. Having little money, we passed out copies to our immediate family and friends in lieu of Christmas gifts.

I knew in my heart that the songs on our albums were too avant-garde and artsy to have any commercial appeal. On occasion, I sold my copies for five bucks apiece at open mics. I used the demo to book my first proper show in town. I assembled a band that consisted of Nate, who switched between drums and mandolin; Jeremy, alternating between electric guitar and bass; our new friend, a painter and writer named Steven Knudson, on accordion; and a fellow Flying Saucer waitress and aspiring musician, Jessi Williams, on banjo and singing occasional harmonies. I made posters and hung them up all over town. My mom came in to see the show, which was held in the attic of Bongo Java on the Belmont campus. The crowd was mostly friends, no more than fifteen to twenty people total. With the five-dollar cover, we only made around seventy-five to a hundred dollars, but it was my first show in the big city with my name on the marquee, and my mama was so proud.

CHAPTER 6

This Town Gets Around (and Around and Around)

One night I went out to play a short set at Norm's River Roadhouse, a dodgy biker bar off of Interstate 40 West and River Road. I played on a small, wooden, *Hee Haw*–lookin' stage in the corner. Facing me were picnic tables of patrons, some of whom resembled Sam Elliott playing a part in a modern western movie. There were lots of men in the room who wore cowboy hats, drank bottled beer, and probably had a hand in the music business as writers or other insiders.

When I got offstage, I sat down at a table alone to watch the next act. Up walked a man in a Canadian tux with long, white hair. He introduced himself with two names.

"Hey there, I'm Larry Short, but everyone around here calls me Doc. Doc Holliday." He held out his hand to greet me.

Now, I knew good and well that the original Doc Holliday was a rambling, gambling gunfighter from the mid-1800s. Growing up, I had watched my fair share of old westerns with my dad. Larry looked old enough to be harmless, but not too old to have a good time. In his hand, adorned with turquoise rings and bracelets, he held an ice-cold Bud Light.

"Great set!" he said with a smile. "Did you write those songs?"

"Well, yes, I did write four of them. Except for that last one, that was Dylan." I laughed.

"Oh, yeah, of course," he bluffed. "Love Bob Dylan. Well, the reason I ask is that I work with a lot of acts in town. A lot of *big* acts. I'd love to hear more of your material. You ever think about writing for other people?"

"No, not really," I admitted.

"Well, you should. There's a lot of money in it. I have a studio and I could get you in to sing some demos. I'm always looking for pretty voices to sing demos for me. Just a few hours of work and you could have a check in the mail. Interested?"

"I guess, maybe. I mostly like to write and sing my own songs. I don't have any aspirations to sing other people's songs or to sell mine." *But I am broke*, I thought.

"Let me buy you a beer and I'll tell you more about it. I think you'd be surprised how easy it is. And then you can use that money to fund your own stuff, ya know?"

I sat next to Doc and he went into his pitch. He claimed to have worked with the Dixie Chicks at some point and casually dropped more artists' names—some I knew, some I didn't. I sat there quietly and listened, keeping one eye on him and another on the door.

"I got a nice log-cabin studio in the city, and I've got a cool jam space out at my house. I live just up the road from here if you want to come check it out sometime." He went on, "There's a barn behind my house that's refurbished. The Grateful Dead used to hang out there—hand to God."

He seemed nice enough, but I wasn't about to go anywhere with a strange man. "That sounds cool." I gathered my purse and guitar. "I do dig the Dead. Maybe I'll come there with my boyfriend, Jeremy, and check it out sometime. He writes songs too." I stood up to leave.

"Here's my info." Doc scribbled down his information on a bar napkin with the waitress's pen. "Why don't you come by my office this week and play me some of your songs? I'll listen and tell you if I think there's potential. We can go from there."

"Sounds good!" I loosened up. "Can Jeremy come too? He's a strong lyricist and has a brilliant sense of melody. You'd love him."

"Sure! Bring your boyfriend. I'd be happy to listen to both of y'all. We need some new blood in our songwriting circle." He motioned to the bartender for another beer, and I shook his hand and said goodbye.

The following Monday, I ended up going by myself to Doc's studio off of Eighth Avenue. It was a rustic log cabin off the beaten path and surrounded by trees. I had given him a copy of my mini album the night we met at Norm's, and I saw it on his desk. He motioned to the CD as I sat in the leather chair opposite him. "I liked the songs, listened a few times. I didn't hear anything that sounded very marketable though. What else you got?"

"Probably nothing marketable, but I do have more songs." I launched into a new one with Travis-style fingerpicking, called "Queen Anne's Lace."

When I finished playing, he said, "These are interesting songs, but they're too personal. And you need to work on your hooks. They show promise but country radio will never play them."

"Well, I don't listen to country radio, so that makes sense." I laughed.

"Honey, then you're in the wrong town." He lit up a rotten-smelling cigar.

"There's other kinds of music being played in this town besides mainstream country. Those songs are one-dimensional and full of terrible clichés. I'm sorry, but I don't write cheesy choruses about pickup trucks and objectifying women in Daisy Dukes, okay? Do you ever go listen to bands at Springwater or Exit/In or the End?" I could feel my blood pressure rising.

Doc was taken aback. "Nah, I'm too old for that scene, but I hear ya. You know, you've got a great voice." He was trying to appeal to me. "But why are you writing songs, and who are you writing them for, if it's not to make money?"

"I'm writing them for me because I like to. Because I want to." I said it as plainly as I could.

"Well, good for you! But I'm telling you, there's money to be made if you follow some simple guidelines. Why don't you try to write something that could be on the radio? Just for fun. And I could have you in for a session to sing some songs from other writers who don't have good delivery. Might be nice to make some money at something other than waitressing, right?"

"I guess I could try it," I said hesitantly. Just the thought of it made me feel dirty, like I was compromising my artistic integrity to make a buck. But how hard could it be to write a stupid radio hit? I started to gather my things to leave.

"Say, you smoke pot, right?" He riffled through his desk drawer and pulled out a giant bag of grass.

"Yeah, I do." I paused from putting my guitar away to judge the quality of the weed.

"Here, take it with you." He handed me the bag. "I don't even smoke that much these days, and my friend sends it to me by the truckload."

I thanked him. It looked like it had been smuggled in the undercarriage of someone's car. But I was broke, so I was happy to take it off his hands, seeds and stems included.

Jeremy met up with him later that week and had a similar experience. Doc didn't care for his songs but saw potential. He set him up with a guy named Aaron for a writing date.

Jeremy and I decided that if we were going to write songs we weren't proud of, we would use pen names. We came up with the monikers Sylvia Slim and Sam Pickens. That way if we wrote something together, the credit would be Slim/Pickens. It was our little inside joke. I wrote a few songs, but I didn't really think they had potential. It was just so hard to gauge if they were good or not, because I wasn't writing from my heart. I don't even remember most of the titles, except for one called "I Need You Like a Hole in My Head." Jeremy wrote a song called "It's Already Been a Long Day." We laughed at how absurd they were.

I went to Doc's office again to play him our new ideas. We had recorded them on the Roland eight track and burned them onto a CD.

"You're on the right track! These are so much better than your first attempts," Doc crowed.

"Thanks. I appreciate that, but I think they're shit, personally." I forced a grin. I was offended that he liked them so much better than the songs I'd written before.

"Oh, now, come on! Don't be so hard on yourself," he said. "What are you doing this weekend? You should come out and cowrite with my buddy who's had a lot of hits. He's staying out in the barn and I think y'all could come up with some strong songs together."

"Well, I'm around, I think. Could Jeremy come? We've been working on some stuff together that's coming along pretty good."

"I think Jeremy would work better with Aaron. The two of you are too similar. You both think outside the box too much. It would be best if you came alone, if you're comfortable with that."

"Oh, okay, well, I guess that would be fine. What's the address?" I asked.

"Just meet me at Norm's Roadhouse and you can follow me. It's hard to describe how to get there."

"Alright! Sounds good." I got up to leave.

"Hey," he said, stopping me. "I know how much you like all my turquoise, so I wanted to give you somethin'." He pulled out an antique turquoise squash-blossom necklace. "You like it?"

"That is stunning, and I do love turquoise jewelry, but I can't accept such a lavish gift."

"Yeah, I have a bunch of these pieces from over the years. Really, I can't wear them all and I don't have a daughter to give them to. It's all yours." He stood up and placed it over my head as though giving me a ceremonial blessing. He wasn't taking no for an answer.

"Thanks, Doc, it's a really beautiful piece." I felt kind of weird about it. Was there some expectation behind it?

"That looks much better on you than it does on me," he said with a nod. "See you Saturday."

That week Jeremy got together with Aaron and tried to cowrite. It did not go well. The song title that Aaron brought to the table was "Whiskey Drinkin', Wishful Thinkin'." Jeremy didn't like it from the start and had nothing to contribute. He reported back that it was "a complete and total waste of time."

When Saturday rolled around, I went out to Norm's to meet Doc. "My buddy's out at the house working on stuff already," Doc said. "He's staying with me for a couple of days. His name's Robert. You'll love him."

I followed Doc in my own car down several winding country roads to his house. It was a pretty big place—it was obvious he had money. He started showing me around. He had a lot of expensive art, including African statues and abstract paintings. There was a vintage motorcycle parked inside his living room, which was full of lavish furniture.

After giving me the grand tour, he said, "I've got a music room upstairs with guitars and a great view of the Dead barn. Come on up. Robert's up there already."

I followed him to the loft and set down my guitar and notebook on the coffee table. There was a sliding glass door and a small patio that overlooked the property. I saw the so-called Grateful Dead barn about a hundred yards away.

"Pretty piece of property you got here," I mused.

I heard a rumble behind a closed door. A disheveled-looking, middle-aged man emerged, and as he did so, he hollered obscenities at a very large and unhappy German shepherd scratching at the door of a metal crate and barking like crazy.

Robert was a stocky man, with curly, salt-and-pepper hair and a haggard face. "Sorry about that," he said to me. He reached into his pocket and pulled out a Zippo lighter to fire up a smoke. "Trying to crate train the bitch but she's stubborn." He reached out to shake my hand. "I'm Robert. Doc's been telling me you got a hell of a voice. And some songs too."

"Margo," I said and gave him a firm handshake. "And same. Pleased to meet you."

"You want some sangria?" Doc inquired. "I just made it this morning."

"Sure, sounds good." I'd never had sangria before, but it sounded refreshing.

"Well, let's get this party started! Shall we?!" Robert was intense. "Bring me that bottle, Doc."

Doc went downstairs and returned with a pitcher of sangria, some glasses, and a liter of Belvedere vodka.

"Want a shot too?" Robert poured himself one.

"Nah, I'm good on vodka. I had a bad experience with it back in college. I can't touch the stuff anymore." Actually, I thought it was a little early to be drinking anything.

Robert handed me a glass of red wine with ice and fruit in it. I sat on the couch, pulled out my guitar, and began tuning it up. I started strumming some old covers just to break the ice. I played "This Wheel's on Fire" by Bob Dylan and the Band and "Shake Sugaree" by Elizabeth Cotten.

"Well, where did you learn them fancy bar chords—you got an older brother?" Robert looked half in the bag already. "You play like a man!" He laughed loudly and took another shot of vodka.

"I'm self-taught," I said dryly. "Why don't you pick one. Got any originals?"

"Yes, I do, in fact." Robert cleared his throat and tried to compose himself. He began to play but his guitar was terribly out of tune. He stopped abruptly and began to fight with the tuning pegs. "Som' bitch always slippin'!"

"I'm going to use the restroom," I said. I went into the bathroom to pee and returned to find him still tuning. I had a good amount of sangria left. I sipped it as he began to play and tried to think of an excuse to leave.

Robert played fragments and pieces of songs, got distracted, and started over again and again. He never remembered any of the words. For half an hour, I sat and sipped my drink as he plowed through several half-assed, three-chord tunes, mumbling many of the words during verses and only really singing the choruses. It was like watching a car crash in slow motion.

My head started to spin.

"The verses are what I need some help with, *help with, help with . . .*" his voice echoed as he explained.

I suddenly felt incredibly disoriented. I set down my drink on the coffee table in front of me. "I don't feel well. What did y'all put in this drink?"

"We poured some vodka in there because we didn't think you were havin' enough fun!" Robert said immediately.

"Why would you do that?" I tried to remain calm as I gathered my things from the coffee table.

Doc shot Robert a look as if to say, *Shut up*, then he said, "No, we didn't put nothin' in there. He's just messin' with ya."

"Well, did you or didn't you?" I demanded. I started to have a panic attack. It was hard to speak, and my own voice sounded far away.

"Can't you have a good time? Relax." Robert's tone had changed. He was no longer smiling. He stood up and walked toward me. "Come on, sit down and let's have one more."

"No, I don't want more. I want to go home." My mother's words rang through my head: "Don't trust everyone you meet, Margo. Never set your drink down. Not all people are good! You're not invincible. *Be careful.*" I was in a secluded house out in the country, alone with two strange men, and my cell phone was dying. No one knew where I was. Jeremy had a vague clue but no specific address.

"What's your address, Larry?" I asked, surprising them both by using his real name. He wasn't Doc Holliday and he knew it.

"I'm not telling anyone my address. I don't want people to know where I live. You're on your own. You got a car, drive yourself." He lit up a cigar and sat back in his leather chair. I realized how little I knew him in that moment. I wanted to go home.

My knees buckled but I stumbled back to the bathroom with my dying cell phone. I locked the door behind me and sat down on the floor.

I sent Jeremy a text, *Please come get me. I don't feel well. At Doc's mansion down on River Road by Norm's. I think they put something in my drink.*

I hit send. I sat there with my head between my legs, trying to remain calm. I was dizzy and felt like I was on the verge of blacking out. There was no way I should be feeling so inebriated from one drink.

Jeremy replied, *Address? Where are you exactly?*

I tried to recite the turns we had taken and explain that Larry wouldn't share the address, but before I could hit send, my phone died. I felt like I was going to puke, but I started to cry instead. I tried to do some deep breathing and stay calm.

Someone knocked on the door. "You okay in there? Did ya fall in?" Robert asked, laughing.

I didn't answer. I just sat there for a long time, quiet as a mouse. I could hear them pacing back and forth outside as I sat with my back to the door, listening to them whispering to each other.

Suddenly I heard the dog start barking again through the wall and some commotion. I stood up slowly and opened the door a little, peering through the crack. Jeremy and our friend Dave Harder emerged from the staircase.

"This is a nice place you've got out here, Larry." Jeremy sounded unusually confident as he approached the two older men from behind, catching them off guard.

Doc jumped out of his skin. He turned around. "How did you get in here? How did you find this place?"

"Hell, that doesn't really matter, does it?" Dave said in his thick southern drawl. "The door was unlocked. Walked right in. Ha!"

"This is private property, you know," slurred Robert. Jeremy and Dave ignored him.

"You okay?" Jeremy asked as he retrieved me and grabbed my guitar.

"Let's just go," I whispered. My legs were weak, but he grabbed my arm and started to escort me out.

Doc was pissed off. "This is trespassing, you know. You can't just walk into someone's house like that."

Dave and Jeremy shot him a look, and they all started to shout. Things got heated, but Robert and Larry were too old and too buzzed to put up a fight.

"Let's go!" I said again. We walked down the stairs and out the front door. Jeremy drove my car home and Dave drove his. I passed out cold when I got to the house and woke up the next day with the worst headache I'd had in my life. I'd only had the one glass of sangria. To this day, I don't know what they put in my drink, but I'm so grateful I escaped. I never saw or spoke to Larry ever again.

CHAPTER 7

Black Water

One gray day, Jeremy and I came home from work to a river of sewage winding through the house. Thick, black water flooded the bathroom and the kitchen, overtaking everything in its wake. The smell was unbearable, our belongings were ruined, and the landlord was in no rush to fix it, so we broke our lease and moved.

For our next digs, we were in a little white house with maroon shutters nestled between a small section of city forest and a train track, at the edge of Sylvan Heights in West Nashville. The rent there was $750 a month, not including utilities—another fixer-upper. There was pet hair everywhere, and the stained, shaggy carpets were infested with fleas. We had the place deep cleaned and made the best of it. I often took walks along the train tracks with Creedence, leaving pennies on the rails and picking them up once the train flattened them.

Jeremy and I were most excited about the basement, which had been refinished and was the perfect place for a studio. There was a little wooden room with a padlock by the washer and dryer. I opened it and was delighted to see a light hanging from the ceiling and a little table.

It was a grow room. I'd always wanted to grow my own weed. I took it as a good sign.

We had made a solid group of friends by this point—many musicians, visual artists, and vagabonds whom we hung out with often. There was Dave Harder, who had helped Jeremy rescue me from Larry's place on River Road. Dave was an upright-bass player and an electrician with sandy-blond hair and shocking-blue eyes. He was from Ohio, on the Kentucky border, and he had the thickest southern drawl I'd ever heard. "*Well, hell,*" he would say, "we could go down and pick up a six-pack and do some pickin'! *Well, hell,* we could go fishin' if y'all ain't busy." Dave was a good ol' boy and a great bluegrass picker. He lived out in Whites Creek and had a home down in the holler, where we often went to play music and sit around a bonfire. He had speakers and old tube radios all over his house that were all set to 650 AM WSM. Being out at his place in the country was always good medicine.

There was Steven Knudson, who'd sat in with me on accordion at my first gig at Bongo Java. He was from Wisconsin and had a nasal speaking voice, but when he sang his tone was deep and he had a strong vibrato. You would never know by looking at him that his voice was so robust, because he looked like a scrawny punk more likely to be playing in a Nirvana cover band. Steven was also a phenomenal painter whose paintings were like his songs—desolate, rural, otherworldly. I met him at an open mic at Hall of Fame Lounge and began hanging out with him, playing music up at Brown's Diner. He was part of a band called the Applewood Threshold. They had a Dylan and the Band *Basement Tapes* vibe going, with lots of mandolin and accordion.

The leader of the band was a guy named Chet O'Keefe, who was also a brilliant songwriter. He had the frankness of Guy Clark, the delivery of Greg Brown, and the humor and wit of John Prine, but a style all his own. Chet was in his midthirties when we met him and a true weirdo— he had a guitar amp he'd made out of a car engine that sounded bizarre. It looked really cool onstage.

Also in the band was someone unknown in the wider world but a

Nashville legend, Susie Monick. Susie played banjo, mandolin, fiddle, guitar, and accordion. She had been around forever and knew a lot of the old Nashville cats. She'd sat in with Townes Van Zandt, Blaze Foley, Nanci Griffith, and Richard Dobson. She had done some acting in her day and made quirky clay figures that were showcased at different bars and music venues all over town. Susie was older but still had a spark in her eye. I idolized her.

Steven also introduced me to a German couple who lived up the street from us, Nadine and René. They had a two-year-old boy named Leopold whom we all affectionately called Lubbie. Nadine was a brilliant photographer who only used old film cameras. One summer evening, she convinced me to let her take some portraits of me. I was makeup free and wore a vintage peasant dress I had bought at Southern Thrift. The photos she took that summer at dusk were some of the first professional photos I ever had taken. My favorite was one of me standing in the middle of the street in our old neighborhood, holding my '56 Gibson guitar in front of Steven's 1985 Chevy Impala.

I was also thick as thieves with a skinny, redheaded girl named Jessi Williams. Like me, she was an aspiring songwriter and a waitress. We met working long shifts at the Saucer. She played not only guitar but also banjo. Jessi was a fellow Aries and had a similar outgoing, fun-loving personality. She was named after one of my favorite singers—an original member of the outlaw gang that included Waylon Jennings and Willie Nelson—the small but mighty spitfire Jessi Colter. Jessi and I spent hours collaborating in my basement studio, swapping our songs, learning covers, harmonizing, and trying to master playing lead on the guitar.

One evening my friend Ross came over to sell me some grass. He pulled out my usual order—an eighth of weed for fifty dollars—and then mentioned that he had liquid acid.

"You want some?" Ross asked with a smile.

"Sure!" I said without thinking, even though I had never done liquid acid before.

"Open wide!" He pulled out an eyedropper and placed a hit on my tongue.

It all happened fast. I became a victim of my own spontaneity again. Jessi was coming over in thirty minutes to play guitar, but I was hoping I could take the ride since I'd accidentally splurged on a ticket.

At first I wasn't sure if I felt any different at all. I kept it to myself, not even telling Jeremy. I tried to play it cool for a couple of hours. Suddenly I got a feeling that was like approaching a big hill on a roller coaster. I felt like I might lose my stomach, but it was also so exciting. Everything seemed significant—every word, every chord, every conversation was meaningful. I tried to play along on the the mandolin to one of Jessi's songs, but the strings bounced and hummed in my hands. Then the neck of the instrument began to feel like rubber. I started laughing hysterically and finally admitted that I was on LSD.

"I think I need some fresh air." I stood up to examine the space, which felt smaller than usual. The cinder-block walls began to close in on me, and I escaped outside into the black of the night to survey the stars and dip my feet in the wet, overgrown grass in our unkempt backyard.

Jessi was both shocked and impressed that I'd held it together that long without telling anyone, but she certainly didn't judge me. "Girl, I've already been there and done that. Power to ya for attempting new chords on the mandolin while under the thumb of the higher power." She laughed between sips of a thick and cheap cabernet. Jeremy didn't judge my decision either and immediately began planning how to set up the perfect acid trip for me.

"You need to watch *Fear and Loathing*! That's the move." He went upstairs to riffle through our collection of movies. He put it on and we all gathered around our small television. I felt the urge to smoke cigarettes inside, and Jeremy agreed it was necessary. He took good care of me and made sure I was comfortable, amused by my reaction to everything. We stayed up late laughing at the insanity and brilliance of Hunter S. Thompson and the world at large. "We were somewhere around Barstow on the edge of the desert when the drugs began to take hold. . . . I tell you man, this is the American dream in action!"

When it was over, we went outside and made a fire. "If you think about it," I said as I gazed into the flames, "the fire was the first TV. I've heard fire stimulates the same part of your brain as a television . . ." My voice trailed off. I got lost in the colors of the burning wood as shadows danced playfully in the thicket beyond the yard.

By this point, Jeremy and I were officially a couple. My family came down to Nashville to celebrate Thanksgiving and fell for Jeremy's charming demeanor and quick-witted sense of humor. One afternoon we took my family to one of our favorite vintage stores on the Rock Block of Elliston Place. We walked into the store, and my dad leaned over to us and whispered, "Now who would wear a pair of old, used boots?" I looked at Jeremy and then at my dad and then back down at Jeremy's feet, clad in a worn-out pair of black Beatles-style boots. I pointed and said, "Dad, I have no idea."

Jeremy and I were also starting to write songs together. Our first cowrite was called "At the Gates." It was a postapocalyptic folk song, a failed but noble attempt at mystic writing. The first lines were, "The devil's got a number, he's takin' to the gate, he's talking to a stranger, who listens for his fate, and although his eyes are open, the stranger doesn't see, the fate that he's been given is the same as you and me."

We were both inspired to attempt full-length, homemade records. I had finally gotten a decent settlement from the woman who had pulled out in front of me on Murfreesboro Road. This and dedicated saving had made for a good nest egg. I was supposed to use the money to get physical therapy, but instead I bought equipment. I purchased a couple of guitar amps, microphones, tape, and a drum kit. The drums came from Nashville Used Music on Nolensville Pike. Five hundred dollars got me an all-natural-wood kit made by Tama. It was the same-sized kit that Dave Grohl used with Nirvana: a giant twenty-four-inch bass drum, four toms, and the cheapest cymbals I could find. I didn't know shit about drums; I'd never taken lessons, and my only experience was sitting in with Jeremy and Jake in our short-lived band River Bottom. I just sat behind them and taught myself.

We also acquired an Otari eight track, a used one-inch reel-to-reel recorder that only worked occasionally. Jeremy's album was entitled *Three Threes* and mine was called *Chrysalis*. We layered everything by tracking the parts one by one and played almost all of the instruments ourselves. We enlisted Nate on drums and mandolin and Steven on accordion. We made the artwork ourselves using photos, homemade collages, and a simple computer program called Paint. The songs were more fully realized than the ones I had recorded on our first EPs. I was constantly reading Sylvia Plath, and a lot of my songs were in a minor key. I had not yet found my true voice and sang much lower in my register during those days. Still, we were both beginning to sound more like ourselves—whoever that was, whoever they were.

Jeremy got a minimum-wage job cooking at a restaurant called Bread and Company. At an hourly wage of seven dollars and some change, it was less than ideal, but he brought home so much free food it helped us survive. Bread and Company had a donation program that delivered fresh loaves of bread to people struggling with homelessness, but the other six days a week, they threw away all of the food that wasn't eaten. Jeremy brought home bread and quarts of soup and chicken salad that we lived on for the entire week. This went on for a year or more, and by the end of it, I was so sick of tarragon-chicken-salad sandwiches that just the thought of them made me nauseous.

It was at Bread and Company that Jeremy first met Dillon Napier, who later became my drummer in our band Buffalo Clover and my solo project. The two of them bonded while smoking grass together in the walk-in freezer during their shifts.

I still worked at the Flying Saucer, but I also picked up a job teaching preschool at a Presbyterian church on Murfreesboro Road. The great thing about the church was the arsenal of instruments at our disposal. I spent a lot of lunch breaks and nap times writing songs on the piano there. Jeremy snuck in during the day while I worked and made good use of a giant pipe organ, an old 1900s pump organ, and a grand piano. Nate mixed the recordings for us and helped us print our homemade covers and sleeves. We sat around the table in our kitchen, folding and assembling them together.

One of the songs that sticks with me from that time was one Jeremy wrote called "Safe and Sound." It was the most pure thing anyone had ever written for me. It was about our unborn children and the life we planned to build together. He played me the recording and I listened intently through a pair of rotting-rubber headphones. I was hopelessly in love.

If you wanna talk a while, I would like to talk a while with you
And if you wanna sing, I'd like to hear a song or two
Oh, you mean more to me than I do to myself
Half the time my head's up in a cloud
You set me down, safe and sound

We frequently had fires and picking parties in the backyard between our splintered porch on stilts and the train tracks. I began growing weed in the basement grow room with starter plants a friend gave me. It was a strain called Sweet Caroline, after the Neil Diamond song. I didn't know the first thing about growing weed, but I was eager, so I started to study and read anything I could on the subject. I told no one, for fear of being busted. It was my little secret endeavor in city farming.

With Jeremy working mornings and me burning the candle at both ends, we were like ships that pass in the night. The preschool job only paid minimum wage, so I had to keep picking up shifts at the bar to make rent. I was on the clock until two or three A.M. most nights, so we sometimes went days without seeing each other, apart from when we slept. We made love in the mornings and left each other love letters on our tiny kitchen table. We lived paycheck to paycheck and scraped by. Eggs for breakfast, PB&J for lunch, and frozen tilapia and edamame for dinner. We bought most of our food up the street at a local mom-and-pop grocery store called the Produce Place. We almost never ate out unless I got a massive tip at work, and when we did it was a celebratory occasion.

When we got a little extra cash, we sometimes had drinks at an English pub called Sherlock Holmes Pub, followed by dinner at Boscos in Hillsboro Village. We loved Hillsboro Village because it felt like our own little slice of what I imagined Greenwich Village to be (although I hadn't been to New York yet). There was a bookstore called Book-ManBookWoman where we would curl up for hours on worn, red-velvet armchairs to read poetry and scribble in our notebooks. Every so often, the owners would come back and scold us when we camped out too long, insisting we were dragging down the property value.

One evening Jeremy took me up to an area called Love Circle off of West End. We went to parks all over the city to write and talk and walk around, so I didn't think much of it until he got down on one knee and asked me to marry him. He had a cheap, little gold ring in his pocket with a peridot stone. He had noticed me eyeing it at the Eighth Avenue Antique Warehouse. I was pretty shocked; even though we had talked about the future and were very much in love, I didn't think he would ever marry again. I said yes without hesitation and started crying. It was a brisk fall day, and we walked arm in arm to stay warm. I remember every detail: he was wearing a sweater and corduroy pants, and I was wearing a black peacoat and French braids in my hair.

We were broke but happy. Later that night, we bought a bottle of petite syrah from the wine shop on Murphy Road, cooked our frozen, two-dollar tilapia fillets and beans, put on a Billie Holiday record, and danced around like fools in our tiny kitchen.

CHAPTER 8

Stealing from Thieves

They say you only fight with the people you love, and Jeremy and I were definitely doing our fair share of fighting. Most of my friends were building careers, pregnant with their first or second baby, and putting down payments on new homes. The specter of failure made me restless, and I lay awake at night feeling worthless, endlessly disconcerted about the future.

The Sylvan Heights house was a fine place for hosting crusty punk parties, but the whole place was infested with rats. They weren't just little field mice like the ones that occasionally occupied my parents' farmhouse—they were the biggest rats I'd ever seen in my life. One afternoon I went down to the basement to do laundry and came face to face with a rat the size of a possum. I jumped on top of the dryer and started screaming. Creedence came to investigate, but even he was frightened. He was usually too brave for his own good, but as the rat hissed at him, he turned and ran back upstairs with his tail between his legs. We could hear the rats crawling around in the walls, and I knew there had to be nests everywhere.

We finished our lease and moved in to a house in West Nashville on Indiana Avenue. It was right across the street from a townie bar called Glen's Den. To the right of us was a convenience store called the Stop-N-Shop Market. It was robbed at gunpoint the first week after we moved in. We were having band practice when we heard shots through the wall. About ten minutes later, we heard an ambulance and saw a man being wheeled out on a stretcher. The owner of the gas station had taken out his own gun and shot the thief. From that moment on, we dubbed it the Stop-N-Rob.

Our neighbors to the left were a middle-aged redneck couple who bickered constantly and kept several mangy dogs chained to the ground like helpless slaves. The mutts barked relentlessly among the rubber tires and birdbaths that littered their lawn. Day and night, the toothless couple got drunk and screamed obscenities at each other and traded punches. The cops visited them frequently.

The Indiana Avenue house was old and had a lot of character. It wasn't nice by any means, but we always found a way to love where we lived and make it our own. It had tall, vaulted ceilings, and we painted each room a different bright, obnoxious color. The kitchen was sunny and yellow, with a black-and-white-checkered floor; the bedroom was pea green, accented with dainty lace curtains; the living room was orange, and the bathroom was hot pink. We left a Sharpie in there and encouraged our friends to write on the wall, like it was the bathroom of a dive bar. At times, it definitely felt like it was.

My mother and father visited, and I could see the disappointment and worry in their eyes. I knew they wanted better for me. My mother later confessed that she cried when she saw the squalor in which we were living. I didn't want to disappoint them, but the way I figured it, we were still young and had time to get our lives together. My parents thought we encouraged each other's bad habits. My mom, despite her typically feminist opinions, feared Jeremy wasn't able to financially support me. I told her I didn't need him to, that I would figure it out on my own. But I didn't really believe it.

For Christmas I bought Jeremy a copy of the Kinks' *Arthur*, and we immediately started listening to and obsessing over everything the Kinks had ever done. We fell in love with their dark humor, their fuck-all attitude, and their descriptive depictions of the world. We devoured *The Kinks Are the Village Green Preservation Society*, *Lola versus Power-man and the Moneygoround, Part One*, and of course *Muswell Hillbillies*. We made a pact to form a band like the Kinks, where we would only sing about the social circles of modern society, governmental control, and the downtrodden losers, underdogs, and outcasts of the world. And so our first proper band, Secret Handshake, was formed.

For the first time, we recorded at a real studio, a place called Big Ears Studio that was owned by Paul Gannon, a middle-aged, baby-boomer, pot-smoking hippie. He was always walking around barefoot, doing yoga, stretching between takes, and eating grapes.

We made an EP called *Listen* that included songs we wrote both sepa-rately and together. I took the vocal on the songs "Here You Are," "Dirty Hands," "Rovin' Line," and "Architects of War." Jeremy sang one called "Animal City." The songs were all about social issues and had themes similar to those of George Orwell's *Animal Farm* and *Nineteen Eighty-Four*. Sonically, they mirrored the tones of the British Invasion, with crunchy guitars and loud amps. Our buddy Luke Amelang played slide guitar on a couple of the tunes, but we did the rest of the overdubs with me strumming acoustic guitar and pounding out percussion and drums while Jeremy played electric guitar, keys, and bass.

"Architects of War" was specifically about the war in Iraq. Jeremy and I were both in opposition to the conflict that had, at that time, claimed the lives of around two thousand American citizens and thousands more Iraqis. In addition to writing songs about civil rights and equality, we wanted to become part of the United for Peace and Justice movement. We wanted to stand against the war on the poor, which was happening in both the United States and Iraq. Hurricane Katrina had also recently pummeled the Gulf Coast, and folks were really struggling. Groups like the ANSWER Coalition embodied a wide range of political views but actually took action. When we were hanging up a handmade poster for a local show in Nashville, we saw an advertisement for a protest happening in Washington, DC, on September 24, 2005. We packed our bags and left the very next day.

We were joined on our pilgrimage to DC by our new friend and short-lived drummer and bandmate, Luke, and his wife, Alex. Before we left I sat in the living room and hand painted two big signs that said "Stop the Violence" and "Bring Them Home." They were simple black words on white poster board, but Jeremy deemed them bold and effective. As soon as we arrived at the Washington Monument, where the march was starting, Luke and Alex got cold feet. They took one look at the police officers patrolling the area and decided they would rather sightsee than risk getting arrested. Jeremy and I took our homemade signs, grabbed each other by the hand, and walked toward the crowd.

I was surprised and moved by the diversity of the protestors. They were all ethnicities, all ages, all denominations, all there for one common goal: to rebuke an administration that had started this never-ending war. We encountered groups of counterprotestors who held signs in support of President Bush and Vice President Cheney. Tensions were high, but no violence broke out.

We chanted in unison, backed by conga drums, hand claps, and foot stomps. When we arrived at the end of the march, we listened to compelling speeches by the Reverend Jesse Jackson, Jessica Lange, and others, but what moved me the most was a speech by a woman named Cindy Sheehan, a California mother whose son had been killed fighting overseas. Tears rolled down my cheeks as I thought about how devastating it would be to lose a child to such senseless violence.

President Bush was away from Washington at the time of the protest, and it felt like he had turned his back on the cries of the peaceful protestors. We raised hell anyway. From the back of the crowd, someone blasted the Vietnam-era protest song "War" through a giant speaker on wheels, and the crowd began chanting in a call-and-response.

"WAR!"

"HUH!"

"What is it good for?"

"ABSOLUTELY NOTHING. Say it again!"

The police formed a barricade around the exit, and my heart started hammering. Jeremy put his arm around my shoulder and said, "Let's split. It's over anyway."

The armed cops formed a human chain and gazed down at us menacingly from atop stoic-looking horses, as if to say, "Go ahead, try it." They forced everyone to file out through their line and to present IDs upon leaving. They scanned people's driver's licenses and wrote down the names of everyone in attendance.

We saw a hole in the crowd and escaped without having to go through the questioning and the runaround. Back in our tiny hotel room, we ate Chinese takeout and took refuge in the comfort of each other's company for the rest of the evening.

When we returned home, we threw ourselves into more advocacy and home recording. In some instances, the two passions intersected in a topical song. One in particular came to life while we were sitting at a coffee shop reading a copy of the *Nashville Scene*. The cover story hit us like a ton of bricks. It was about a man named Paul House who had been incarcerated for murder for twenty-two years on Tennessee's death row before forensic evidence stirred rumors of his innocence. We hung posters around town with his face and story on them. We passed out flyers with information urging people to call the federal court system to beg for his acquittal. And we wrote a song for him, "Free Paul House," which was partially inspired by John Lennon's "John Sinclair."

Our record was completed in the same sort of manic and loving way as our previous projects. All of the album artwork was resourceful and homemade; the constraints on us sparked more creativity than having a big budget. My photographer friend, Nadine, took the photos for the cover. My grandmother had given Jeremy and me a tiny kitchen table for our house, and we hauled it out into an open field of tall grass to take some portraits. We both wore bright yellow and no shoes. The photos turned out really lovely, but we left covered in chigger bites.

After we released the album, we sent it around to anyone and everyone we thought might care. Jeremy and I got our first-ever radio play on a local college station called 91.1 WRVU with the song "Here You Are," and we were on cloud nine when we received our first-ever write-up in a local music paper, *All the Rage*. A journalist named Dave Paulson graced us with our first-ever review in print, which described our "penchant for sneering social commentary." That was good enough for us. We were so proud, we clipped out the review and put it in a scrapbook.

Lyrically, "Here You Are" was our version of the Kinks' "Dead End Street" meets "Sunny Afternoon."

> *Here you are coming home in dirty rags just some poor fool*
> *Life is cruel and you're the one who really knows that nasty rule*
>
> *Here you are, working so hard, day after day, for minimum pay*
> *With none left to save, and bills on the way, you can't live this way,*
> *The working-class slave that you are*
>
> *Sun arrives you're looking at the classifieds through black-hole eyes*
> *All you see are other people's luxuries being advertised*
>
> *Here you are working so hard, takin' out the trash and scrubbing*
>   *at the stalls*
> *And when you get home, you're there all alone*
> *With cigarettes and beer to help you forget who you are*
> *Every day the story gets retold, 'til you wake up once and you're old,*
>   *la da da da*

We were living those words, mopping the floors, cleaning the toilets, living paycheck to paycheck. I eventually got sick of waitressing long hours at the Flying Saucer and picked up fewer shifts. Even though I was still working full-time at the preschool, money was always tight. Jeremy and I never argued about money, though. We always pooled everything we made and never kept tabs on who was earning or spending more. For better or worse, we were in it together. Eventually, I left both jobs and applied for a position at the Belcourt Theater. It was a minimum-wage gig with minimal tips. I worked the booth, selling movie and concert tickets and popcorn, candy, wine, and beer.

The theater itself was historic to the city of Nashville. It was built as a silent-movie house in 1925 and was home to the Grand Ole Opry from 1934 to 1936. It also hosted concerts, which was a definite motivation for landing the job there. I wanted to work at a place with culture, music, and class. The whole establishment felt very European; it showed foreign films, indie films, and music documentaries, and it served as an art space and showcased local visual artists. The paintings on the wall in the lobby changed monthly. Everyone who worked there was quirky and hip. Having free rein to watch all of those films inspired me to write stories and lots of songs. I felt tapped into culture and creativity, taking it all straight into my veins and pouring it out on the page.

One of the first films I watched there was the 1970 documentary *Gimme Shelter* about the Rolling Stones' concert at Altamont Speedway in San Francisco. The Hells Angels had been hired as security, but violence broke out and a fan was tragically killed. One of my coworkers, Manda, convinced me the best seat in the house was sitting on the stage behind the screen. We both quickly shotgunned a beer and then walked up the small wooden staircase to the stage. The screen was translucent, and you could see the entire audience through the projection of the film. Mick Jagger was up there shaking it like a Vegas showgirl. I gazed through his image to see the crowd's reaction. It was exhilarating and terrifying.

"Can't they see us?" I asked.

"No, they can't see a thing but the movie in front of them. Isn't this fun?" Manda smiled and pulled a joint out of her cigarette pack. "We smoke back here all the time." She pulled out a lighter and sparked it up.

We sat cross-legged on the floor and puffed away as we watched the film unfold in front of us. I had found my dream job. I mean, I still had to mop the floors, scrub the toilets, wash the glass doors in the entryway, empty the ashtrays, drain the water in the hot-dog steamer, and clean the popcorn machine with crazy chemicals. But I figured all the work was building character.

The paycheck was meager, but the change from the restaurant business was refreshing. Plus, I could see all the movies and concerts I wanted for free and eat all the watery hot dogs and popcorn covered in sriracha I wanted. In my time working there, I was able to see Lucinda Williams, John Prine, Ben Folds, and a slew of other artists I adored. I even got the chance to meet Emmylou Harris and to pour her a glass of white wine one evening at a benefit. I followed her around all night, making sure she was taken care of.

Jeremy and I hit a new level of poverty. We rode our bicycles everywhere to save on gas. We scrounged for our meals. There was a sandwich place where we could score a free lunch every now and then. You ordered by writing your name down on a piece of paper and picking all of the ingredients. Then you sat down and ate and paid before you left. It was a flawed system, and we took advantage of it. We used fake names and alter egos. I was "Alice" and Jeremy was "Henry," but we didn't keep the names for long; we always switched it up. I'm not proud of it, but hunger will make you do all kinds of things.

We had both read Abbie Hoffman's *Steal This Book* and felt inspired to live as far outside the law as we possibly could. We adopted the mindset of near anarchists: the system was screwing us, so we should screw the system. We walked into department stores, grabbed a shopping cart, threw in whatever we needed or wanted, and walked right out the front door. We were young and careless, and the crazy thing is we never once got caught.

Our music reflected our punk spirit at the time. We assembled a four-piece band. I played acoustic, Jeremy played electric, my friend and Belcourt coworker Andy Holmes was on bass, and Luke Amelang was on the drums. Our first gig was at our old stomping ground, Cafe Coco. The cover was five dollars and the sound guy cost us fifty bucks. No one came except for a few close friends whom we had put on the list. Only three people whom we didn't know came and paid, including a guy named Jason White, who would eventually join our band as our bass player. So we made about fifteen dollars, but then we had to scrounge up thirty-five more dollars for the sound guy. The night was pretty humiliating, a total waste.

We were slowly working our way through the list of clubs I had written down in my notebook. Through word of mouth, we procured a gig at a dive called the Springwater Supper Club and Lounge. It is the most notorious of shithole venues that Nashville has to offer, but I mean that in the best way. It smells like stale beer and urine, the microphones shock your lips if you touch them, and you could probably pick up tetanus if you walked around barefoot—but boy does it have charm. Giant velvet paintings of naked women adorn the walls. The beers are cheap, and you can smoke inside. People are always locking themselves in the bathrooms to do cocaine and God only knows what else. The underground rock scene there was thriving, and we tried to fit in to it, but our band stood out like a sore thumb.

We worked on songs for a full-length album but only ever made demos, because we didn't have the funds to record it properly. It was called *Black Flowers* and the songs were working-class, antiwar protest tunes. We booked more shows around town but had a hard time finding a scene that accepted us. We were too country for the rock scene and too rock for the country scene.

CHAPTER 9

Floating

In 2006 our lease at Indiana Avenue ended. Jeremy and I didn't want to get into another lease right away. We were immersed in our writing and felt unmotivated to get better jobs that might be more lucrative. We had played a lot of small gigs in town, but we felt chewed up and spit out, disenchanted with Nashville. A lot of bands in town had a good buzz going and could draw fans to their shows, but we sure weren't one of them. Aside from our one write-up in *All the Rage*, we had no local press. We were outcasts and pariahs, and we were burned out on living this hand-to-mouth existence.

Around every corner was a bill we couldn't pay or a debt collector calling us. The heavy load of dereliction weighed us down. We made the decision to sell everything we owned and travel out west to Colorado. Some fresh air, open space, and a change of scenery was what we needed.

We dragged our belongings onto the front yard. In the too-bright light of day, our ragged possessions were exposed, on display for the entire neighborhood: a few priceless antiques, but also my peasant dresses and thrift-store clothes, Jeremy's sweaters and corduroys, our couches and chairs. We also sold all the music gear we had collected over the years: our beloved piano, microphones, our reel-to-reel recorder, amplifiers, radios. Everything must go. We planned to live with nothing, like monks, and thought about how good the mountain air would be for our souls. We'd live off the land, become one with the moon cycles, and find a group of people to belong to. And we would write the best songs we'd ever written. Just me and Jeremy and Creedence, living like hippies in a tent down a dead-end road, in the foggy foothills of Boulder.

We made about $2,500 from our yard sale, and it felt like a fortune. We rented a small storage unit in Nashville for the remainder of our sentimental belongings, mostly our photos and records, and left town. As the Nashville skyline disappeared in the rearview mirror, I felt sad and defeated but still hopeful about what lay ahead.

We headed to Illinois to visit my family first. When we arrived at my parents' house, they lit up the grill and my dad cooked us steaks. My sisters greeted me warmly; we all wrapped our skinny arms around each other for a big group hug. I missed them both dearly and was amazed at how much they'd grown. Both of them were taller than me.

I borrowed what we could from my parents. They were happy to help us on our adventure, as they had really warmed up to Jeremy. Since we had started living together, my mom had become less overprotective, and she no longer demanded to talk to me on the phone every day. My dad helped us pack and supplied us with a machete, a fire starter, a cooking pot and pan, sleeping bags, flashlights, batteries, and other supplies, including a cooler full of deer sausage. He even took us to a sporting-goods store and bought us both pairs of brand-new hiking boots, because Creedence had chewed about every pair of shoes I owned. My dad took one look at Jeremy's thrift-store boots and laughed. "Those aren't gonna cut it."

I don't think my folks understood exactly what we were doing, but they supported us as best they could. My mother worried about my safety, as any mother would—it was hard to let her firstborn grow up. She pulled me aside the night before we left. "You know I absolutely adore Jeremy—he's very nice—and I'm glad you have him so you're not alone out there, but I just don't know how he is going to take care of you without a decent job."

"Mom, I don't have a decent job or a college education either, and I don't need anyone to take care of me. I'm going to take care of myself." I tried to sound confident, even though I was also uncertain. "Remember what you said when I was little? Women can do anything!"

"I know, Margo, but it's just so hard to see you struggle, and..." Mama began to lead herself down that endless trail of worry that she knew so well before I cut her off.

"We'll figure it out. I promise."

She laughed and cried and finally hugged me. The two of us rejoined the rest of the family at the kitchen table to imbibe and play a game of spoons. The next morning, Jeremy and I woke up early, for a change, and set off.

As we drove toward the mountains, we blasted Ralph Stanley, Hank Williams, Alice Gerrard, and Hazel Dickens. We played the new album by Loretta Lynn and Jack White, *Van Lear Rose*, and sang "High on a Mountain Top" as we made the long drive. With some of the money from the yard sale, Jeremy had bought me a cheap mandolin for my birthday. I wore a straw cowboy hat and sat in the passenger seat, picking out chords and singing songs, my dirty, shoeless feet tapping the windshield. Creedence was squeezed between us, perched up on the glove box, curious where we were going.

We made the trek in just a couple of days and stopped in Boulder to take in the scene and grab a bite. We dined like royalty at a fancy log-cabin restaurant that overlooked snow-covered mountains. We feasted on a single steak split two ways and some red wine. The new surroundings and the altitude made us euphoric. We were drunk on love and adventure. That first night we cuddled together under a heap of blankets in a cheap motel outside the city. We made plans to wake early and hit the road the next day. It was a two-and-a-half-hour drive to Grand Lake, where Jeremy knew of a secluded camping spot.

We stopped on the way to buy more supplies, including eggs, rice, canned beans, soup, dog food, and toilet paper. When we arrived around noon, the sun was shining bright, illuminated by the snow on the ground. A red-tailed hawk flew over my head as we walked from the car to the middle of a thicket on a dead-end road. I took it as a good omen. I loved the simple beauty of the untouched spot, and best of all, it was incredibly secluded. There was only one other person camping, in a small tent far away from where we set up our camp.

We found the perfect place to build our makeshift home, among the massive pine trees next to the Fraser River. Creedence was happy to be out of the car and immediately began smelling the scents and marking his territory. Jeremy and I went straight to work, assembling a tent we'd stolen from a department store in Kentucky. We dug out a spot for our firepit and placed two little folding chairs on either side.

The temperature dropped quickly as the sun faded away into the slate-colored rocks. Jeremy started a fire and cooked some beans and rice with hot sauce as our first meal. We took out our guitars and played until well past midnight. Then we crawled into our tent and snuggled into a single sleeping bag, talking of what was to come and dreaming with all the stars in our eyes.

For the first week or so, we stayed in the forest and made no plans to see anyone in town. In the mornings, we boiled water for coffee and cooked eggs in a cast-iron skillet over the fire. We read poetry and our favorite passages from books to each other before splitting up to write songs and compose melodies in separate corners of the woods.

Many afternoons, the sun grew warm and peeked through the tops of the trees, and I would sunbathe naked and pick the guitar. It was so nice to work uninterrupted. We had all the privacy we needed to create.

I was strumming on my old Gibson one morning when I heard Jeremy cussing up a storm in total disgust. "Dammit, Creedence! You little bastard. What the hell?!"

I walked back through the forest, following his voice to a clearing. "What on earth is going on?"

"He rolled in something that smells terrible," Jeremy said.

Creedence had a big goofy grin on his face, and flies swarmed around his head. He was covered in feces. I started to laugh hysterically.

"Oh my God! He's covered in poop! I told you that you had to dig the hole deep. You can't just shit and cover it up with a couple of leaves." I was laughing so hard, tears rolled down my face.

"Yeah, I know. It's too late now," Jeremy said angrily.

There were no showers nearby, no running water, no toilets. When we needed to shower, we'd planned to go to the YMCA to a private family bathroom.

"I don't know . . . not my shit, not my problem. How about you bathe him in the river?" I suggested.

"It's freezing cold! And do we even have liquid soap?"

"I have shampoo! I'll grab it for you." I went to the car to grab my bath supplies and a towel.

Jeremy rolled up his jeans and pulled Creedence to the edge of the river by his collar. "It's so, so cold! Dear Lord. Creedence, be still!" Creedence fought the bath with all his spastic might. I sat on the bank trying not to giggle. After about ten minutes, Jeremy sat down on a rock and let go of the leash. "This is terrible. I can't get him to sit still. He won't listen to me. He's still got it on him."

I got up and walked into the frigid water. I finally got Creedence to sit still and got our ornery pup clean. It was a messy morning. We had to visit a laundromat and the YMCA shower afterward.

Most mornings we stuck to our routine, but some days we treated ourselves to a nice breakfast at a little cafe called Rosie's. It had a breathtaking view, strong coffee, and the best honey-butter pancakes I'd ever had.

After a couple of weeks of seclusion and writing, we made our way to the towns. We were running low on money and weed, so it was more out of necessity than desire. Pearl Street in Boulder was a special place for us. All different kinds of people gathered there, and it felt like a carnival of sorts. There were minstrels with violins, drummers, fire twirlers—

all playing on the street with their tip buckets full of paper money. After a stroll up and down the street, we looked at each other and knew what we had to do.

We decided we would busk rather than try to find jobs. We opened our cases, got our guitars out, and began to play. We played originals, but usually covers got better tips because people recognized the melodies. We worked up "One More Cup of Coffee" and "Oh Sister" by Bob Dylan and peppered in some Simon and Garfunkel, Beatles, Joni Mitchell. We cased people as they walked by and played what we thought they might want to hear. "House of the Rising Sun" always got people to open their hearts and wallets. They threw in quarters, nickels, and dimes, dollar bills, five-dollar bills, and sometimes a ten or a twenty. Occasionally we found flowers or joints sprinkled in there. Busking became our part-time job. We didn't have a schedule, and best of all, we didn't have to answer to anybody but ourselves. Once we had enough money for dinner and a bottle of cheap wine, we packed up, filled our bellies, and went about the business of getting drunk.

We made friends with a hippie couple we saw often on Pearl Street. Michael and Marybeth were street performers and fire spinners, and they had the whole routine down to a science. Not only were they very talented at the art of fire poi but they knew how to work a crowd. They started by chanting loudly and drumming on five-gallon plastic buckets. Then they turned the buckets over so people had a place to throw their tips as they started the real show. They poured lighter fluid on ropes and set them ablaze. Marybeth twirled and danced, spinning the fire as flames circled around her. Michael did flips and jumps, cheating death. For the finale, they spun fire around each other and performed lifts and tricks—all of their most dangerous moves. They took the bucket around one more time and thanked everyone for taking time to enjoy the show. They lived up in a mountain town called Nederland in a little shack. Aside from the fire spinning, they hadn't worked in five years.

One day I had a brilliant idea. "Jeremy, what if we made a sign, something that says, 'Just married, need money for rings.' People will love that! And, I mean, it's not too far from the truth. We don't have money for rings, and we would get married if we could afford to."

"I love it," he said. We got a piece of cardboard and a marker. We set the sign up in our guitar case. We played love songs all day. People walked by and smiled at us and the sign.

"Isn't that romantic?" they whispered. "Adorable!" "Congratulations!" The tips were extra generous with our new hustle.

After a few weeks, we were hungry for proper gigs and more spotlights.

"We should try to get a couple real shows out here," Jeremy suggested. "I mean, we have CDs to sell, so why not?"

We started looking in the paper to see where there was live music. We walked into restaurants and clubs, asked for the owner or booking agent, and introduced ourselves. We handed them our CDs, but they wanted to know what our online presence was. Neither Jeremy nor I really had much interest in putting ourselves or our music online back in those days. In our humble opinion, Myspace and Facebook were just more ways to be owned and tracked by the Man. A lot of people said they would call us back, but a lot of other venue owners just flat-out said no.

"Ah, it's mud season right now. We're not really doing live music." "Oh, we'd love to have you, but we need bands with more of a following." "Folk duo? Nah, that ain't gonna sell tickets. We only have jam bands play here."

Finally, we found a coffee shop called Burned Toast that said we could do a set, but we would have to do the sound by ourselves. "No problem!" Jeremy said enthusiastically. We played separate sets and sang a couple of songs together at the end. We made some tips, sold a couple of CDs. There weren't many people in attendance, but it boosted our confidence.

We were told by a guy we met at the coffee shop that there was a lodge up in the mountains called the Millsite Inn. It was in a small town called Ward. We called them up and asked if we could play sometime. "Well, sure!" said the woman on the phone. "We love havin' some live music up here! If y'all can make the drive, you're welcome to play as often as you want. How does next weekend sound?" We confirmed the date and started working up new material.

The drive up there was slightly treacherous. It was still mud season, so the roads were slippery, and we had to watch out for rockslides. We got lost on the way, and I could see why no one else wanted to play a gig there. It was nine thousand feet above sea level and in the middle of Nowheresville. After taking a few wrong turns and getting into an argument about the best route to get there, we finally arrived.

The Millsite was a log-cabin hotel with a restaurant and bar attached. It had a lot of rustic charm. There was a wood-burning stove in the corner and stained-glass chandelier lamps hanging above the tables. The place had opened sometime in the early '80s. The bartender filled us in on the history as we loaded in. There weren't many people in there, and those that sat drinking were no doubt locals. A few old men huddled in the corner playing poker and smoking hand-rolled cigarettes, and a couple of rival biker gangs drank beers together outside in the parking lot. The inn was supposedly haunted by a ghost named Carl.

The sweet couple who owned it offered us a free meal of pizza and some beers. We accepted and ate quickly, as we were famished. They also let us bring Creedence in to roam around freely. As night grew near, we checked the microphones and got the mix right. A fur trapper came over to talk.

"I heard there was live music tonight. What kind of stuff do you play?"

"Folk, blues, country, rock and roll—roots music. All sorts of different stuff," Jeremy said with a smile.

"I'd love to sit in. I brought my harmonicas," the man offered.

"Well, feel free to jump up if the mood strikes ya. We love to play with other folks," I said.

He was bearded and dirty, and he wore a fur hat and animal hides. He was also barefoot and explained that he hadn't worn shoes in twenty years. "People don't need 'em. Shoes make your feet soft. If you go without them, you build up calluses. Better for the spine."

We began to play. The fur trapper jumped up immediately and joined us on a Neil Young song. He ended up sitting in for most of the night and even accompanied us on our original songs. The evening rolled on and on. We played every song we knew and some we didn't. The locals were gracious and so were we. Jeremy and I both sold some albums, made some tips, and were fed twice. We couldn't ask for more. With full bellies and happy hearts, we went back down the mountain to our campsite near the river. By the time we got back, it was the middle of the night and much too late to build a fire. We parked on the dirt road, walked out to our tent with nothing but a flashlight, and crawled into bed.

About twenty minutes later we heard a stirring in the woods. Something big was walking around out there, and we lay as still as we could, afraid to even breathe. We held on to each other and whispered into each other's ears.

"What should we do?" I asked.

"Don't move," Jeremy said.

Even Creedence, who normally barked at every single sound, sensed the fear and sat in total silence, sniffing the air. It could have been a moose, a mountain lion, a bear—we didn't know and didn't want to find out. This went on for about thirty minutes, until whatever it was finally left the area. We made up our minds the next day that we needed protection. We went to buy a gun.

There was a little town called Tabernash that sold firearms, so we drove there with a handful of cash. The owner gave us the hairy eyeball when we walked in. I'm sure he was thinking, *What the hell are these hippies doing in here wanting a gun?* But a sale is a sale, and he graciously showed us his selection. We finally decided on a shotgun that had a twenty-two-inch barrel.

"Now, this is typically used for duck hunting, but it sounds like you just need it to scare off predators. If that's the case, I can grind it down for you. It's pretty long to be toting around," the old man explained.

"Yeah, something shorter would be nice," Jeremy said. "Go ahead and take some length off of it."

The old man took the gun to the back room and came out about twenty minutes later with four inches shaved off. "It's only eighteen inches long now. It's gonna be illegal in most states, but if you're staying here, it's not a problem."

Jeremy and I looked at each other and shrugged. "Thanks," we said hesitantly. I handed the man my ID and he gave me the gun. I was now the owner of an eighteen-inch sawed-off shotgun.

"Be safe out there," warned the old man, eyeing Credence. "Those mountain lions will kill your dog if you ain't careful. And they'll hunt you too."

"I sleep with one eye open," I said with a Cheshire grin and threw the gun over my shoulder.

We drove out to a remote canyon to fire some shots into the void. The sun was at high noon and it was hotter than a scorpion pepper up on the ridge. I could see for miles, but the heat made the landscape look wavy and surreal, like a Dalí painting. Jeremy fired the gun first. Creedence jumped out of his skin and ran to take cover under the car.

"Woah, this thing has a really intense kickback." Jeremy rubbed his shoulder. "I don't know if you're gonna want to shoot this."

"Bullshit I'm not gonna shoot it. It's *my* gun." I was offended. "In case you forgot, this isn't my first rodeo. I grew up shooting guns! My daddy taught me how to shoot skeet when I was ten years old."

"I'm not saying you can't, but it's hard for me to shoot and I'm experienced too. Not to mention you only weigh 105 and this gun has a lot of force."

"I'll be just fine." I grabbed the gun from him and walked to the edge of the rocks. I aimed at a tree far off in the distance. Lining the barrel up with a branch, I took a breath and fired. The gun kicked back so hard, I spun around on my bootheel in a near three-sixty.

Jeremy dropped to the ground. "Holy shit! I thought you were gonna kill me."

"Woah, you weren't kidding. This thing has some serious kickback!" I laughed. It scared the crap out of both of us, but no one was hurt, aside from my bony shoulder and my pride. "Let me give it another try. I'll hold on to it tighter. I promise."

Jeremy took cover behind the car and I put a giant sweater on my shoulder to pad it from the gun. I was determined to shoot it properly. I loaded another shell and took aim a second time. When I fired, I didn't spin around like the first time, but it felt as though my shoulder had been ripped out of the socket. I gritted my teeth and refused to show that I felt any pain.

"Nice! You feel satisfied now?" Jeremy asked.

"Yep, I do. At least I can handle an emergency if it comes our way." I got down on my knees and tried to convince Creedence to emerge from under the car. He was gun-shy and wasn't having any of it. I had to drag him out by his collar.

Jeremy and I stayed a few more weeks in the mountains. We continued showering for free at the YMCA, busked most days on Pearl Street, and returned home in time to light a fire and fall asleep in our cozy little tent. I loved everything about being there and felt rejuvenated by the mountain air and the howling call of the wilderness. I was exactly where I wanted to be.

Heaven can't last forever, though, and we caught word that Jeremy's dad had fallen ill again. He'd had serious health problems in recent years because of an ulcer surgery gone awry. He had also undergone multiple surgeries to remove his esophagus and replace it with a piece of his intestine after a negligent nurse had punctured a hole in his throat, causing him to contract sepsis.

"I need to go be with him," Jeremy said one morning after he got off the phone. "He's not well."

I understood, but I was sad that our time in the mountains had come to an end. I wasn't finished soaking up the inspiration of the Wild West yet. Plus, I had nothing waiting for me back in Nashville. No home, no job, and I couldn't bear to go back to waiting tables. The thought of it drained me spiritually.

As we packed up our campsite, I picked a handful of Indian paintbrush wildflowers. I held them in my lap as we merged onto Interstate 76. Gazing upon the silhouette of the snow-capped Rockies in the rearview, I cried all the way back east.

Even harder than leaving Colorado was the thought of being separated from Jeremy. "It's gonna be fine, babe," he assured me as we trucked along. "I'll go visit my folks for a month or so, and we'll make a plan to meet back up in Nashville." He was being realistic but still sympathetic.

I wanted to go with him, but we weren't married, and his parents wouldn't have us "living in sin" under their roof. So I moved back in with my parents temporarily, like the college-dropout-loser I felt I had become. It was humiliating. My parents didn't make me feel unwelcome, but it's easy to sense disappointment. I lay around in my childhood room for a couple of days, but it made me even more depressed. It looked exactly as it had the day I'd left for college. The shelves held my dance trophies, dried carnations, petrified rocks, found arrowheads, the sash and rhinestone crown that had once belonged to a homecoming queen. Pink paint covered all but one wall, which was papered in a delicate flower-patterned wallpaper.

Being home and in that room made me anxious. Little in there seemed to reflect who I had become. I went to the local hardware store and bought some cans of sunny-yellow paint. I put away most of my childhood relics—the trophies, the porcelain dolls, the ribbons and bows. I gathered antique photos of my grandparents and decorated the room with salvaged antiques I found in my folks' basement.

I made a plan to return to Colorado on my own, which my mother despised. But I had my dog and my gun, and I longed for the freedom to roam. I didn't want to be tied down to a job, and I was looking for some distraction to escape the loneliness I felt because of Jeremy's absence. I eyed my parents' beat-up Jeep Grand Cherokee that was rusting away in their yard like a lawn ornament. It had 276,000 miles on it; they were less than thrilled that I wanted to take it up and down mountain passes, but at the end of the day, they knew nothing was going to stop me.

A few days before I planned to make my escape, my friend Kate called me on the phone. We had met while working at the mall in Antioch, and she was my closest friend in Nashville. Kate had thick, dark hair and cerulean-blue eyes. She didn't have aspirations to play music for a living, but we had similar musical tastes and she had a beautiful singing voice; we often harmonized together. She was also feeling stifled back at home in Tennessee and had never traveled much. When I told her my plan, she begged to come along. "I'll head north tomorrow. Don't leave without me," she pleaded.

She arrived in Aledo and we packed the car and drove out west. We must have played Johnny Cash's version of "I've Been Everywhere" at least a hundred times, more than enough to learn all of the words. When we arrived, we went straight to singing on Pearl Street. We had worked up harmonies to Bruce Springsteen's "I'm on Fire" and a bunch of my originals. We wore peasant dresses and walked around barefoot. People graciously tossed money and cannabis flowers into my open guitar case. It was late summer and perfect weather, but Kate wasn't much for camping, so we spent the first few nights in a dingy motel. We knew we would soon run out of money and had to make a plan so we could continue to live off the income of two street performers.

We found a gig up in a mountain town at a bar called the Lariat. It was full of rustic charm despite being one of the smallest stages I had ever played. The two of us shared a mic, and Kate accompanied me on my new songs. We brought the house down with a yodeling version of "Long Black Veil." When we finished we headed to another bar called Pancho and Lefty's after the Townes Van Zandt song. As soon as we sat down at a crooked little corner table, a couple of guys came up to us.

"Did we just see you two perform at the Lariat? Those were some pretty impressive song choices."

"Nope, that wasn't us," I said.

Kate kicked me under the table. "Why, thank you, yes, it was! Please excuse my rude friend."

"Do you want to come play some music with us at our cabin?" one of them asked. "We live just fifteen minutes up the mountain from here."

"Sure! That sounds fun!" Kate replied before I could answer. I was wary of strange men, especially after my experience with Doc. But they assured us that a large group of people were going, both women and men.

We followed them through the dark to a beautiful cabin at the edge of a dead-end road. There were other houses around too, spread out among the trees. The house was nice; it didn't seem like a place where a couple of young bachelors would live. One of the guys, Chester, explained that they were house-sitting. He and Kate took an immediate liking to each other, and he seemed nice enough, so we accepted when he said we could stay there for the night if we wanted. Chester played music too and got out a couple of guitars to pass around. We got drunk on beer, and soon everyone left one by one. I passed out on a pull-out couch in the living room. Kate and her new beau slept upstairs in his room.

The next morning I gathered my things to leave.

"What are you doing?" Kate asked.

"Well, we don't want to be intrusive. Shouldn't we go?"

"Go where? We have nowhere else to go. I'm going to make breakfast. Chester said I could." She made herself at home in their country kitchen, preparing eggs, bacon, and yerba maté tea.

Chester came downstairs shirtless and took a seat at the breakfast table. "I could sure get used to this!" In addition to frying up some food, we had cleaned up the remnants of the party from the night before. "So, what are your plans? Where are you two staying?" he asked as he took a bite.

"Funny you should ask," Kate started.

"We're on the no-plan plan," I interjected.

"We're couch surfing until I get a proper job out here," Kate said.

"Oh, well, feel free to stay here if you want. I'm actually going to be taking a trip and could use someone to look after the house for me. Are you ladies interested?"

"Seriously?!"

"We would love to," Kate said. "We can get the mail for you and take out the trash, anything you need."

"Well, then it's settled. You'll stay," Chester said. "Did you see the hot tub yet?"

For the next couple of weeks, Kate and I enjoyed the luxuries of free living, rummaging through the cabinets for cans of food and boxes of macaroni. We continued to perform on Pearl Street, and I explored the neighboring hot springs and went hiking and rock climbing often.

After a few weeks, we felt like we were wearing out our welcome. Kate and Chester's fling had run its course, and we realized we had nowhere to go but back to the cockroach-infested motel. I would rather have camped, but the motel was cheap and they let Creedence stay, so we dealt with the crummy conditions.

One evening after our shift on Pearl, we took our tips into a little Thai restaurant, and Kate started making eyes at another customer during dinner.

"You see that guy over there that looks like Bob Dylan?" she asked under her breath.

"The dude with the curly hair who looks like the 1966, too-many-amphetamines version of Bobby? Yeah, how could I not?" I laughed.

"Well, is he looking at me?"

"Yeah, he is. You gonna go talk to him?"

"No, I can't. I'm nervous."

"Just write down your name and number on a napkin, put it on his table, and we'll walk out the door," I suggested.

She scrawled her information down, but before she had a chance to give it to him, he walked over. He set down a napkin with his phone number scrawled on it and walked away.

"See? What a great move." I laughed. "You gonna call him?"

"Yep, you better believe it."

The next day she called him, and they talked on the phone for about an hour.

"Robbie. His name's Robbie," she said dreamily after they hung up. That evening, we went to his one-room apartment and played guitar for a few hours. He was a really nice guy, and his songs weren't too bad either. After songs were swapped, two bottles of wine were consumed, and the cigarettes were burned down to the filter, it was plain that Kate and Robbie wanted to make out. The apartment was so small, there was only one other room, and that was the bathroom.

"You can sleep in the bathtub!" Robbie joked.

"Ah, I'm fine. I'll sleep in my car," I said.

"You sure?" Kate asked, slightly worried.

"Yeah, it wouldn't be the first time." I left and drove out to Vasquez Road, where Jeremy and I had stayed. It was much too late to set up my tent, so I just reclined the seat and slept in the car with the window cracked.

I woke up with an aching back and decided I should set up my tent and camp again. For protection, I slept with the shotgun next to me. I kept it unloaded but kept one buckshot shell under my pillow. I didn't like the thought of keeping it loaded all the time, so I practiced loading and unloading it quickly before locking it into place. I liked the sound it made and figured that alone might scare away intruders.

Creedence was also a good lookout, and although he was only thirty-five pounds, he had the confidence of a lion. I have no doubt he would have fought a grizzly bear for me if he came face to face with one.

I enjoyed mornings the most, with my boiled coffee and two fried eggs. I stared up at the mountains and the vultures circling the trees. The most fitting tune I wrote during that time was called "Twelve Gauge." It was a minor-key dirge that told a classic story. I based it loosely on a film I'd seen about a man who went off to war and left his woman behind, leaving her to fend for herself out in the Wild West with a newborn. I weaved in my own experiences while living there alone in the mountains.

I always sleep with a gun beside the bed
And a shell under the pillow when you're gone
It's been cold, and it's getting colder yet
And while you are off at war, the night is long

And while you're alone, lying in some dusty trench
Drinking whiskey from your flask to keep you calm
I've been at home, sitting on the front-porch steps
And I'd rather see your face than the sun

(Chorus)
Oh, oh, oh, the night is long
Oh, oh, oh, the night is long
Since you been gone, time is dragging on
And I'd rather see your face than the sun

I had a dream, that I saw your silhouette
Stumbling over snowy peaks and mountaintops
The child I conceived on the day before you left
Has grown before my eyes and time goes on

Every now and then, a stranger comes on in
Lookin' for a little something he can own
They try and lay their head down upon my feather bed
But I shot them one by one and sent them home

I hid out on Vasquez Road for a few more weeks, but it wasn't as much fun without Jeremy. I missed him terribly, and I was even starting to miss Nashville. I called him on the phone, crying.

He didn't like that I'd been camping alone. "Come to Texas and stay here for a couple days," he said. "Then we'll head back to Nashville together. We can start over." He said his father was finally doing better. Tom was a fighter and had been through a lot, but he had proved to be tougher than the rest, beating the odds again and again, in true marine corps fashion.

I told Kate, and she was understanding. She had been gathering job applications all over Boulder and had some leads. I was happy for her. I promised to come back to visit.

We hugged each other goodbye, and I drove through the night to Texas. I was so excited to see Jeremy that I stopped only briefly to sleep in a Walmart parking lot. I made it in just a day and a half.

When I arrived in Dallas, Jeremy met me at a restaurant. We ran to each other in the parking lot, and he picked me up and spun me around in his arms. We went inside to fool around in a bathroom stall.

"You're too skinny! Have you been eating?" he asked.

"Yeah, I've been eating," I lied. "Just been a little depressed and a little broke."

Jeremy, on the other hand, had been working in the produce department of a grocery store called Market Fresh in McKinney, Texas, and had actually saved a little money. "Well, enough of that!" he said. "Let's eat and be merry."

We sat down and had a meal together and caught up on all we had missed, which was mostly each other. He had sustained himself on Bob Dylan's recently released record *Modern Times* and Leonard Cohen's book *The Favorite Game*. He gave me his tattered copy of the novel, which I would devour almost immediately.

"What's the plan, Stan? Where do we go from here?" I asked between bites of food.

"Back to Nashville, I suppose."

"I guess I'm okay with that," I said. "I don't want to let that town beat me. I've still got venues to cross off the list."

"Damn straight we do, baby."

We stayed through the weekend with Jeremy's parents. We pretended to sleep in separate rooms so as not to make them uncomfortable, but we secretly snuck into bed together during the night. It was frustrating, to say the least, and we packed our bags and headed east come Monday morning. Nate said we could stay at his house out west of Nashville in Fairview if we helped take care of his dogs.

Nate was always a rock in our life, and when we fell on hard times he took us under his wing. He also hired us to work at his self-owned company, Handy Giant Services. Nate was skilled at *everything*. He did interior and exterior painting, tiling, siding, and any other type of remodeling you could think of. Jeremy and I worked for him on and off over the next couple of years. Nate taught me skills I never thought I'd have. I learned how to paint perfectly with no tape by cutting in with an angled brush. Thanks to him, I can mud walls and do siding, roofing, and a bit of tiling and grouting. It was fun to work with him; we would get super stoned, turn on a record, and work the day away. He paid us both a great rate and was flexible with our schedules—and our flakiness.

Life in Fairview was nice as well because it was a slower pace than life in the city. I went to Bowie Nature Park every morning and hiked with Creedence. I took care of Nate's three giant dogs—two hardheaded pit bull mixes who were sweet but didn't listen worth a shit and a half-wolf breed named Kiowa. On many mornings I chased them around the neighborhood in my bathrobe.

Nate had a girlfriend moving in soon, so we knew it was time to make an exit. I was packing up my beat-up Grand Cherokee when Dave Harder drove by. He was doing electrical work on a house in the neighborhood. I caught up and he asked where we were moving.

"We don't know," I said. "Don't have anywhere to go, but we can't stay here any longer."

"Really?" Dave's piercing blue eyes were incredibly empathetic. "Well, hell—y'all could come stay out at my house. I've got a whole refinished basement and a one-room cabin with a wood-burning stove on the property. Been thinking of getting some roommates anyway to help with the bills."

"Oh, jeez, Dave. I appreciate the offer, but you don't have to do that. We'll find somewhere, we always do."

"No, I'd love to have y'all. It wouldn't be putting me out at all. I mean it," he said in his simple way. Dave sounded a bit like George W. Bush, though his accent was Southern Ohio/Kentuckian rather than Texan. "At least come check it out."

Dave lived in Whites Creek, an area I'd always loved. It was just a little bit north of Nashville, and the town was unincorporated and all about simple country livin'. The idea of a one-room cabin on a hill intrigued me. I went inside to tell Jeremy about the offer, and he agreed, since it was our only prospect at the moment. We packed up our things once again and followed Dave out to the rolling hills of Whites Creek.

The whole setup was perfect. Dave's house was settled down in a holler. There was a giant bonfire pit out back with a wooden stage and a small barn for pickin' parties. Dave played upright and electric bass and had a great love of bluegrass and country music. He had a collection of old tube radios and, being an electrician, had speakers wired all over the house, even outside and in his carport, that blasted out 650 AM twenty-four seven. There was a wood stove in the main house, and mornings were always cozy. We fried up bacon and ate breakfast family style before Dave headed off to work. Jeremy and I spent the rest of the day writing songs and half-ass applying for jobs. Eventually, I got my job back at the Belcourt.

Jeremy got some work through my friend Erin, a waitress and coworker from the Flying Saucer days. She was an incredible cook and had started working at a business called Dream Come True Catering. The truth of it was, it was anything but a dream. The owner ran it out of a dirty trailer in West Nashville, but they had a decent reputation and booked events all over town. One was a monthly gig out in Whites Creek at a place called Cowboy Town. It was right up the street from Dave's, and they had shoot-outs, barrel racing, rodeo stuff. Dream Come True cooked classic cowboy fare: barbecue ribs, chicken, corn on the cob, baked beans, corn bread. Sometimes I picked up a shift or two doing prep or washing dishes, but it was menial work. I'd come in on a Monday and scrub dishes after an event or wedding. The faucet was leaky, so there was no water pressure, and the plates and platters were covered in dried, crusted food. I wasn't much of a cook, but sometimes Erin needed help making six hundred crab cakes, so I'd roll up my sleeves and pound them out.

Jeremy and I were still eaten up with the dream of music and the sickness of writing. We stayed at Dave's for several months but ultimately felt we needed our own space. We found a cute little place up on the hill behind Centennial Park on West End. It was on Parthenon Avenue, a three-story brick home with a bright-red door. There was a beautiful Japanese maple in the front yard. It was right across the street from the dog park, so Creedence would have a place to run free.

The house was split into three separate apartments, and we had half of the main floor and the upstairs. Jake and Sarah gifted us their small, brown spinet piano, and we treasured it so, even though it was slightly out of tune. We displayed it proudly right by the front door. The kitchen was bright and cheery, with a giant window for plants and herbs. We got our furniture and records out of storage and set up a music room in the upstairs. There were skylights on the second floor. We put our antique bed in the corner nook with an old paisley tapestry to soften the sun's glow where it poured in above us.

I took on yet another job, giving tap, ballet, and gymnastics lessons at the YMCA. I eventually worked my way up to be the director of the dance department there, but even still, it wasn't much dough.

The rent was modest, but we had to scrape together every cent we had to make it work at the Parthenon house. We could afford the deposit and first month's rent, but there was also a deposit for the gas to run the furnace. We had no savings whatsoever. I remember calling my parents and telling them about our predicament, and although they were sympathetic to our plight, they offered no money. Let's face it, I was a grown-ass woman and shouldn't have asked in the first place. When we moved in it was warm, but the seasons changed quickly. We spent that winter without heat to save money. It was the longest, coldest, most brutal winter of my life. We had one tiny space heater, and I dragged it all over the house with me. We wrote songs while wrapped up in heavy blankets and shivering in the freezing cold. All we could do was wait for spring to come.

The Prices, left to right: Steve,
my father Duane as a teenager,
Grandpa Paul, Gary, Flint, Linda,
and Grandma Mary outside on
the farm (1972).

My mother, Candace,
and me by the pool (1983).

When I was three and a half years old, my parents gave a tiny organ to my sister and me at Christmas. It came with sheet music, and I immediately taught myself how to play "Auld Lang Syne" (1986).

Three sisters, left to right: Britni, Kylie, and me (1995).

Jeremy took this photo of me playing mandolin at our campsite on Vasquez Road in Winter Park, Colorado (2008).

Standing in front of our 1986 Winnebago before our show at Cafe Boogaloo in Hermosa Beach, California (2008). Left to right: me, Jared Braucht, Aaron Latos, and Jeremy. Photo by Morgan Pence.

Performing at Carousel Lounge, Austin, Texas. Left to right: Jared Braucht, Aaron Latos, me, and Jeremy (2008). Photo by Karen Landon.

During the "Maybe We'll Make It Tour," back row, left to right: Jared Braucht and me; front row, left to right: Aaron Latos and Jeremy. We somehow procured a convertible for running errands while in Nashville and picked up a box of CDs to sell on tour (2008).

Right after Jeremy and I tied the knot, in White's Creek, Tennessee (October 26, 2008).

We scored some free studio time at the Tracking Room in Nashville. I was sitting in my guitar case, going over the lyrics of a song I was about to record, when Jeremy snapped the photo (2009).

Jeremy took this photo of me backstage in the green room before a Buffalo Clover show at the End, a rite-of-passage venue in Nashville located on the Rock Block (2009).

Jeremy and I often corresponded through little notes we left on the kitchen table. When I was working night shifts and he was working morning shifts, we saw very little of each other (ca. 2010).

Jeremy, I love you
I'm sorry
Here is my apology
I didn't mean for this to happen
Take it or leave it.

Love,

Margo

I'll take it
I'll make it
I'll shake it
I love you
so never mistake it

Jeremy

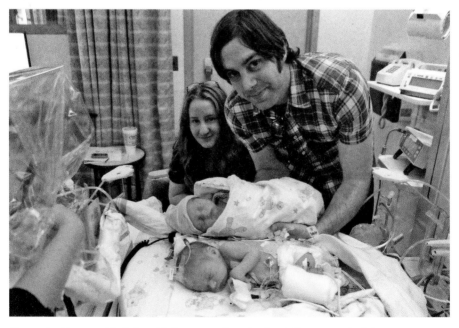

Our twins Ezra and Judah, with Jeremy and me in the NICU at Vanderbilt University (July 6, 2010). Photo by Candace Price.

Buffalo Clover, hanging with our van outside a gas station on Dickerson Pike, East Nashville (2013). The sign above us reads "Patrolled Area, No Drug Dealing, No Prostitution, No Loitering Here." Top, left to right: Jeremy, Houston Mathews, and me; below, left to right, Jason White, Matt Gardner, and Amaia Aguirre. Photo by Melissa Madison Fuller.

Jeremy giving me a good luck kiss moments before I stepped on stage to make my SNL debut at NBC Studio 8H (April 9, 2016). Photo by Bella Bronson.

The Pricetags and me backstage at The Tonight Show Starring Jimmy Fallon. *Back row, left to right: Jamie Davis, Dillon Napier, Kevin Black, and Luke Schneider; front row, left to right: me, Jeremy, and Micah Hulscher (2016). Photo by Danielle Holbert.*

Backstage at The Late Show with Stephen Colbert *(2016). Photo by Danielle Holbert.*

Kris Kristofferson and me backstage at the Newport Folk Festival right after we sang "Me and Bobby McGee" (2016). Photo by Greg Giannukos.

Working out a song while recording at Creative Workshop Studio in Nashville, Tennessee (2017). Photo by Danielle Holbert.

Willie Nelson with me (holding Ramona) onstage while singing gospel songs at Farm Aid, at the Alpine Valley Music Center, Wisconsin (September 16, 2019). Photo by Joey Martinez.

The family in 2020: Ramona, Judah, Jeremy and me, with our kitten, Shadow, and our pup, Zephyr. Photo by Danielle Holbert.

CHAPTER 10

Pearls to Swine

It came to our attention that the name Secret Handshake was already taken by an electronic artist with a much bigger following. We finally accepted that we needed an online presence if we wanted to book gigs. Everything was being done that way, and we had to move with the times, regardless of whether we wanted to or not. We started thinking of band names, and the phrase Buffalo Clover came to my mind. My grandmother had always talked about the plant and its resilience; it popped up wherever buffalo trampled the ground. Buffalo had become more rare on the prairie, and so too had the clover. I mentioned it to Jeremy, and he loved it.

I met a violinist from Memphis named Abigail Wilensky. She attended Vanderbilt University, where she studied violin performance at the Blair School of Music as well as the Suzuki method. Abi had bright-red roses tattooed on her collarbone and dreadlocks down to her waist. She began coming over for late-night jams and played along to my songs. I booked more shows in town, and she agreed to sit in with me.

When Buffalo Clover first started there was no set lineup. Aside from me on acoustic guitar and Jeremy on electric, we had random people play with us all the time. Jason White, whom we had met at our first gig at Cafe Coco, sat in from time to time. Nate played auxiliary on keys or drums, depending on what we needed.

We got a gig at Windows off the Cumberland—not to be confused with Windows *on* the Cumberland, where Jeremy and I had our first date. The owner went by the name of Boots. Boots had been forced out of his downtown building and relocated to a dive bar on the outskirts of town. He had a reputation for being unpredictable; sometimes he got too drunk at work and fought with the talent. Nonetheless, he was always kind to me, and I knew that deep down he had a good heart. Boots was a character; he had long, gray hair and always wore a cowboy hat. It was rumored that he used to be buddies with Townes Van Zandt back in the day. I seemed to be chasing Townes's ghost all over this town, and this time it was to Boots's new venue, a rundown shack that was once a biker bar and strip club.

There was a band on the bill called Darla Farmer, along with a song-writer named Lilly Hiatt whom I was really excited to meet. I listened to some of her songs prior to the show and they were so well written. I also knew we had several mutual friends.

The show was a lot of fun despite some technical difficulties and a bad PA system. Mariachi music and CB radio frequencies came through the monitors, and you could hear truckers talking back and forth to each other in between the songs. The microphones weren't grounded, and they shocked you if you touched them with your lips. All that aside, it was a great night of music, and we got the crowd up and dancing by our last song. I considered it a win.

Lilly's performance was really great—her songs and her voice blew me away. I remember feeling jealous of how effortless she was making it look up there, but that wasn't going to stop me from being her friend. The two of us got to talk and hang out after the set, and I liked how spunky she was right off the bat. Besides my new hippie violinist, Abigail, most of the crowd I ran around with at the time were men. I was so happy to have another songwriting girlfriend.

Jeremy and I continued to struggle and scrape to make ends meet and frequently overdrew our bank account. I can't count how often the electricity and water got shut off, or how many debt collectors and rent collectors were after us. We cared more about recording our songs and paying for studio time than having a full fridge or new guitar strings. Every spare cent was spent on studio time at the Bomb Shelter in East Nashville. The engineer and producer who worked there, Andrija Tokic, was a local legend in town and recorded exclusively with analog tape machines. Andrija operated on a whole other frequency. He was a young, hip, crusty punk genius who was covered in strange tattoos. The son of immigrants who had moved from Croatia to the United States, Andrija grew up in Washington, DC, and moved to Nashville to chase his dream of making incredible records. He built his studio from the ground up, from a combination of refurbished wood scraps he had bought from the Amish community and recycled materials he had salvaged from the trash while dumpster diving.

Andrija knew we were just a couple of poor kids looking to make a record, and he gave us a fair rate, promising he would work around the clock to finish the album. We had a collection of eleven songs, some of which Jeremy and I had cowritten, some that I'd written on my own. The whole album had abstract, mystic lyrics and a wanderlust vibe, inspired by Bob Dylan's *Desire*, Karen Dalton, the Velvet Underground, and poets like Sylvia Plath and T. S. Eliot, whom we'd read during our time in Colorado. The songs were drifting further from the blunt social and political themes of our previous work and more toward poetry, travel, and lived experiences. It was more earthy and folk centered, and our songwriting was definitely improving.

The instrumentation was simple. Jeremy and I played all of the guitars, Abi Wilensky played fiddle, Jason White played bass, Trey Gunther was on pedal steel, and my cousin Steve Maule was on drums. Steve was only seventeen years old but he was a complete prodigy. He had been playing drums since he was three and had won competitions as a toddler against teenagers. Steve mostly played in punk bands, and my stuff was definitely not that, but he was eager, versatile, and within our meager budget.

"What are we gonna start with today?" Andrija would ask excitedly as he bounced around the kitchen and made a pot of coffee. He had so much energy that at times it seemed he might spontaneously combust into a million pieces.

Jeremy, directing and producing in his own easy way, suggested "Luck," a sarcastic song that had definite remnants of our love affair with the Kinks.

I can't get well on what the doctor takes
Cheap wine and pills help to settle my shakes
Oh if I could, I would sail to the moon and fall asleep
Far from this tomb of debt and doom and misery

Oh Luck, you never knew me that well anyway
But when you came by, you never came by to stay

I've got a hole, in the wall of my town
A cup of rain and the highway sound
If it seems like I am losing my mind I just might
All my friends quit calling and they don't stop by

Oh Luck, you never knew me that well anyway
But when you came by, you never came by to stay

I burned the streets to every place that I pass
Black flowers bloom in a garden of trash
It's a wicked wasteland when you're out there on your own
But you can't feel the judgement when you're throwing all the stones

Oh Luck, you never knew me that well anyway
But when you came by, you never came by to stay

We threw ourselves into the recording process. Being in the studio made us both so happy. It was important for us to get our songs down properly and professionally, even if nobody else cared. We thought maybe we would be discovered long after we were dead and become cult heroes like Karen Dalton, Sandy Denny, or Vincent van Gogh.

We filmed ourselves on a little handheld camera and made homemade music videos and shorts to kill the time. I had a good collection of film cameras, and I took lots of photos with a thirty-five-millimeter Canon that my mom had passed down to me. Jeremy and I saved poems, little notes we left for each other, pressed flowers, and other sentimental tokens of our affection in photo albums: scrapbooks that were shrines to our love. I began decoupaging things and making avant-garde collages in my spare time. We spent hours together cutting photos out of old issues of *Time*, *Rolling Stone*, *National Geographic*, and other vintage magazines to make stop-motion animation for homemade music videos. My favorite one was for a song called "Ashes and Sand" from our lost album *Stealing from Thieves*. There wasn't a moment or a shred of creativity wasted. We were making do with what we had. As they say, necessity is the mother of invention, and invention was what we lived for.

I was trying my hardest to book shows with our new online press kit, but we weren't having much luck. We had no management, no booking agent, no label, and no real fan base to speak of. We'd reached out to a few people around town but hadn't had a single reply. It was pretty apparent that no one wanted to work with us.

"We need representation," I said one morning over coffee. "No one's going to take us seriously if we're reaching out ourselves and writing the venue owners personally."

"Yeah, you're probably right," Jeremy agreed. "What do you suggest we do?"

"Well, we could make our own booking agency. You know, create someone to manage us. I think people would take me a lot more seriously if I were a man."

"Obviously they would." Jeremy laughed. "But I'm not sure I know what you mean."

"We make a website, an email, a Myspace page, and say we're represented by this guy. He can write venues and book shows on our behalf."

"Actually, that's a brilliant idea. What will we name him?"

"I don't know. We need something that sounds professional." I scratched my head. "Something generic, like John."

"How about Sirota? John Sirota! I knew a guy in high school with the last name Sirota," Jeremy said.

We brainstormed how to fabricate this elaborate scheme. We wrote down a bunch of different ideas for what the company would be called and finally settled on Little Button Booking. We made two separate Myspace pages, a personal one for John and a business one for the company. We also created an email account.

Once we'd established our alias, I began writing to venues around Nashville as John Sirota. The difference in response was immediate—like night and day. Club owners said, "Sure! We'd love to book them. What date? Do they need support?" It was our best heist yet. Little Button Booking was the Trojan horse that opened those previously unlocked doors.

With John's help, we booked shows at 3rd and Lindsley and 12th and Porter. If we showed up and the club owner was frustrated about something—easy! We blamed it on John Sirota. He was our imaginary scapegoat. We gained a little ground in the scene, but progress was slow.

I enjoyed teaching dance and using my creativity to help children. The mothers of Green Hills weren't always easy to please; they wanted their children to perform to the classics like *The Nutcracker*, but I was choreographing routines to avant-garde songs like Brian Wilson's "Vegetables," the Beatles' "Being for the Benefit of Mr. Kite!," and Fiona Apple's "Extraordinary Machine." I even put together a year-end recital at the Belcourt Theater. It was good for my soul but it barely paid my bills.

One day I was giving my friend Steven a haircut at our house. It was late and Jeremy went out front to let Creedence do his business.

Suddenly, my overly energetic shepherd darted across the road to the hill toward the dog park. He must have spotted an animal or something. At the same time, a car came flying by. It nailed Creedence midstride. The driver pulled over to the side of the road when he realized what had happened. Creedence took off running and disappeared into the dark. The guy who hit him was a nurse from Vanderbilt. He felt terrible about it. Jeremy and the nurse finally found Creedence lying down, panting heavily, by a tree. He didn't appear to be injured too badly but he was not being his normal self. He had a glazed look in his eyes.

Jeremy rushed in to the house and told me the news. "He looks okay, but I know he can't be. The guy was driving so fast and hit him really hard. We should take him to the vet."

There was a twenty-four-hour animal clinic over in Berry Hill. We rushed there, but they turned us away because they were out of syringes. They directed us to Franklin Animal Hospital. It was about a thirty-minute drive, and along the way Creedence started to get lethargic. He lost control of his bowels in my lap, and I looked at his abdomen. I could see the bruising starting and knew he was bleeding internally. I began to cry. I loved that dog so much. He was so smart and protective. He had been there with me through my early twenties, and at times it had felt like he was my only friend.

I didn't have much money, so Erin offered to let me use her credit card. They hooked Creedence up to a bunch of machines and promised to do what they could, but thirty minutes and $2,000 later, he was dead. They handed him to me in a cardboard box. I was heartbroken. I knew it wasn't Jeremy's fault; Creedence had a mind of his own and didn't listen to anybody but me when it came down to it. Still, I was angry and took it out on Jeremy. I didn't get out of bed for three days. I buried Creedence out on Dave's property in Whites Creek, just downhill from the little one-room cabin.

After a year of living in the Parthenon house, our restless spirits longed again for change. And the neighborhood was changing too. Gentrification was creeping in all over Nashville. They tore down an entire block of homes next to us to build a giant condo development called the Acropolis. The construction was maddening. We stayed up late, and the workers started drilling and blasting at six or seven A.M. The entire house rattled so intensely, our paintings and portraits were shaken off the walls. Once again, it was time to leave.

Our record, *Pearls to Swine*, was finally mixed, but we had no label connections to help put it out. We could burn a few copies and give it to our friends, but what was the point? We needed to get out and play shows and sell it to the people. We needed to tour and play in other cities besides Nashville. Playing local was great, but it wasn't going to get us anywhere.

"We should book a cross-country tour," Jeremy suggested. "You and me. Coast to coast!"

"Exactly!" I agreed. "Like Festival Express or the Rolling Thunder Revue!"

"John Sirota can book it," he said. "We can get a van or an RV and just split."

"Yes, I need to travel. I need to see the world! I feel suffocated here!" I cried.

"We should have another yard sale. Make a little money for the lost highway."

Which is exactly what we did. Purging our belongings became the norm, so we both learned not to become too attached to anything. We took part of the yard-sale cash and pressed proper CDs this time. Jeremy ordered three hundred copies of *Pearls to Swine*, which included professional cardboard sleeves with our humble designs on them. The cover was a photo I'd taken on the thirty-five-millimeter camera in front of an 1800s farmhouse. It fit the spooky-gothic-folk vibe of the record. The title was a biblical reference, and it felt fitting to our plight. To cast your pearls to swine meant to offer something beautiful, valuable, or good to those who didn't understand it, and we truly felt misunderstood.

CHAPTER 11

Hell in the Heartland

Progress was slow, even with John Sirota's help, and booking a tour for a completely unknown band across America proved to be harder than we had thought. So we made a plan to temporarily move in with my parents and find jobs in the Quad Cities area. We would save money on rent, and then when the tour dates were finalized and we had enough cash, we would make a run for it.

"It's only temporary. We just need to make a nest egg," I explained to my mother. "We won't be here long."

My parents said we could stay as long as we needed. My mother and I did butt heads a little bit while I was there. I was feeling pretty free in those days: I was not into wearing a bra or much makeup, and I had grown out my armpit hair as a fuck-you to the patriarchy. My mother offered me $200 to shave my armpits. We didn't talk for a week.

Jeremy and I both found jobs in Davenport, Iowa, at the 11th Street Precinct Bar and Grill. He was a line cook and I was a waitress. It was less than ideal, but they did have live music. We thought we could maybe play a few shows there. We both worked forty-plus hours a week, pulling doubles, earning tips, and getting overtime when we could to make as much money as possible.

The place had been recently renovated, but the food was standard bar trash. They were famous for their tenderloin sandwiches. The smell of them made me gag. The manager was a chauvinist pig with a bad temper who had not worked in a restaurant before, and it showed. He was completely ignorant of how to run a restaurant. Sometimes paychecks were weeks late, and things rarely ran smoothly. To top it all off, the customers barely tipped ten percent and complained about everything.

Jeremy and I tolerated it as long as we could and told ourselves it was only temporary. But one day during a brunch rush, the shit hit the fan. Everyone on the kitchen staff was pissed off because payroll had messed up and the employee checks were nearly two weeks late. The waitresses were frustrated too, but at least we were walking off with some tip cash every day. To make matters worse, someone had robbed the cash earnings from the manager's office the night before by sticking their arm though the mailbox-like slot where they were deposited nightly. I had a funny feeling some of them thought it was Jeremy and me, because we had skinny arms. But we didn't do it.

During that hellish Sunday brunch, a fight broke out between Jeremy and the lazy owner-manager. Tickets were piling up and customers were growing restless. The manager was never around when you needed him most, and in that moment I needed him to reset the POS machine. And two of the line cooks hadn't even shown up. Jeremy and I decided then and there to cut our losses and we threw down our aprons. Like Gillian Welch says in "Everything Is Free," we didn't mind working hard—it was who we were working for.

We walked out hand in hand. Before I shut the door, Jeremy yelled over his shoulder, "We'll be back for our last couple checks!" We eventually got them and excitedly added to our pile of cash. We were more than ready to make our break from the Midwest before this mundane life swallowed us up.

With the help of John Sirota, I had booked shows in Illinois,

Tennessee, North Carolina, Louisiana, Texas, Arizona, and California. My childhood friend Jared Braucht was a like-minded soul and up for adventure. He agreed to come along as our bass player, but we struggled to find a drummer. We posted an ad on Craigslist and finally got a reply from someone who appeared sane and talented. He was a jazz drummer in Louisville, Kentucky, and he seemed to have pretty good credentials.

The only missing piece was a tour vehicle. With the money we'd earned at the last yard sale and working at the restaurant, we bought a 1986 four-cylinder Winnebago LeSharo, also found on Craigslist. Our parents said it was a money pit and a cop magnet, but we didn't listen. It had two full-sized beds, a table and chairs, a working stove and refrigerator, and a toilet. Most important, it ran. We picked it up in Sandwich, Illinois. It was freedom on wheels—freedom from rent, hotels, regular jobs, regular life. Freedom to tour and travel and live like wanderers.

We decorated the inside of the Winnebago with hippie beads and tapestries. We printed photos of our favorite paintings from the internet—Klimt, Frida Kahlo, Van Gogh—and hung them on every wall with sticky poster tack. Jared's parents bought us a generator from Farm and Fleet so we could run the AC when the engine was off. We stocked the fridge with groceries and planned to cook all of our own meals to save money. I finally gave in and shaved my underarms to appease my mother and collect my $200. I'd take all the money I could get at that point.

In June of 2008, we packed up our belongings and waved goodbye to my folks. For our first gig as Buffalo Clover, we traveled to DeKalb, Illinois, as a three piece. It was a small show at a modest little coffee bar called the House Cafe. Because I had friends there, the turnout wasn't terrible—some forty to fifty people who were actually engaged and listening. We played mostly original songs, but we also peppered in a lot of cuts from Bob Dylan's *Desire*, including "Oh Sister" and "One More Cup of Coffee." And we always covered "Meet Me in the Morning."

From DeKalb, Jared, Jeremy, and I made our way down to Louisville to meet up with our Craigslist drummer, Aaron Latos. We were taking a total gamble on him. The RV was small, but we needed someone to hold down the groove. It was a risk we were willing to take.

When we pulled up at Aaron's house we were greeted by a very young man. He looked like a teenager. He was tall and lanky and had light-brown, shaggy hair, baby skin, and an honest face. He shook our hands as we walked through the door to his duplex to set up for an audition and rehearsal.

"If you don't mind me asking, how old are you?" I asked.

"I'm nineteen. But I've got a lot of experience." He flashed me a smile.

I kept things upbeat but wondered if we would have a hard time getting him into the bars and clubs because he was not yet twenty-one.

We set up and started going through the songs. Aaron knew all the parts and had his own style. He played underhand, which impressed me. He had the feel of Charlie Watts and the swing of Ginger Baker, but he looked like a young Ray Manzarek. I knew after playing just two songs that he was the guy. Hell, he had to be—he was the only choice we had! But I was genuinely relieved at how well he played.

With one practice under our belt, we packed up Aaron's stuff into Winnie Cooper (the nickname we had given the Winnebago). On our way out of Louisville, we stopped at Cox's Smoker's for a carton of cigarettes. We also grabbed a six-piece fried-chicken bucket and made a pit stop at a drive-through liquor store. Then we headed south to play a gig in Nashville at our favorite watering hole, the Springwater.

When we arrived, we parked in Steven Knudson's driveway; he was our songwriter-painter friend whom we had met years back at the Hall of Fame Lounge open mic.

"Woah! This thing is pretty neat," Steven said in his Wisconsin accent as he looked around our new living quarters.

"Yeah! It's our home on wheels," Jeremy said. "And we don't have to pay rent!"

"We're gonna be living in trailer parks with people named Ethel and Hank, eatin' lots of canned goods, and talkin' about the weather." I was only half joking.

Playing at the Springwater was always fun; it was also probably the only place that would host us. We were early, so we played a couple of games of pool and darts and pregamed with some cold beers. My friends from the Belcourt and some from the Flying Saucer crew showed up. We reminisced and proudly showed off the Winnebago. It was our make-shift greenroom, since the Springwater only had a roach-infested mop closet of a bathroom. It was also the perfect place to smoke weed with a large group of people.

Steven opened the show for us. His dark voice and strange songs were a great match for our style. He had a homemade record called *Parsboro* that we listened to often in those days. It was like Dave Van Ronk mixed with Johnny Cash. During live shows, I sometimes sang harmony with him. He launched into his set of folk tunes in a minor key, and I joined him on my favorite song of his, "Let's Get Married (In the Morning)." Next was a band called Mountain Goats, with my friend Elle from the Belcourt fronting it with a ukulele. Her songs were fragile and bizarre and she had an awkward stage presence that I found endearing. Elle was a doe-eyed beauty, tall and thin and delicate like her songs. She played, and then we got up to do our thing. Lots of buildup to play last, but I welcomed it. The Springwater always brought out the punk in me, and Nashville amplified my competitive side. *One last show in Nashville before I head to California*, I thought. Somewhere in this great wide countryside I'd find a place where I belonged, and maybe, just maybe, it was out there on the West Coast.

I played like I had something to prove, because I did. I sang my guts out, pronouncing every word so that I could be understood through the dive's muddy speakers. The microphone shocked my lips several times, but I didn't let it faze me. I strummed my '56 Gibson like a maniac, treating it like more of a percussion instrument than a guitar. I shook my tambourine like a singer in a gospel choir. I was wearing a headscarf, like *Hard Rain*–era Dylan. Jeremy had donned a black, wide-rimmed hat with feathers tucked into the band. It was the band's first show together, and I'm sure it sounded rough around the edges, but it felt right.

The next day we were all struggling and ordered burgers to soak up our hangovers. It helped a bit, and then we went back to Dave Harder's place in Whites Creek to rehearse before we hit the road. We used the basement and even set up the camera to record ourselves. We had decided to film everywhere we went and had plans to release a documentary, tentatively titled "Maybe We'll Make It." After running through our material, we packed up and headed east for North Carolina.

Maybe we'll make it across the country without this ancient vehicle wearing out. And maybe we'll make it, break out, and get discovered. We were green and hopeful and deluded.

CHAPTER 12

Everywhere

The mood on the drive to the East Coast was light and happy. We talked and got to know each other. Of course Jeremy, Jared, and I were already pretty well acquainted, but Aaron was new to our tribe. We all took turns playing music through the speakers of the Winnebago. It was only equipped with a tape player, so we had rigged a Walkman to it so we could play CDs.

When we arrived in Wilmington, North Carolina, it was gray and overcast, but a warm ocean breeze floated in the air. The sleepy little beach town was charming, but the Juggling Gypsy was in a worn-down part of town.

Jared pondered, "Where are the jugglers? Where are the gypsies?"

"They come out at night," the bartender said.

"Perfect. We'll be here," Jeremy said. "We're the band. Where should we load in?"

It wasn't much of a stage, really—maybe just a six-to-twelve-inch raised area in the corner of the building. A bench lining the side wall was covered in cushions and pillows of deep reds, oranges, pinks, and yellows. A little sectioned-off table back in the corner had the vibe of an opium den beneath a canopy of silk and tapestries.

I pulled out a crisp twenty-dollar bill from a pile of cash I kept hidden deep inside my boot in the closet of the motor home and ordered the band some hookah. The four of us sat and smoked as the customers slowly started to come in.

"This is delicious!" I puffed out a smoke ring like the caterpillar from *Alice in Wonderland*. "Who . . . are . . . you?" I exhaled more smoke and worked on my French inhale.

Jeremy looked green. "I don't feel so good. I think I'm done. I'd rather just smoke a cigarette." He passed on his turn the next time around and lit up an American Spirit.

"All this smoke is too much," Aaron agreed.

Jared and I kept puffing away until the embers burned out.

"I just wish I could have dropped a big fat nug in there," I said.

"Green pouch time?" Jared looked at me with a knowing grin. He was referring to the stash of weed and the pipe we kept hidden in a tiny sack. We walked outside to get our minds right.

The small venue was pretty well occupied by the time we took the stage. There were freaks and weirdos everywhere—tattooed punks with brightly colored mohawks; women in midriff tops, with hennaed hands and nose rings; surfers; stoners; burnouts; goth girls; and everyone in between. We took the stage and channeled mystics, sang like a tortured canary. We always started the set with "Luck" and ended with "Midnight Circus." I tried my best to win over the crowd, who had surely never heard of us. Jeremy wore a vest and his wide-rimmed, black hat. I wore a head wrap and a pair of low-rise, light-brown corduroy pants and a tiny tank top. By the end of the set, sweat was dripping off my body, and my right hand was bleeding from strumming like a lunatic.

We went outside, where there was a firepit in the middle of a junk pile. Tires and trash lined the back of the building, and people gathered around talking and drinking and smoking.

It was a full moon, and everyone made plans to drive out to the beach and swim in the ocean. I was intrigued. We gathered our small amount of merch, took inventory of what we'd sold, and collected our door money—which wasn't much, but was better than nothing. Then we piled in the Winnebago and drove to a remote beach blanketed in moonlight. We removed our shoes and ventured through the tall grass, walking toward the roaring ocean. The leader of the group of locals hushed us, and I realized we were probably trespassing.

"Where is everyone from?" a surfer with dreads and a hemp necklace asked.

"Illinois, Kentucky, and Texas," Jeremy replied as he walked quickly to the water.

"Where are you headed next?" someone else wanted to know.

"Everywhere," I whispered.

"'Into the great wide open,'" Jared quoted Petty.

"The French Quarter," Aaron explained.

We came to a clearing in the tall dune grasses. Without discussion, the locals began undressing and waded into the ocean under the glow of the full moon. Jeremy and I looked at each other and shrugged. We had left our swimming suits in the Winnebago, so we surrendered to the night and the circumstances. The water was surprisingly warm, and the moon cast a dreamy haze on the Atlantic. We walked out into the tide, the waves gently meeting the shore with a low hush. Suddenly I noticed something strange below the surface of the water, an electric glow that looked like jellyfish moving around my body.

"Something's glowing in the water!" I panicked.

One of the girls laughed. "It's just moon plankton. They won't hurt you."

I looked down again. The plankton were beautiful—one of the most surreal things I'd ever witnessed. I swam out farther. The warm salt water cleansed my skin and hair and lungs. I felt reborn, new, and free.

We sat on the beach for a long time talking with our newfound friends before we returned to the Winnebago and fell asleep in the parking lot. We woke at dawn and drove west, our sights set on Louisiana.

Jeremy and I took turns driving. Jared also drove occasionally, even though he wasn't insured. It was a twelve-and-a-half-hour drive, so we stopped in Georgia for the night and stayed in a mobile-home park just outside of Atlanta. The redneck couple who owned the place showed us the ropes and made us feel right at home. It was a lot like camping, but there was a slab of concrete to park on and a place to plug in. We set out folding chairs and grilled some food.

Jared had a banjo he'd bought in a pawnshop in Davenport, Iowa, before we left town. It was a cheap old thing but it was his pride and joy. The headstock was adorned with the words "Riverboat Queen." He'd put new strings on it and was constantly working hard to learn chords and to integrate it into our set. When Jared played banjo, Jeremy switched from guitar to bass—he was versatile like that.

I could tell by the look on Aaron's face that the droning banjo was starting to wear on him, but he kept it to himself. Aaron had a jazz background, while the rest of us were self-taught and played straight from the gut. Nonetheless, we all sat around and picked songs while Aaron drummed away on an empty peanut can. Eventually the owner of the trailer park told us to put out our fire and wrap up the singin'. "Sounds like a bunch of hillbilly nonsense," I heard him mumble as he walked away. We put up the instruments but continued to party quietly, telling stories about the ghosts of our childhood and staring at the sky.

On our way out of Atlanta, Jeremy drove us by Newnan, Georgia, where he had lived as a kid. He had experienced supernatural and spiritual occurrences there and later found out the home was built on an Indian burial ground. He told me stories about wild bobcats with gold eyes staring through the windows at him, tales of demonic possession, priests, and exorcism. He talked of mysterious intruders that disappeared like shadows and haunted him before his family eventually moved back to Texas. I loved hearing about his past lives; Jeremy had a baby face and was only twenty-nine, but in my eyes he was as ancient and wise as Georgia pine.

After two days of driving, we arrived in New Orleans to find it still in something of a shambles. Hurricane Katrina had torn through the city only three years earlier. The poorer parts of town were still in pieces, and boarded-up buildings lined roads covered in debris. The skeletal remains of factories were evidence of a once bright and thriving city. In some parts of town, colorful painted homes were marked by floodwater stains, and folks sat out on porches looking defeated and disheveled. On the other side of the tracks, we found beautiful mansions with thriving gardens and sophisticated French architecture, neatly protected by wrought-iron gates and security systems.

We managed to find a Cafe du Monde. I ordered four black coffees to wake us up for that night's show at the Zeitgeist Theater. And I got a bag of beignets for us to share; we were all starved from the drive.

The evening's bill was not exactly your normal lineup. Instead of another band, the club owner had found a burlesque troupe to join us. The Zeitgeist was still being renovated after flood damage, but nevertheless it was better than the first two places we had played on our ragamuffin tour (we had also played a gig at the Springwater in Nashville). It actually had the feel of a proper venue.

The burlesque troupe was already in the dressing room getting ready in the yellow glow of the lightbulb-lined mirrors.

A half-naked women wearing fishnets and a top hat walked over to introduce herself. She was obviously in charge.

"Hello, darling! You must be Margo." The leader of the troupe gave me a warm hug. She was about four-foot-eleven and had bright-red hair. "I'm Lydia. Thanks for having us!"

"Thanks for doing this!" I said. "It's so great to meet you."

The other girls and a couple of drag queens all scurried about applying makeup, combing wigs, and taking curlers out of their hair. Some did it with a cigarette hanging from between their teeth. They were all different sizes and shapes, but they all wore a uniform of matching black sequin outfits and classic red lipstick.

"We've got something extra special worked up for tonight." Lydia shot me a devilish grin.

"Really? What is it? I've never seen a burlesque show before. I'm excited," I said.

"Oh, this isn't just any burlesque show. This is gonna be wild!" Her eyes flashed. "We're doing fire tassels."

"Fire tassels? What's that?"

"Oh, you'll see," one of the ladies said. They all began laughing and went back to the mirrors to apply their cat eyeliner and rouge.

I grabbed my guitar and serenaded them with a few songs while they got ready. It was nice to be around women, and I spent a couple of hours in the dressing room playing guitar and warming up my voice. I wasn't wearing much makeup in those days, and the only thing I did to get ready for the show was to put on a long, flowered peasant skirt that I got at a Goodwill, paired with a spaghetti-strap tank top. The skirt, a pair of corduroys, and my bell-bottoms pretty much made up my stage attire for the entire tour.

The owner of the Zeitgeist was up-front about how attendance had been since the flood. "People are still struggling. Not many folks even know we're open and doing shows because of all the construction and renovations."

"Well, that's okay, we don't have any expectations. We're just happy to be here and to help," I assured him. The band and I had agreed to donate any proceeds to the theater to help them rebuild.

"We've only presold three tickets," he said glumly.

"That's better than I would have thought!" I said, trying to cheer him up. "I don't even know three people in New Orleans."

He forced a smile and walked back to his office.

The walls inside the theater were painted jet black. The whole space had a lonely, ominous feeling about it. The stage was bare and the lighting was simple, just a few white can lights that shone down on the wooden platform in the back of the room. There were folding chairs set up in rows facing the stage.

The doors opened and a few stragglers entered. It was a standard five-dollar cover, and we had two people on the list. One was a friend of

Aaron's; the other was a guy named Clayton whom we had met online when setting up the tour. Clayton had been living in Los Angeles but had moved back to New Orleans a few months ago. He claimed to have connections in the music world and promised he could help get us a gig at the House of Blues in LA.

When Clayton walked in, Jeremy and I were slightly taken aback. It was clear he had recently been beaten up: his face was badly mangled. He had a black eye, a bloody lip, and a nose that looked to be sliding off his face. His head was shaved and covered in bumps.

"Hey! How goes it?" Clayton reached out to shake our hands. "I know, I know, I look bad. Got into it with my ex-roommate the other day. He hit me in the face with a mic stand."

"Oh, no worries, I can hardly tell," I lied.

"Good to meet you. I'm Jeremy." Jeremy was trying not to stare at him.

"Looking forward to seeing your band play!" Clayton slurred. With his facial injuries, he had a bit of a lisp—or he was already drunk. It was hard to tell.

"Yeah, we're happy to be here! First time playing in New Orleans," I said.

"Well, welcome! I hope you enjoy it here! Although, I'm trying to leave. I want to get back to Los Angeles. Hoping I might be able to catch a ride west with you guys."

"We're kind of crowded, but we can talk about it," Jeremy said.

"For sure, for sure. Well, break a leg!" Clayton slapped Jeremy on the back sort of aggressively before taking his seat.

We went back to the backstage area, which was just a black curtain that divided the room.

"I'm not getting good vibes from that guy," Jared offered.

"Me neither," said Jeremy.

"Yeah, same," I said.

"Who?" asked Aaron, who was busy tuning his drums.

"Clayton," Jared said.

"Clayton who?"

"Oh, I have a feeling you'll find out soon enough," Jeremy predicted.

The crowd was thin, but it was dark, so it was hard to get a head count. I didn't let it bother me. I was just happy to be in a new city, playing music for people who needed it. The night rolled on, and we did our thing. The burlesque troupe got up and danced to our songs, grabbing strangers' hands and pulling them onto the empty space in the center of the stage to spin-dance around like lunatics.

When we finished, we went outside for a smoke before the burlesque performers started their set. Clayton seemed floored.

"That was amazing! I know my friend Jacqueline will be happy to book you at the House of Blues in California," he said. "I know I can help you guys make some solid connections."

Little did Clayton know, John Sirota had already been in contact with the House of Blues. We were in the middle of picking a date to play. And although Clayton was trying to make a case for why we needed him, we knew we didn't.

"I can totally hook you guys up with some great shows. This place is a shithole. You deserve to be playing the best venues—not dumps like this," he said loudly as he drank from a thirty-two-ounce can of Miller Lite wrapped in a paper bag. He had brought his own booze to the venue. "Trying to save some money for the move," he'd explained when I'd eyed the beer.

"Well, I don't know about that," I said. "We're just getting started, after all."

"No, you do. Don't sell yourself short. I can manage you—you *need* a manager. Someone to help you connect the dots. I'd only want ten to fifteen percent." He was dead serious.

"Ten percent of nothin' is nothin'." I laughed uncomfortably.

"Well, maybe now, but later . . . you'll be raking in the dough and you'll need someone to keep you in line."

"I doubt anyone can keep Margo in line." Jeremy took a drag of his cigarette.

The burlesque show was about to start. We snuffed out our butts, took our seats in the audience, and waited for Lydia and her troupe to take the stage. The single bulb was low; the music started. I recognized it immediately. It was one of my favorite songs by Françoise Hardy. "Le temps de l'amour" pumped through the house sound system. The dancers came out single file and faced the black curtain; they swayed side to side in unison and slowly turned around. The moves were reminiscent of Bob Fosse. They flashed jazz hands and popped their knees to the rhythm.

For their next act, they deployed the fire tassels. Only three of them were brave enough to try it. Lydia and two other women took down their bras and revealed pasties with ropes attached to little marshmallow-shaped balls. Assistants seductively lit matches. Lydia and the others bent forward, their breasts dangling. Then, *poof,* the fire was lit, and the three women shimmied and swung their boobs left to right, right to left. People leapt to their feet and cheered at the dangerous spectacle. I had never seen anything like it. Everyone was whooping and hollering. As the song ended, the women threw blankets around Lydia and the others to put out the flames. The audience erupted in applause. It was a night we would not soon forget.

There was no money to be made that night from the cover at the door, since we donated it to the theater, but we did manage to sell a few copies of *Pearls to Swine* and to make a few fans. We pulled the Winnebago up to the back entrance of the building to load out our gear. Clayton followed, now clearly intoxicated.

"What are you guys up to? We should go drink!" he yelled into the void of the night sky.

"I imagine we'll probably partake in some of that," Jared said in his soft-spoken way.

"Well, where are you goin'? Let's *do this*!" Clayton clapped his hands together.

We were all getting a creepy feeling from him, but there didn't seem to be a way to shake him at that point.

"I heard about a local bar in the French Quarter that serves food late. I'm hungry," Jeremy said.

"Okay, great, I'll ride with you guys." Without being invited, Clayton climbed inside the sacred space of our RV. We exchanged looks and then got in behind him without a word. It was clear we would need to figure out how to ditch him.

The neon glow of the bar sign shone bright on the dark street. It was now nearing midnight, but we were just getting started. We ordered the cheapest beers on the menu and a couple of shrimp po'boys to share. Our budget was strict and our lack of money kept us thin. We sat out in the street smoking and drinking, sharing our food.

Clayton clung to us like a piece of toilet paper stuck to a shoe. He talked incessantly about his experience in the industry as he swayed back and forth.

"I used to be in a band, but there's just no money in it, ya know? And I'm much more productive on the business side of things." His voice slurred and his eyes were at half-mast. "The House of Blues is gonna love you."

"Yeah, I think they've already been talking to our booking agent," I said.

"Well, you'll still need me to put in a good word," Clayton bullshitted. "They don't do anything without my go-ahead." He went on, "You guys really need someone representing you. That's why it will work out great that I come along with you to California. It'll be perfect." As he said this, he was starting to pass out right there in the street, midsentence.

We made a plan to exit through the back of the bar and make a run for it. Slowly, one by one, we all left and piled in the Winnebago.

"Go! Go! *Go!*" Aaron screamed as we closed the door.

Jeremy started the engine and we sped off to Aaron's rich friends' house in the bougie part of town. They said we could park in their driveway and not be robbed or towed. We made up the beds and fell asleep.

The next morning, as we pulled away from the city of New Orleans, we sparked up a joint, blasted Led Zeppelin's *Houses of the Holy* through our crummy speakers, and headed for the interstate. We were bound for Austin, Texas.

I have a vivid memory of leaving Louisiana and driving over the twenty-mile-long Atchafalaya Basin Bridge. It stretches between Baton Rouge and Lafayette for more than eighteen miles. As we passed over muddy water and swampland, I imagined what might lie beneath us. I was sitting in the back of the RV, staring out the window and scribbling. I had a moment where I thought, *If these wheels ever stop rolling, I might die.* I was addicted to the road, to traveling, to meeting new people, to seeing new things. I knew I had to find a way to do this for the rest of my days.

Austin was a blur. We played at the Carousel Lounge, and again the crowd was thin. One of the guests in attendance was Jeremy's birth mother, Karen. She had given Jeremy up for adoption when he was born, and we had met her a couple of years earlier. Their relationship was and still is a complicated one. From the moment we saw her, it was clear they were blood. Karen had long, dark hair, a wiry frame, and beautiful olive skin that had been worn and weathered by her years working beneath the Texas sun. She lived in a trailer outside of San Antonio in a town called Canyon Lake, deep in the Hill Country, with just her dogs and her horse.

When we first met Karen, she was very open about why she gave Jeremy up for adoption. She'd been young and poor, and Jeremy's birth father, Alan, had abandoned her, leaving town on his motorcycle without a word. Karen's folks were deeply religious and threatened to take Jeremy away from her after he was born, so she went to a home for unwed mothers called the Buckner Baptist Benevolence. She was not only financially unable to care for him but also addicted to various substances—booze and hard drugs—and that alone made her completely unfit to raise a child. She later regretted putting him up for adoption, but it was probably for the best.

The crowd at the Carousel Lounge was nothing to write home about. Aside from Karen, her sister, and several drunk cowboys they had hauled along with them, it was a lonely Tuesday night. We played there in the dark room decorated with giant ceramic elephants and other circus creatures. Karen and her wild hippie family waltzed around drunk on the dusty dance floor as we played every song we knew well past the midnight hour.

Around two A.M., we drove about an hour south to stay the night on Karen's property in Canyon Lake. She was so excited to show Jeremy where she lived. It was a modest double-wide on a beautiful piece of property. She had it decorated so cutely—it felt like an old-time saloon, all wood and leather and delicate lace curtains and cowboy wisdom on the walls. A plaque above the stove read, "Never miss a good chance to shut up." We each drank a Lone Star Beer and bedded down for the night.

I awoke earlier than the guys the next morning and stepped out into the blistering Texas sun. The view was breathtaking. The terrain was rocky and dusty and covered in sagebrush. There was danger in the air; you knew there were rattlesnakes and scorpions lurking around somewhere.

Karen had made plans for us to ride horses that day. Her horse, Blues, was already on the property. Blues reminded me of my dear old Indiana, and I immediately climbed up on his back to do some rodeo rider stunts. Karen's neighbor brought in four other horses for us to ride. She saddled them up and we circled around the ridge and through the trails behind her house. The solitude was spectacular.

When we returned to the trailer, we watered the horses and fed them carrots and apples. Although we needed to get on the road to Arizona, Karen insisted we go up to her favorite bar, the legendary Devil's Backbone Tavern near San Marcos.

We piled in Karen's truck. She drove like a maniac, going seventy to eighty miles an hour on a thin, dusty highway the entire way there, puffing her cigarette and drinking her beer, which was tucked in a koozie that rested between her tan, muscular legs. She seemed to always wear the same uniform: cutoff Wrangler shorts, a pair of cowboy boots, a straw hat, and a tank top. At one point she leaned over and said, "Honey, you're gonna love this place." At least that's what I think she said; she was blaring Pinetop Perkins through the speakers and I feared for my life. But Karen was confident, and I was sure it wasn't the first time she had driven to the bar with a buzz on. I looked out the window and saw a road sign that said Purgatory Road and laughed to myself.

The Devil's Backbone was your typical roadside tavern for cowboys, hippies, bikers, and road-worn drinkers. I couldn't believe how cheap the beers were—$1.50 for a Lone Star! The entire joint was covered in defaced money, dollar bills stapled to the walls and ceiling, each one with a name or a quote on it in black marker. Along one wall was a shuffleboard table, and in the back was a pool table. They only served beer, but you were allowed to bring your own bottle of hard liquor as long as you kept it in a bag and set it down on the table if you weren't drinking it. Karen's sister, Kathy, met us there and brought some Crown Royal. We took turns pulling straight from the bottle, and I threw all my money in the jukebox.

I spotted Guy Clark's *Old No. 1* and began playing all his songs I'd never heard before. I was familiar with "Desperados Waiting for a Train" and "L.A. Freeway," but I'd never heard "Rita Ballou" or "She Ain't Goin' Nowhere." I was instantly transfixed. I got up and waltzed around the place by myself, until an old, random cowboy took my hand and spun me around the dirty dance floor. The locals had been wary of us at first, but by the time we left, we had made some great friends. I bought some Mexican dirt weed off an old hippie who said his name was Sheriff Marshal, but he wasn't a sheriff and he definitely wasn't a marshal. The band and I smoked with him out of his metal pipe back behind the bar.

After we had our fun with the jukebox, Jeremy and I sat down at the piano and played songs and sang at the top of our lungs. I played the low notes and he played the high ones, adding leads here and there. After singing Bob Dylan's "Winterlude," we decided it was time to go.

It was hard to say goodbye, but we had to hit the road. It was a fourteen-hour haul to Arizona. We drove for about six hours along Interstate 10 until we spotted a rundown trailer park. It was late and dark—no lights anywhere except for a blanket of stars and the constellation Orion and his dog, Canis Major, shining in the night sky.

The next day we continued down I-10, headed for the Goat Head Saloon in Arizona. Aaron took a shift driving, as the rest of us were burned out, but that only lasted ten minutes before he accidentally drove down a frontage road and nearly buried us in a ditch. I took over for the rest of the day after that and carried on strong into the night. Jeremy and Aaron eventually lay down in the back to sleep for a while, and Jared and I cranked the speakers and lit up a joint. We were nearing the Texas border town of El Paso when I spotted flashing lights and what looked to be a roadblock up ahead.

"Oh shit! What's that?" Jared pointed at a line of Border Patrol cars. I instantly felt paranoia kicking in.

We had reached Sierra Blanca, one of the most notorious Border Patrol checkpoints in the country. Willie Nelson and Snoop Dog had both been busted there. I threw the joint out the window. "It looks like they're doing a stop and search." I rolled down the windows and sprayed some perfume I kept in the glove box for such an occasion.

I slowed down as we approached the officers. My heart pounded in my throat. We had a pretty good stash of weed, and the van reeked from the freshly lit J we had just put out. My hair was a windblown tangle of curls, and I was barefoot and in need of a shower. Jared had a red bandana around his shaggy, light-brown hair. Jeremy and Aaron were passed out hard on the beds in the back.

"Hello, ma'am. How are you doing tonight?" an officer asked as we rolled up.

"I'm fine!" I replied nervously. "How are you?"

"Oh, we're doing well, thanks for asking." He smirked. "Where are you kids headed?"

Just then, Jeremy poked his head up from the back. "Where are we?" he asked sleepily.

That didn't look or sound good. Jeremy was shirtless, and his dark hair was hanging down in front of his eyes. We all looked suspect, no doubt.

"I hope you know where you are, son." The officer shined a flashlight straight into Jeremy's bloodshot eyes. "Where are y'all headed?" He sounded stern.

"Mesa, Arizona, sir," I said. "Actually, our navigation system has us going the long way—do you know the best route from here?" I flashed him a sweet smile, but I was sure my eyes were cashed, both from the weed and the lack of sleep. He most likely knew what I was doing; I liked to send police officers into civil-servant mode at any opportunity I could by asking them questions.

"Well, you're on the right trail. You've got a long ways to go . . ." He stopped midsentence. "You don't have anything or anyone illegal in this vehicle, now, do you?"

"No, sir. We were all born and raised here in the States. All proud American citizens," Jared somberly noted.

"Good . . . good. Could I see some identification?"

"Yes, sir. Of course, sir," I replied.

Everyone passed me their licenses and I handed them over. The officer took them back to his booth, ran our info, and kept one eye on us as he talked to another officer. He walked up to my side of the vehicle and returned our IDs.

"Alright, you're free to go, Ms. Price. Safe travels."

My heart was beating out of my chest. A huge wave of relief washed over me. Thank God they hadn't searched the Winnebago.

"Thank you, Officer. Adios!" I put the van into drive and didn't look back.

"That was a close one." Jared laughed nervously.

"No shit! And it killed my buzz." I cranked up the volume on the speakers again. "Let's roll another one!"

"Green pouch!" Jared yelled.

We lit up a joint and drove straight through New Mexico and into Arizona. The desert stretched around us as far as we could see.

CHAPTER 13

Mesa Boogie

Mesa was so hot, we literally fried an egg on the hood of the Winnebago as an experiment. We stayed for a night at my friend Tyler's mother's house. Jeanie, his mom, had a lot of money and lived in a pristine home inside a gated community. She offered us clean beds, the opportunity to do laundry, and much-needed showers.

They had immaculate landscaping with beautiful white and pink stones, aloe plants, and cacti. The roof of their house was covered in solar panels, and they hung all their laundry out to dry. They were retired hippies living their best baby boomer life among a much older generation of blue-haired retirees. They also had a pool, which we took full advantage of. Spiny desert lizards crawled around the stucco architecture, and I watched them as I sunbathed in a lawn chair by the garden in the early morning hours.

It felt great to recharge. We set up and rehearsed some new material before going to the Goat Head Saloon to load in. Our gig there was the most poorly attended yet. Some of the staff seemed to be on hard drugs and they were all cold to us, aside from an extra-chatty soundman who showed me the proper way to wind my cables and shared a mantra that went "Its shape will reveal itself." When the promoter gave us our thirty-dollar profit at the end of the night, we all blamed John Sirota for not promoting us well enough. That bastard.

"Are you guys touring an album or what?" the promoter wanted to know. "You need a publicist if you're going to travel all this way. You should at least have a write-up in a local paper or something."

"Well," said the acid-casualty soundman, "this *is* a college town and it's summer. No one's even in town to go to a show. You need to come back when school is in session. This place is usually packed."

We didn't dwell on it. What was the point? After all, I was only twenty-four and it was my first-ever tour. Plus, we were California bound the next day, and I had hope in my heart. I'd never seen the West Coast, and I was beside myself with excitement.

That night, Jared and Aaron planned to get their own beds. Normally they begrudgingly shared a bed in the Winnebago, but we got an offer to stay with a friend named Corinna. She was not only hospitable but also had a large supply of mushrooms that she offered to give us, free of charge. Corinna had curly, brown hair and almond-shaped eyes. She was a student at Arizona State University and a belly dancer in training. Jared and Aaron fought over her affections, and you could tell she didn't mind one bit.

At one point, Corinna and Jared made their way into a bedroom and shut the door. Aaron came outside looking discouraged. In one hand, he carried a pillow and a blanket, in the other hand, a pint of beer. He was obviously intoxicated and in a sour mood, realizing he would be getting the pullout couch and not the bed with the beautiful girl. He lay down on the sidewalk with his blanket and pillow.

"I'm sleeping out here tonight," he slurred. "This is total bullshit." He stretched himself out on the pavement and started to drift off.

"Aaron, you should go sleep inside. It's not safe out here," I said softly.

"Yes, it is. The entire community is over seventy-five. You think some old retiree is gonna come rob me?"

"True, true," Jeremy said. "But it's gonna get so hot here in just a few hours when the sun comes up. Just go sleep inside. You'll be more comfortable."

Finally, Aaron allowed us to help him to his feet and inside.

Jeremy and I had been excited to sleep in the Winnebago alone for once. But when we pulled in, the sunroof was still propped open, and we wrecked it on the awning of the apartment complex. We couldn't fit into any of the parking spots and began to fight like an old married couple, each blaming the other for an honest mistake.

Eventually, angry and embarrassed, we decided to leave in search of a campground. We finally found a place that had openings. It was nearing two A.M., so we just grabbed an envelope from the check-in desk and filled out the info, put the seventeen-dollar fee inside, and hung it on the outside of our RV.

It had been a while since we'd been intimate with each other, since we were living in such close quarters with the rest of the band. The whole point of them staying at Corinna's and us staying alone was so we could make love, but we'd ruined the mood by arguing. We went to sleep mad at each other and were awakened at six A.M. when someone banged on the Winnebago door.

"Dear Lord, who is it at this hour?" Jeremy moaned.

I threw on my kimono and answered.

"Just what I thought," the old man standing outside the door said in greeting. "This is a *seniors'* campground. You're not old enough to stay here. Pack up and move along!"

"This is ageism!" I cried as he walked away.

"We're old souls in young bodies!" Jeremy hollered.

"I'm so tired. I need more sleep!" I crawled back into bed for a moment.

"It's so early, and I think we're out of coffee." Jeremy took me into his arms. We started kissing and making up for lost time, but the grumpy old man came back and started pounding on our camper again.

"I told you to get out of here! You're not wanted."

"We're leaving!" we screamed in unison. We put on our clothes and climbed into the front seat.

"At least they didn't take our money!" Jeremy said, finding the silver lining. "Free rent!" He took the money out of the envelope and shoved it in his pants pocket.

"Old farts," I laughed as we drove into Mesa in search of caffeine. We killed as much time as we could before driving back to Corinna's to pick up the guys. She gave us all hugs and sent us off with that large bag of powerful mushrooms.

We put on some Joni Mitchell and headed to the coast. I had butterflies in my stomach and flowers in my hair. I imagined we were headed for the gold rush and that maybe in California all my dreams would come true. Maybe someone would discover the band and our music, maybe I would become an actress . . . so many possibilities awaited us. I drove faster and faster, unafraid of being pulled over, unafraid of anything. I couldn't wait to see the Hollywood sign, the palm trees, the Walk of Fame. Most of all, I couldn't wait to get to the ocean.

The heat melted the highway and the entire desert was rippled, like a watercolor painting. About halfway there, the Winnebago started to overheat. We pulled over to investigate. Jared had the most knowledge when it came to engines, and he informed us that not only was there a bird's nest beneath the hood but the radiator was low on water. We removed the nest, added water, and sat for a while to let it cool down. We piled back in and kept driving.

About fifty miles farther along, the Winnebago started to shake. Something was wrong with the wheels. We pulled over again. The trees along the road were black and charred, signs that a fire had recently swept through. We got out and looked at the front passenger wheel. It was bent and crooked. We took the hubcap off and tried to assess the damage. All the bolts were rusted on, and there was no removing them. We had a spare but couldn't get the old tire off to put the new one on. We were stranded in the desert in the midday sun at the peak of summer. We had very little food and only a small amount of water.

"I'm calling AAA," Jeremy said. "It's time to phone a friend. And we haven't done it yet."

"I'm going up to that ridge to stretch and do some yoga." I took my yoga mat and began hiking off into the distance. My legs were feeling stiff and my back was aching from the drive. I fell asleep after a few poses and woke up to vultures flying overhead. I went back to the RV to find the guys playing cards and guitar with the generator on. It wasn't really keeping up, but it was cooler in there than it was outside, and they were definitely making the most out of it.

"Y'all playing poker? Let's at least put some money in and make it more interesting," I suggested. We sat for another half hour before an old guy finally showed up to tow us to a service station at the next exit. The mechanic, a middle-aged man with grease-stained hands, told us they could have it fixed by the next day at ten A.M.

"Would it be possible to sleep in the Winnebago on your property?" Jeremy asked the secretary behind the desk.

"I'm not sure," she said slowly as she chewed her gum. "You ain't got nowhere else you can go?"

"No, ma'am. We're vagabonds," I told her.

"Vaga-whats?" she asked.

"We're traveling across the country. We don't have much money. This RV is our home," I explained.

"Lemme ask my manager." She sighed and picked up the phone, dialing with her long, fake, hot-pink fingernails.

Jared sat outside the shop smoking a hand-rolled cigarette. "Damn, so close."

"We haven't even made it out of Arizona yet," Aaron pointed out.

"Don't worry," Jeremy assured me, "We'll make it."

That night we slept in the broken-down Winnebago in the parking lot and woke early so that they could weld our tire together. The four of us walked next door to a local diner for breakfast. The coffee was weak and the bacon was limp, but we ate some eggs and counted our money. We weren't sure how much the repair would end up costing and we didn't have much. The shows had been less than profitable, with merch sales the only thing keeping us at breakeven, and our nest egg was getting smaller by the day.

The mechanic understood our plight. When we returned to pick up the vehicle, he gave us a quote. "How does $150 sound?" he asked, brow raised.

"Great!" Jeremy was shocked. "Are you sure that's enough?

"It'll cover the parts. I had to weld together a makeshift tire, but I think this oughta get you at least to California. I didn't charge you for the labor."

"Thank you, sir!" Jared shook his hand.

"No problem. Hope you guys make it to Los Angeles. Just keep putting water in that radiator when it gets low, and watch the tire." I could tell he thought we were crazy, taking such an old vehicle on such a long trip. "Maybe I could get one of those CDs signed from you, as a tip. Ya know, in case you make it big someday." He looked at me and smiled.

"Anything! You saved us. We're eternally grateful." I grabbed a copy of our album and signed it with an ink pen.

Jeremy paid the secretary with the hot-pink fake nails. She counted our dirty money—paid in cash, every cent—and we were on our way. California or bust.

CHAPTER 14

C for California

When we finally hit the California state line, we howled out the window and honked the horn for at least a mile. None of us had been out west before, and it was exhilarating. We passed Joshua Tree National Park, Palm Springs, Banning, Beaumont, Yucaipa, and San Bernardino. We kept driving and driving until we saw the water. The sun was still up when we arrived.

We camped at Docweiler Beach in Los Angeles. It was magnificent. We stared out at the Pacific Ocean as it glistened, all navy and silver, like the world's largest unminable diamond.

We kicked off our shoes and felt the sand on our bare feet. We rushed into the water. Although it was cold, it felt like something we all had to do, an unspoken ritual of sorts to baptize ourselves in the ocean of the opposite coast. We had been in North Carolina just a couple of weeks ago, and now we were on the other side of the country, in another body of water. It was much colder than the Atlantic, but we paid it no mind. I submerged myself completely, clothes and all.

"Time to cook up some grub!" Jeremy said. Each campsite had small grills and a little faucet with fresh water. It was twenty bucks a night to stay and they had public showers. That alone made the price worth it.

We ate a decent meal and decided to set up in the parking lot to play some music. Jared played some bass scales, and Aaron turned to him and snapped, "Could we *please* keep the noodling to a minimum?" The weeks of living in close quarters were starting to wear on the group.

We began playing and soon drew a small crowd. Random campers and beach bums circled us, dancing barefoot in the parking lot while we played. Pretty soon an officer approached us and told us to shut the whole thing down. We packed up and went to bed. We had a pretty big gig the next day. We were booked at the House of Blues.

We woke early and started preparing for our show. I boiled water for coffee, sat down at our tiny kitchen table, and wrote a proper set list—something I didn't usually do in those days. I lay out on the beach for a while, took a run next to the ocean, and then went to use the amenities. It had been a while since I'd shaved my legs, and that proved difficult in the public shower. The water was freezing cold, the pressure was terrible, and you had to push a button every ten seconds to make the water come out. I couldn't get the shampoo to wash out of my thick hair, but I pulled my hair back into a sleek ponytail, put on my finest black dress, and tried to look respectable.

We were only a mile and a half from the venue, but by the time we left, it was rush hour. We piled in the RV and started to make our way through LA traffic.

"The navigation says an hour and a half!" Jeremy noted.

"Seriously? We're gonna be late for sound check," I grumbled.

"Wouldn't be the first time," Aaron smirked. He was the most prompt of all of us, and he tried his best to keep us running on time, since of course there was no tour manager to do it.

"Something's wrong with Winnie Cooper," Jeremy said. "I think she's overheating again."

"Just drive slowly and put it in neutral or park whenever you get a chance to stop," Jared instructed.

"That will be easy. We're basically not even moving," I moaned.

Several carloads of rich, hip LA types drove by us, gawking at our ride. We looked out of place among the fancy cars. A group of beautiful girls stared as they approached in a BMW and began to laugh. I showed them my favorite finger.

As the hour passed, the Winnebago began making unusual sounds. Something was terribly wrong. We finally arrived at the House of Blues and let out a sigh of relief.

"I need a drink. That was stressful," I said. We walked up to a little bar outside on the patio.

"Two Jack Daniel's on the rocks, please." Jeremy reached into his pocket for some cash.

The bartender started pouring the drinks. "That will be twenty-four dollars."

"What?!" we exclaimed.

"Twenty-four dollars," she repeated slowly.

"Well, we're playing here tonight," I said. "Do we get any drink vouchers?"

"No, I don't believe so." She stopped pouring.

"We'll just take one, in that case," I said.

"Whatever." The waitress rolled her eyes and passed us a single, tiny drink with an embellished napkin.

We paid her and went off to find a place to share the drink and smoke a cigarette.

"Here's to you, LA! You greasy bastard!" Jeremy said as he took a sip from the plastic cup and passed it to me.

Inside, there were several different rooms with stages. The manager brought us to the smallest of the three. There were plaster faces of blues singers mounted on the walls and ceiling, and the lighting was blue and purple. Although it was predictable, in a way, it wasn't what we had envisioned. It felt more like a plastic shrine—a letdown on all accounts. Our set was early, six o'clock, and there was obviously no one there to see us.

"Can we push back until more people arrive?" I asked the sound guy.

"No, absolutely not. We've got a full night. You're the openers," he snapped.

We'd been playing empty rooms all across America, but we'd had high hopes for this show. I was beginning to realize it was going to be harder than I thought to make any headway in this industry. I felt like I was screaming into a void and no one was answering back.

"How about we start with 'Over the Weather'?" Jeremy suggested. It was a song we cowrote.

"That's too slow. We need to draw people in here," I stressed.

Jeremy turned on his vibro pedal and launched into the beginning riff of the song anyway. I shot him a dirty look. I started angrily singing the words:

> Three days without sleep, has got me so uptight
> Staying up on the poison, swatting flies in the night
> Staring at my breakfast, I got no appetite
> I'm going ten miles down, with no end in sight

The show went on, forty-five long, awkward minutes of playing for the blues faces on the wall. A couple of my friends who lived in LA did show up, but I couldn't wait for the set to end. When we finished, I walked outside and lit up a smoke while the guys packed up. I turned the corner to go sit by the Winnebago and ran into Clayton.

"Well, well, well," he started. "How was the show, you ungrateful bitch? Thought you'd never see me again?" He had a wild look in his eyes.

I turned around and ran straight back into the venue. My heart was racing. I searched for my bandmates. Finally I saw Jared. I said only one word—"Clayton"—and he turned white as a ghost.

We decided to get the bouncers to help us load out our stuff. Clayton stood at a distance, watching with a menacing eye. As soon as the van was packed, we took off as fast as we could—which wasn't very fast. The RV was sputtering and shaking all the way back down the road.

We met up with Jessi, my old picking partner from Nashville who had moved out to LA several months earlier. My friends Amber and Billie also met us at a fancy restaurant. I was feeling low from the under-attended gig and shaken from the run-in with Clayton, but that wasn't gonna stop us from partaking in as many alcoholic beverages as our budget would allow. We ate dinner and headed back to Docweiler Beach to start a campfire and play guitar.

When we got there, Jared pulled out the bag of mushrooms Corinna had gifted us and started passing them out like candy. Jeremy and I ate only one apiece. We wanted to wait to have a full trip when the tour was over. We planned to visit the Redwoods.

The rest of the evening was euphoric. We sat on the beach staring at the fire contentedly, until we were all compelled to get in and swim in the ocean one more time. Once we had our fill, we started walking back to the Winnebago. We passed a small, triangular tent that had been abandoned on the sand.

"Let's sleep in this!" I said to Jeremy.

"Seriously?"

"Yeah! It will be romantic, sleeping on the beach. We never get any privacy these days." I pulled him close to me.

"Alright. I'll get our pillows and some blankets."

We made love to the ocean's roar and slept like babies.

The next morning we were abruptly woken by an angry beach patrol person who was sweeping the sand of trash. He peeked his head into our tent and hollered, "Get up, get moving, you lazy bums! If I catch you out here again, I'll give you both a ticket."

We hurriedly dressed, rushed back to the Winnebago, and lay back down for a couple more hours of sleep.

For the next few days we lived on Docweiler Beach and soaked in the beautiful weather. We ate fish tacos and went shopping with Jessi down on Melrose. She took us thrifting and I found so many one-of-a-kind vintage dresses for really cheap.

Our next gig was up north in Hermosa Beach at a place called Cafe

Boogaloo. It was the last official show of the tour, and for the first time there was a decent crowd. We were shocked. About one hundred people were there, all drinking and eating; I'm sure none of them had ever heard of us, but they were attentive and gracious. The owners fed us a healthy meal and treated us well. It was a breath of fresh air and a good show to go out on. Aaron left the next day on a flight back to Kentucky. Jeremy, Jared, and I embarked on the spiritual leg of the journey.

We jumped in the Winnebago and headed north on the Pacific Coast Highway, the ocean chasing us on the left side of the RV as we made our way north. There was only one problem, and that was Winnie Cooper's engine. With no real idea of what was wrong with it, we took the drive slow. Cars passed us left and right as we drove up the coast, but we didn't care. I was in no hurry to get back to Nashville, and had started thinking about staying out west. So we had nowhere to go and no real agenda other than to explore the countryside.

We used a paper map to look for any landmarks we might want to stop at, as none of us had smartphones yet. We saw a sign for Morro Bay and several state parks and stopped to camp at Montaña de Oro for a night. In the morning, we drove to a remote island that was a bird sanctuary. When the tide was low, you could walk out on the rocks and access the island. It was a beautiful place, home to thousands of shorebirds. I had never seen so many birds in one place before. It was a holy moment but also kind of ominous, like a scene out of Hitchcock's *The Birds*. The three of us climbed all over the jagged cliffs as the waves beat the rocks around us. Later that afternoon, we went into Morro to find sustenance.

We passed a shop window that had a neon sign out front: Palm Reader. Jeremy was dead set on visiting a fortune teller and getting a tarot card reading, but the woman was elusive. A couple of dark-haired, dark-eyed children answered the door.

"We're all booked for today. Come back tomorrow. She can see you tomorrow," the oldest daughter said.

"We'll be gone tomorrow," Jeremy explained. "It's almost my birthday. Can't she squeeze me in?"

"Not today. Today is no good," the girl replied.

"Tomorrow may never come," Jeremy argued.

"We shall see," said the daughter.

I could tell it broke his heart, but we didn't want to stay in Morro Bay for another night. It was time to move on. Plus, a reading was expensive, and we were just barely getting by as it was. He convinced himself he didn't want to know what was in store for him anyway. "The future should be uncertain," he insisted. We went to eat our one meal for the day at a cafe next door. With bellies fed and palms unread, we traveled onward.

August 27, 2008, was Jeremy's thirtieth birthday. We crossed the Golden Gate Bridge and spent the day and night in San Francisco. We went to the legendary intersection of Haight and Ashbury Streets and smoked a joint in broad daylight. Good luck led us to a coffee shop, where we hung out and scribbled in our notebooks to kill time. During our stay, we got to talking to the barista behind the counter.

"Are you in a band?" he asked.

"Yep. How could you tell?" Jeremy asked.

"You just look like musicians," the barista said, smiling. "Are you hungry?"

"Always," I said.

The owner gave us a garbage bag full of day-old bagels that we feasted on for at least a week, until they started to mold. That evening we went to a bar called Whiskey Thieves and made it our mission to get Jeremy loaded. I vaguely remember playing the Doors' "Alabama Song (Whiskey Bar)" on the jukebox and drunkenly dancing on the tables, causing a proper scene. I think we left around three in the morning with no plans of where to stay. We ended up parking the Winnebago on a steep hill on a city street shortly after. We would have to leave before six, according to the sign on the road, but Jeremy sat up chain-smoking out of the air vent of the RV long into the night, enjoying the last hour of his twenties and one of his million "last cigarettes."

After three hours of restless sleep, I climbed into the front of Winnie and drove us north. I could have slept all day, but I knew we would get a ticket if I didn't move us on out of the city. I watched the sun come up as Jeremy and Jared slept off the booze. We trucked along the Pacific Coast Highway. The terrain was hard on our ancient wheels. I could only get the speed up to thirty-five miles an hour before the RV started making a terrible noise. Jared woke up and noticed the sound.

"I don't think Winnie is getting up to third gear anymore," he said sadly.

"Well, she still moves, so I'm gonna drive her 'til the wheels fall off," I said with an evil grin. "To the redwoods!"

"Time for a vision quest!" Jared declared.

It was a three-and-a-half-hour drive up to Humboldt Redwoods State Park, but with the engine just barely pushing forty, we made it there in seven. During most of the scenic drive, I looked out of the window at the lush landscape. I was truly in heaven in the Rockefeller Forest; it was one of the most breathtaking places I'd ever seen. We had a staggering view of the coast as we entered the Avenue of the Giants. Rust-colored trees ushered us in, and I knew we were in the perfect place to escape from the monotony of civilization.

There was no planning ahead, so we just showed up at the office of the state park and asked the ranger if there were any available campsites. Thankfully, there was room. We paid for a week.

In heading for our campsite, we drove straight through a tree, one of the hollowed-out redwoods that had been made into a tunnel. Finally we pulled Winnie Cooper up to a shaded spot that was surrounded with brush and shrubs. It was our temporary home and it was perfect. There was a power outlet to plug in to, a picnic table for meals, and a small grill. The best part was a firepit half-enclosed by the dead trunk of a redwood. The weather was perfect. The air was clean and cool. We cooked a meal and sat at the table together.

Afterward, Jeremy got out a guitar and began picking a tune. I started making a fire. Jared pulled mushrooms out of the green pouch and popped several in his mouth. "Delicious." He passed them to me.

Grabbing two stems and a couple of caps, I chewed them up, gagging at the wretched taste, and handed the bag to Jeremy.

We sat and waited, but it didn't take long to feel the effects. The patterns of the trees became mathematical. I saw equations in the leaves.

"I feel all booby eyed," Jared exclaimed.

Jeremy agreed. The forest had grown dark, and we all sat around watching the flames of the caveman's TV. I could hear the wind rushing through the sequoias. I could hear the neighbors on either side of us talking quietly in the distance. We sat up talking all night about God, nature, life and death, hopes and dreams, mythology, poetry, and philosophy.

The next week was spent macro dosing, writing, and playing songs. We had little contact with the outside world, aside from the several people who came by, drawn to the sound of music. A couple who was celebrating their marriage anniversary visited with an offering of a dandelion salad they had foraged. A family with children snuck up on our campsite by accident and startled us. We all busted out laughing and went on dosing ourselves with more psilocybin before taking a walk around the forest.

The three of us bonded that week in a way that is difficult to describe. I felt like I had found a community in our traveling band. I felt oddly at home on the road—being an unknown, living in a junky van, playing songs for ourselves and occasionally for a small crowd.

We finally ran out of mushrooms and headed to Eugene, Oregon, the Anarchist Capital of the World. We hung out downtown, visited art museums, bought weed off some locals, and headed up to Portland. The entire time, the Winnebago was only going thirty-five miles an hour. It was painful, but we got lots of sightseeing in. The cars on the interstate zipped by as we clung to the white line.

People in Oregon said we should go to Bend because it was beautiful and there was a folk festival going on. Jared was restless. He wanted to get back to Illinois. "Driving at this pace is a little bit ridiculous," he argued. "I need to get back and help my dad on the farm."

"Well, you can get a plane ticket because I'm not leaving. I like it out here," I said stubbornly.

"You guys said you were going back. That was the plan," he insisted.

"Plans change. This RV wants to die out here, and the way I see it, it's a sign from God. I don't want to go back east. I'm staying right here in this van." The conversation was getting heated.

Jeremy jumped in. "We can figure this out."

I stormed off to a coffee shop alone. Jeremy came to meet me. "Margo, we need to take him back. That was what we decided when we left."

"I don't ever remember agreeing to anything," I said. "I don't want to go back to Nashville or the Midwest again. We could live in LA. I would even go farther east. I mean, I know New York is cold but it might be welcoming." The truth was, going back to Music City felt daunting. It was easier to float around in limbo, daydreaming inside the wood-paneled walls of our make-believe tour bus.

"Well, don't fight with him. He's one of your best friends," Jeremy said softly. "It wouldn't kill us to go back to Tennessee."

"Yes, it could," I said with tears in my eyes.

We busked on the street in Bend but found no work at the actual folk festival. What we did find was a group of hippies who were part of the Rainbow Gathering. They noticed us sitting outside of the Winnebago and came up to admire it.

"Bro! This thing is awesome," one of them said as he walked circles around our ride. "We need a space machine so bad, dude!"

"Oh, really?" Jeremy said. "Well, we might actually be selling this." I shot him a look, but he didn't pay any attention.

"Seriously? For how much?" The straggler's eyes grew wide.

"Well, hoping to get a couple grand out of it, at least," Jeremy said.

"Man, we don't have that much money, but we could get it to you later."

I finally spoke up. "How much could you get right now?"

"Probably like five hundred or something," the hippie replied.

"So, like a down payment?" Jared chimed in.

"Yeah, man! A down payment. We can get the rest to you in just a couple weeks, no problem," he assured us.

The three of us talked it over and agreed that it was in our best interest to get rid of the Winnebago. It was only a matter of time before the engine went out completely. We could use the money to get a U-Haul to drive back home. I was heartbroken, but at two to one, I was outnumbered.

We met the burnouts the next morning. The ringleader came up with a stack of dirty, crumbled-up cash in his hand. "All we could come up with was $375, but we promise we'll get you the rest as soon as we can."

"That wasn't the deal," I said angrily. "You don't get the title until you send the rest of the money."

He looked taken aback. "Harsh. Dang, sister. We'll get you the rest of the money."

Jeremy stepped in. "It's fine. We just need to write up some sort of agreement. I'll get a piece of paper." We worked up a simple contract on a page from Jeremy's notebook, and both parties signed with a Sharpie. The hippies went on their way in their new space machine, and we went about the business of renting a U-Haul and driving back east.

"You know they're gonna trash that thing. We'll never see a cent of what they promised," I said.

"Joke's on them," Jeremy pointed out, "because they never even test-drove it."

CHAPTER 15

Aimless Fate

Jared went back to work on his parents' farm in Illinois, and Jeremy and I hung out there for as long as we could. We knew we should return to Nashville and set out on the daunting task of finding jobs and a place to rent. Instead, we headed next to my folks' house, where we stayed for a couple of weeks, writing songs at a little place in Davenport called Coffee Dive. The place was, exactly as its name suggested, a dive that served coffee. You could also smoke inside, so in an upstairs corner booth we drank endless amounts of caffeine and puffed on one-hitters of weed, then smoked cigarettes to cover up the smell.

Jeremy's parents called to check on us. They knew we were having trouble finding our footing as a young couple. They made us a deal: if we got married, stopped living in sin, stopped playing music and touring and "aimlessly running around," they would help us put down a deposit on a house in Nashville. I was resistant.

"It's our only option right now," Jeremy said. "Where else are we gonna go?"

"I don't know," I said. "But I can tell you one thing, I'm not going to quit playing music and I know you won't either. Promise?" We locked pinkies.

We decided to get married in Nashville on Sunday, October 26, 2008. It was already the middle of September at that point. I immediately called my sisters to tell them the good news.

Jeremy's and my parents helped with the cost of the wedding, since we were flat broke. We found a place called Cedarwood out in Whites Creek that did weddings with everything included: the cake, the flowers, the decorations, the preacher, the music, a champagne toast, the tables and chairs. The venue was a big, old, white farmhouse with a beautiful red barn out back for photos. We decided to have the ceremony and reception outside.

With the help of my younger and extremely organized sister, Britni, we planned our wedding and invited our closest family and friends, about thirty people total. We had our bachelor and bachelorette parties the night before, which was probably not the smartest idea. I hung out at our new rental home and smoked weed with my girlfriends. Jeremy had a party with the groomsmen out at Dave Harder's house, where they had a bonfire and drank moonshine until three or four in the morning.

At nine-thirty A.M., with the wedding set to start at ten, there was still no sign of Jeremy or the groomsmen. "Where is he?" I cried as I paced the floor.

"He'll be here," my sister Kylie assured me.

"What if he got cold feet? He told me when we met that he would never get married a second time." I kept pacing.

"He's probably just late! You're *both* always late." Britni smiled.

Just then, Jeremy's parents popped their heads into the room where the bridesmaids and I were getting ready. "He's here! Don't worry," Jeremy's mother, Sandra, said. I hugged her and breathed a sigh of relief.

It was a beautiful fall day, a Sunday, with not a cloud in the sky. Jeremy was a sight for my sore, sleepy eyes. He had on a vintage brown suit he'd bought at a Quad City thrift store called Trash Can Annie's. I had gone dress shopping with my mama and sisters and found the most perfect strapless, beaded white gown and a long veil. The dress cost $500, which I definitely didn't have. My mother and father generously bought it for me.

We had our champagne toast, but our wedding party was shameless and wild. We couldn't afford a bartender or booze, but our guests had brought their own and began pouring it themselves. They lit up blunts and cigarettes behind the barn. The owners of Cedarwood were not amused; soon it was time to take the party elsewhere.

We went down to Lower Broadway. At Layla's Bluegrass Inn, our friends the Howling Brothers were playing a set.

"Margo and Jeremy! Congrats!" our friend Ian cheered. "Do y'all wanna come up and sing one?"

Jared passed the guitar to Jeremy, and I took the mic. Dave Harder jumped on upright bass. We played Bob Dylan's "You Ain't Goin' Nowhere," still dressed in our wedding attire, for a small afternoon crowd.

We continued to drink, pausing only to eat a cheap dinner at a hotel Applebee's, and then continued to party through the night. The weekend was a whirlwind.

We had no money for a proper honeymoon, so we rented a cabin at Cedars of Lebanon State Park in Lebanon, Tennessee. The cabin was a one-room shack with a tiny kitchen, a living area with a wood-burning stove, and two single beds that we pushed together. The mattresses were hard and covered in plastic. It was fifty-six dollars a night, and we made the best of it. We spent three days recovering from a hellacious hangover, writing songs, and watching the last of the fall leaves fade.

CHAPTER 16

Ball and Unchained

We were newlyweds. I was twenty-five and Jeremy had just turned thirty. Despite my wishes, we had wound up right back in the city we had fled from. But now we were there with rings on our hands. Our new house was a cheap place over in East Nashville, a small brick home on a half acre in Inglewood. It was a two bedroom, with a half-finished basement that made a perfect studio. The best thing about the house was the big back porch that overlooked a nature preserve. It was a marshland, and nobody could build back there.

Jeremy had told me from the moment we started dating that he couldn't have kids. When he was about five years old, he'd had tonsillitis and a terrible fever that reached 105. At the hospital, they'd packed him in ice. He'd nearly died. The doctor told his mother that there was a strong likelihood he would be infertile as a result. I had always dreamed of having a huge family and brought it up often, begging Jeremy to eventually adopt a child with me, but he was against the idea of adopting. He said he had always felt so out of place being adopted, he either wanted his own blood family or none at all. He tried to convince me that children would be too hard for our wandering lifestyle and reasoned that, without offspring, we would be happy, untethered, and free to travel anywhere. I settled on getting another dog but still felt a pang of sadness anytime I saw a young couple with a new baby.

I went out one afternoon, telling Jeremy I was going to the bank, and came back with a puppy that we named Annabella. She was part Australian shepherd and part border collie. She immediately began tearing up the house and chewing on everything in sight: the walls, the doors, my shoes—you name it, she destroyed it. But I loved her and was happy to have canine company again. I also rescued a wild Maine coon kitten we found in the backyard. She was incredibly sick when we found her and had one eye that was gouged out and badly infected. We took her to the vet and got her eye stitched up and nursed her back to health. I named her Edith Piaf. She and Bella got along like peas and carrots.

The home was quaint, not too rundown but not too fancy either. I didn't feel like it reflected our personalities, but deep down both of us were happy to be back in Nashville. We made it our own by painting the walls. I chose bright colors again; the living room had a white brick fireplace, so I offset it by painting the room a deep currant red. We chose a robin's-egg blue for the simple country kitchen. Pale green and gold accented the front sitting room, and I covered the walls of our studio basement in mustard and black. In the middle of the room was a gift from Aaron Latos, a refurbished Pearl drum kit covered in a furry leopard print. It was my pride and joy.

We had basically no furniture, but Jeremy's family gave us hand-me-downs, and the rest we bought at the local Goodwill. Many of the pieces, including the couches and chairs, didn't fit our style, but free was free, and we were beggars, not choosers.

Jeremy's great-grandmother, Katie Mae, mailed us a care package. She was getting on in years, and her hands were riddled with arthritis, but she had crocheted baby blankets for every single one of her grandchildren and great-grandchildren. She sent us a delicate white blanket with mint-green trim and a little note that read, "Dear Jeremy and Margo,

I know you were only just married and don't have a baby on the way, but I won't be able to knit much longer. I hope this blanket brings you love and fertility. Love, Katie Mae."

I stood in the kitchen sobbing and clutching the blanket. I grieved the thought of not having a daughter or a son. Jeremy read the note over my shoulder. We stood together in silence, not knowing what to say. I buried the blanket deep in the closet and tried to forget about it.

Jeremy took a job up the street at Mitchell Delicatessen in Riverside Village. I took on various jobs, but had a harder time holding on to them. For a time I was a hostess at Rosepepper Mexican Restaurant, but the owner, Ernan, was a total creep and started coming on to me, so I quit. Then I got a job at a fine-dining restaurant called Taste over on Hillsboro Road. I wasn't much of a fine-dining sort of waitress and only lasted a couple of weeks before heading down to Broadway and finding work slinging bottles at Layla's Bluegrass Inn. I enjoyed hearing classic country music while I worked, but I wanted so badly to be onstage. I thought about getting some people together to play down there once a week, but the idea of doing only covers didn't appeal to me. A friend of mine once told me that Broadway was where dreams go to die, and I couldn't forget it.

That year, 2009, we focused on building a solid band. Jeremy and I put out ads on Craigslist and found a bass player named Matt Gardner, who worked as an English teacher. We also found a drummer, Casey Smith, who looked a lot like the Band's Levon Helm. Nate was still playing with us, but he only sat in on the keys occasionally. He was too busy with his home-renovation business to play with us full-time.

Our new band recorded an EP called *Strong Medicine* with Andrija at the Bomb Shelter. Matt ended up being such a great guitar player that he switched from playing bass to lead guitar and banjo. Jason White came back and played bass.

On the EP were seven songs, all cowritten by Jeremy and me, except for "The Well Wisher," which I wrote on my own, and "20 Tons of

Blues," which Matt sang and wrote. Our sound was changing again, more toward groovy folk rock—think Fairport Convention meets Janis Joplin, or Big Brother and the Holding Company meets the Rolling Stones. At least, that's what we were going for. Matt loved the blues, as well as 1960s and '70s psychedelia, just as much as we did. He was a white dude with soul, and he changed the vibe of the band with his playing. When he was on, really on, he could sound like Jimi Hendrix.

Strong Medicine was a self-released endeavor. I made a collage and drew the fonts for the cover, and we printed the copies ourselves. John Sirota was still booking us gigs, and we played around town at 3rd and Lindsley, Mercy Lounge, 12th and Porter, and the 5 Spot.

The 5 Spot was our local watering hole, and we spent a *lot* of time and money there over the course of the next six years. At one of our early shows at the 5er, we met a couple of young dudes who had recently moved to Nashville from upstate New York. Their names were Gary and Garrett, and they approached us about being on their new indie label, Palaver Records. Garrett had a thick New York City accent and rattled off words like a machine gun. Gary was the opposite; he talked real, real slow. They didn't know what the hell they were doing, but they were young and eager—just a couple of good old boys who had a trust fund and a dream. And no one else around town had shown interest in us. We met them at 3 Crow Bar in Five Points during happy hour to talk about how they could help us jump-start our career.

It was exciting to be there talking with them and making plans. My mind was racing, my heart was full. That evening we celebrated as though we had just hit the big time. First, they bought a round for the band, and then I bought a round for them. The rounds of beers and shots just kept coming. The contract with Palaver Records did not come with a big bonus; it didn't come with any money at all. But they promised to help us fund the vinyl pressing if we made a full-length record, and that was big-time enough for us.

Our spirits soared. We started writing daily again and schemed to get back in the studio at any cost—even if that meant selling plasma again. It was like an addiction, and we worked and saved every penny so we could start recording again as soon as possible.

We also had tentative plans to travel to the UK. Matt had met a musician in Liverpool named Mike Badger who wanted to help us book a tour of England. We were beside ourselves with the thought of it. I just knew the folks over there would understand and appreciate our music.

In the meantime, I began playing drums in Lilly Hiatt's band. Lilly was a firecracker with a heart of gold. She had the face of a sprite, tattoos on her forearms, and a mountain of long, curly hair that trailed down her back. Her songs cut to the bone; they were personal and had memorable melodies. Her father, John Hiatt, was a wildly successful singer and songwriter, but she wasn't given any handouts. Lilly stood out from the pack and I gravitated to her.

At first it was just Lilly on acoustic guitar and vocals, her friend Beth Finney shredding on electric and lead guitar, and me on drums and background vocals. The vibe was Lucinda Williams meets Neko Case. No-bullshit tunes, a little country, a little rock and roll. The band eventually enlisted Jeremy to play bass, and together we had a great rhythm section.

Lilly was wild and liked to party just as much as I did. We hung out in her dingy upstairs apartment and swapped songs and shared a bottle before retiring to the fire escape to feed scraps of food to a local possum we befriended and named Biscuit. We enjoyed going out to the Villager to play darts and raise hell, occupying H-Cue's pool hall for vodka drinks, and hanging out with the crusty punks at Springwater. We tore up the town together and were quite inseparable for a while.

Lilly booked some shows in Texas; we were dying to take our act out on the road. Jeremy stayed home to work at Mitchell's and care for our pets, but Lilly, Beth, and I made preparations to embark on our own for a miniature tour. I didn't have proper drum cases, so I just wrapped my drums in moving blankets and put my hardware and sticks in an old golf bag I bought at a thrift store.

The three of us took off driving in my car. After trucking along at eighty miles an hour for several hours, we stopped at a big-box store for some junk food. I cased the place and decided it was time to do a heist. We were in the middle of nowhere and I was sure we could get away with it. I walked around the store and pocketed a bag of Sour Patch Kids, a pair of heart-shaped sunglasses, and some ridiculous fur hats. Lilly and Beth were shocked at my brazenness, but after I reminded them that corporations can be evil, they were easily persuaded. Lilly stole a bag of plastic farm animals, and after that, as a joke, we left the tiny plastic figurines in random spots everywhere we went: a plastic pig perched on the toilet paper dispenser in a service station bathroom, a miniature cow on a gas pump, a chicken at a counter in a restaurant. Like a trail of bread crumbs.

We carried on until we were halted by the hard rains of a hurricane about to hit the coast and were forced to stop at a hotel on the Texas-Arkansas state line. When we parked under the overhang to check in, a plastic pony fell out of the car onto the ground. "Dropped ya pony," a redneck hollered at us, pointing at the ground. We died laughing. It wasn't even that funny, we were just stoned.

"The Dropped Ponies! That's our band name!" Lilly exclaimed.

"I dig it!" I said. "And 'I dig a pony, well, you can celebrate anything you want!'" I sang the Beatles lyrics as we took our bags into the hotel in the rain.

After we checked in, we decided to go out on the town.

"There ain't shit else to do!" Lilly said.

Beth decided to stay in the hotel room to study and rehearse, having no interest in tearing up the town with us. We stopped down at the front desk to inquire about the closest local watering hole.

"This is a dry county," the man at the reception desk told us. "No booze for miles around. Gotta go to the next town over."

Lilly pulled the car around, and we went to a townie bar about thirty minutes away. It was a classic dive—neon sign in the window, pool tables, jukebox. The clientele was ninety percent men. The few women there looked haggard and at least twice our age. When we walked in, everyone turned to look at us. You could tell they weren't used to seeing many out-of-towners. We didn't have much money to burn, but Lilly had a plan.

"We're gonna take these cowboys for everything they're worth," she whispered as we sat down at the bar. We bought our first round ourselves: two whiskey shots with two domestic bottles. Then we proceeded to hustle the locals in pool, make small talk, and flirt with a couple of lonely men at the bar. We got a solid buzz on and never paid another cent to the bartender. We put some dollars in the jukebox and picked our favorite songs, but someone else's selections played before ours.

"The Eagles suck!" Lilly yelled. I could see things might go in a bad direction, so I pulled her into the bathroom and we snuck out the back door. We got in the car and headed straight to the liquor store, then back to the hotel. While Beth studied for her finals, Lilly and I walked around an abandoned car lot taking pulls from a bottle and howling at the moon. Finally, we returned to the hotel, stopping on the way to get Lilly some Taco Bell. I passed out on the couch and Lilly ended up sleeping on the bathroom floor, hunched over the toilet.

The three of us woke the next day, drove to Austin, played a gig at a Mexican restaurant called Jovita's that evening for about twenty eager listeners, and then drove back to Nashville.

When we arrived back in town, I went straight to the 5 Spot. I met up with Jeremy and stood down at the end of the bar in our usual spot. Something didn't feel right. I ordered a beer and lit up a smoke, but both made me feel sick. I looked down at my breasts and noticed how unusually large they looked. *Could I be pregnant?* I wondered.

"Is everything okay?" Jeremy asked when I turned down a shot of whiskey.

"I'm not sure. I think I might be coming down with something," I lied.

"You wanna go home?"

"Yeah, I do." I set down my beer, he grabbed my hand, and we left.

In the days that followed, I ignored the signs. I felt nauseous and was incredibly emotional. I remember reading an article about the death of John Lennon and crying my eyes out.

Jeremy was confused. "What's wrong? You've known John Lennon's been dead for years."

"I know. But it's just so terribly sad. Why did he have to die?"

That following Sunday was overcast. Jeremy had to work at the deli and I was home alone. I went up to the drugstore on Gallatin Road and grabbed a pregnancy test. I didn't even wait to get home; I took it into the dirty, dimly lit bathroom and hovered above the toilet as I peed on the plastic stick. Two little lines showed up: it was positive. I stared at it in disbelief. We had been carelessly having unprotected sex for five or more years by this point, and I truly thought we couldn't conceive.

I went back to the drugstore counter and bought another pregnancy test and took it home. About an hour later, I took it again: positive. I started to cry. I was happy but also scared. I was so young, I hadn't accomplished anything with my career, and I wondered how we would afford a baby. Had I known we could get pregnant, I would have been more diligent about using birth control.

I walked up to Mitchell Deli, where Jeremy was working behind the sandwich counter. When I got there, he was laughing and joking around with his fellow employees. We made small talk and I ordered a pimento cheese sandwich. He gave me the employee discount and I walked back home. Several hours later he came home, and without saying a word I handed him the positive pregnancy test. He stared at it.

"Is this . . . ? Are you—seriously?!" he stuttered.

"Yes, I am." I began to sob uncontrollably.

"Baby, what's wrong? Aren't you happy? I thought you wanted to be a mother. When we first met, you said you wanted five children!" He put his arms around me.

"Well, I did . . . I mean, I still do, but not now! I'm not ready. And we can't afford it!"

"Oh, babe, please don't cry! Don't worry, we'll make it work . . . this is great news! I've never had blood family." He picked me up and spun me around our small living room. "This is incredible. I'm gonna be a daddy!"

I started to smile. He always had a way of making everything seem like it was going to be okay. He hugged me for a long time and we stood there, a family, between the pale-green walls.

CHAPTER 17

New Mama

In the days that followed, I battled morning sickness with peppermint tea and went on frequent walks with Bella around the neighborhood, reflecting on my new situation. I made an appointment with the Vanderbilt midwives, and they confirmed that I was indeed pregnant. They put a microphone up to my stomach, and I heard a heartbeat that sounded like the flutter of a hummingbird's wings. It was the most amazing sound I'd ever heard.

I scheduled a sonogram at the doctor's request. I didn't have insurance, and our annual income was below the poverty line, so I signed up for TennCare and food stamps. It was humiliating to pay for my groceries with WIC checks, and most of the food you could get with them was pretty terrible. We lived off of government cheese and whatever leftovers Jeremy brought home from the deli. I was prideful and never let on to my family that we were accepting handouts. But we had no other choice.

By Christmastime, I was definitely showing. My mother was shocked to see my growing tummy. "You must be pretty far along! You might have more than one in there," she said with a nervous laugh.

January 2010 came, and Jeremy and I went in for our first sonogram. The room was quiet and calm. A thin nurse instructed me to lie down on the table.

I lay down, unzipped the top of my jeans, and lifted my shirt. She put a cool jelly substance on my round little tummy. The swishing, staticky sound of the equipment filled the room.

After about five minutes, she began to stare more closely at the screen. "Well, well . . . this is exciting." She smiled.

"What? What is it? Can you tell the sex?" I strained my neck to look at the screen.

"No, not yet, it's still too early to determine that." She kept circling around on my stomach. "I think you're about eleven weeks along."

"So almost three months?" I asked.

"Yep . . . and, well, yes, I do believe there are two of them in there." She peered over at me to judge my reaction.

"Two? You mean twins?! No way."

"Yes indeed! Twins. See, here is one sac and then another right here." She began to type on her computer, labeling them Twin A and Twin B.

I glanced at Jeremy. He was pale and looked as though he might pass out. He sat there in shock, completely quiet, with his legs crossed and his hand on his chin.

"Baby! Twins! We're having twins. Can you believe it?" I could barely sit still for the rest of the sonogram.

He finally spoke. "How will we afford it?"

"Baby! Remember, we will make it work! Don't worry!" Now I was comforting him. I grabbed his hand, and happy tears came to my eyes. "We're having twins!" I screamed.

"Holy shit. Twins?" Jeremy was excited now too.

The technician chuckled. "Congrats, Mom and Dad!"

She printed out the photos for us, and on our drive home I kept staring at the two little beans, there in black and white. Twin A and Twin B, eleven weeks along.

I fell into a routine of waking up and walking the dog up to Sip Cafe for a peppermint tea with honey and foamed milk. I sat and read a book, wrote a little, and went back home to play guitar or piano. I felt incredibly inspired while I was pregnant. I was creating life and simultaneously composing music, nesting, and settling into our new home. It all felt very natural. Jeremy and I decided to make solo albums on a reel-to-reel in the basement. We were still writing for Buffalo Clover and had plans to go back into the Bomb Shelter to record another full-length record with Andrija. The band came over and played often, working on the new songs and even planning to go to South by Southwest that spring to play a few shows in Austin. We had Palaver Records helping us book gigs as well as occasional assistance from John Sirota. I would be six or seven months along by March for SXSW, but it didn't mean I couldn't still play guitar and drums and make albums.

Because it was a twin pregnancy, the hospital visits were frequent. I seemed to be in there constantly. It was disappointing, but the midwives told me they would no longer see me since I was having twins, so I began seeing a regular doctor at Vanderbilt. Around sixteen weeks, we found out we were having twin boys.

I was so thrilled. I had always wanted a boy, and now we were getting two. I started to daydream about all of the adventures we would have as a family. *How amazing that they'll have each other to play with*, I thought. I went home and wrote them a poem, "A Brother for a Brother." We started coming up with names immediately. At first we chose Ezra and Eliot, from the Bob Dylan song "Desolation Row." I loved the verse with those names in it. Eventually, though, we settled on Ezra and Judah. Our firstborn would be Ezra Alan. Alan was my father's middle name, and it was also the name of Jeremy's biological father. The second boy would be Judah Quinn, just because we liked it.

I was growing like crazy. I had been about 105 pounds when I got pregnant, with small breasts, skinny legs, narrow hips, and a flat stomach with a belly-button ring. Halfway through my pregnancy, I could hardly recognize my body. My breasts were overflowing my bras, having quickly grown from an A cup to a full C. I felt unexpectedly liberated, but I was also uncomfortable. I was tired and swollen, having a lot of back problems and sciatic pain. Carrying two babies was a lot of work. I just kept giving myself pep talks: *Your vanity doesn't matter. These bodies are just temporary homes for the soul. Everything changes. Stretch marks are the battle scars of warriors.*

Most importantly, I reminded myself, *This will all be worth it when you hold your babies in your arms.* I kept my eyes on the prize.

It was a normal, gray, overcast day in February when I went to the new Vanderbilt hospital in Berry Hill for the anatomy scan. I was nineteen weeks pregnant. I went alone because Jeremy was working on overdubs at the Bomb Shelter that day. We had started tracking our new album, and I had plans to join him after my appointment to track some guitar and vocals.

The new building was sterile. A lady at the information desk pointed me in the right direction, and I made my way through the winding maze of beige walls and dull carpets until I arrived at the prenatal care office.

"Margo Price," called a nurse in kitty cat–patterned scrubs. "Are you all ready for this?" She gave me a warm smile and led me into the dark room.

I lay down on the exam table and lifted my shirt, revealing my basketball belly. She placed the cold metal rolling ball on my stomach and started searching for all the parts: fingers, toes, eyes, nose, kidneys, lungs. I watched wide-eyed as she circled, clicked, and checked off all the boxes.

Then suddenly she paused. She kept going back over the same place on Twin A. She peered at the screen, the wrinkle in her forehead growing deep with worry. When she turned the screen away from me, I started to freak out.

"Is everything okay?"

"I can't say." She pursed her lips.

"Well, you probably have an idea," I pressed.

"I honestly can't make any assessments until I talk to the doctor." She was quiet.

Panic set in. The worst thoughts imaginable ran through my head. She left and came back with another nurse. She pointed at the screen, and they both cocked their heads to the side, examining it. I sat silently for what felt like hours, waiting for them to finish.

Finally, she looked at me with sympathy and said, "I'll send the doctor in to see you soon." Another twenty minutes went by, and finally a man in a white coat came in. He was holding a pile of papers and a few pamphlets.

"Are you here alone?" he asked.

"Yes, my husband is busy. Is everything okay?"

"Well, it's complicated. After reviewing the photos from the sonogram, we have assessed that Twin A has a condition called hypoplastic left heart syndrome." He handed me some papers. "Basically, your son has half a heart. While he is in your womb, he is completely safe and protected. But after birth, he will have to have a series of surgeries to reroute the blood flow in his heart. The survival rate is very good. Nine out of ten survive the first surgery. It's hard to say how many surgeries he will have to have in his lifetime, but he will not be able to do things like most normal children—"

"You might be wrong," I interrupted. "His heart might still be developing. Maybe he just needs more time. I would like to get a second opinion." Tears welled up in my eyes, and my heart rate quickened. I couldn't think clearly. I stared down at the pile of papers in my lap spelling out my boy's fate.

"You can certainly do that, but Vanderbilt is second in the country when it comes to this kind of surgery and this specific heart defect." He put his hand on my hand. "I know this is hard to hear, but sometimes these things just happen, and we don't know why. It's a genetic defect that is fairly common in twins."

Tears started to flow down my face. "What do you mean, he won't be able to do things like most 'normal' children?"

"Well, his heart is small, and physical activities will be difficult for him. Running, playing sports—those kinds of things will likely not be possible for him. If he does survive the first series of surgeries and make it through his childhood, he will probably only live to be in his midthirties."

I lost it. *How can he be telling me this? What does he really know about my son?*

He handed me a box of tissues. "Ma'am, I know you're upset. This is a lot to take in, obviously. We'll make plans for another sonogram to track your progress."

I was hysterical. I gathered my things to leave. I had to get out of that tiny room. Everything was making me angry: the doctor's phony sympathy, the terrible, puke-colored paint on the walls, the florescent lights that flickered above me, and most of all, the bad-news pamphlets with deformed human hearts on them.

I ran out of the hospital. When I finally reached my car, I got in, slammed the door, and screamed. I cried for a long time.

I dialed Jeremy's number and tried to explain to him what they had told me, but I was so frantic and upset that the words wouldn't come out right.

"Baby, baby, slow down. I'm sure everything will be okay." He tried to calm me.

"No, it won't be okay. It's terrible, it's really terrible." I tried to tell him the details, but it seemed impossible to make sense of it. "He may only live to be thirty years old! It's so fucked up, Jeremy. I can't handle this. I'm going to the house."

"Okay, I'm leaving the studio now. I'll tell Andrija what's going on. Are you okay to drive? Please be careful, Margo."

"Yes, I'll be okay," I lied. The truth was, I was not okay. I continued crying when I hung up the phone and as I drove down the interstate. Looking back, I don't know how I made it home in that state, but when I arrived, I walked down into our basement where the guest bed was. It was completely dark. I threw myself on the bed and lay curled up in misery until Jeremy got there.

When he finally arrived, I walked him through what the doctor had told me. I showed him the papers and he read them. He lay down next to me, and we stayed there together in the dark. I didn't get out of bed until the next day. The news had thrown me into a spiral of deep depression, and from that day on, nothing in my life was ever the same again.

The following months were a blur, an endless series of appointments and sonograms and specialists with more sour news. The only things that distracted me were writing songs or disappearing into a good book.

We had plans to go to SXSW with both my band and Lilly's. At first, we debated canceling the trip, but Jeremy thought it might be good for me to get out of the house. I was apprehensive, but I also agreed that it might help boost my dark, isolating moods. Aside from working on music and staying busy in the studio, I was pretty reclusive. Most of the places I had gone before my pregnancy were off-limits to me now. The 5 Spot and 3 Crow Bar were still smoking establishments, and I didn't feel like I fit in there in my current state anyhow. Everywhere I went, people said things like, "You look like you're ready to pop!" and "Wow, you must be due yesterday!" I brushed off the remarks but was growing increasingly tired of rude comments and assumptions from complete strangers.

We made our way down to Texas and were excited to be a part of the annual music ritual. The sad thing was, Buffalo Clover hadn't actually booked an official showcase at SXSW, instead booking a smaller festival, RedGorilla Fest, that was going on at the same time. The band and I made our way to Austin anyway, arriving deadbeat style in a worn-out, early-'90s Chevy Astro van that Matt owned. I kept my feet propped up during the twelve-hour drive to keep them from swelling, but it didn't really work. I was puffy and exhausted by the time we arrived.

Our gigs were laughable. We played a couple of shows, all of them a complete and total wash. Sure, there were people there, but they weren't there to see us. It was crowded chaos—small spaces, bad sound equipment, and hordes of drunk folks, all talking over one another to promote their own shows. We blended in to the background, and although I sang my heart out, no one listened. If I stood out at all, it was only because of how close I looked to going into labor. Holding my guitar in front of my stomach was impossible, so I slung it over my shoulder and played it on my hip.

Lilly's gig was much better than ours. She opened for her father at a proper venue in an official showcase. I was sitting in for her on drums and Jeremy was on bass. When I got onstage to set up my cymbals and snare, the sound guy looked at me, clearly shocked.

"*You're* the drummer?" he sneered in disbelief.

"Yes, *I'm* the drummer. Is there a problem?"

"No, I mean, it's not because you're a girl, it's because you're so . . . well, so . . ." he stuttered.

"Pregnant?" I snapped back. "Why don't you worry about your job and I'll worry about mine." I took off my boots and sat down behind the drum throne.

We sound-checked and kicked off the event with a fever. My blood was boiling from the interaction, but I used it as fuel. Lilly sounded great, and Jeremy and I locked in and played our asses off. It felt good to perform for an attentive audience. I was slightly jealous that I hadn't had the opportunity to play a better show, but I was happy to be involved in Lilly's project and proud to back her up.

Buffalo Clover's tour might have been a complete and total wash, but we made the best of it. Walking around downtown Austin and listening to all the bands was inspiring and overwhelming. It made me realize how much work we had to do to stand out. By the end of the week, we were ready to get back home.

At one point, we sat down on the corner of Sixth Street and Lavaca in the middle of the chaos and ate tacos on the curb. My feet were killing me. I tried to take my boots off so I could walk the streets barefoot, but they wouldn't come off. Jeremy pulled and pulled, but they were stuck. We ended up cutting them down the sides with a pocketknife to get them off my feet. I was pretty upset. What was even more upsetting was getting on a scale. I had gained seventy pounds and still had a couple of months to go. I barely recognized myself from the weight gain, but even more than that, from the infinite sadness that had taken over my eyes.

Back in Nashville at the Bomb Shelter, we finished our record, which never saw the light of day. We didn't self-release it or anything—I don't really know why. Lack of time and money, I suppose. We definitely put money into making it, but getting it out there in any sort of a physical format was another story.

Stealing from Thieves was recorded entirely on tape. My vocals sounded pristine because I hadn't been smoking weed or cigarettes during the pregnancy. There were some decent songs on it, but no real direction as far as genre went. It was a half-acoustic, half-electric collection of songs. We also did a cover of the Kinks' "Big Black Smoke," a song I had always related to personally. I actually tap-danced on it for the percussion—one of Andrija's avant-garde ideas when he heard I possessed the skill.

We also completed both of our solo albums. Jeremy's was entitled *Peppermint Weasel,* a collection of nine songs best described as *Heart-worn Highways* meets the Beatles' *White Album,* but somehow stranger. Mine was entitled *Bird in the Thorn* and had a folky-country vibe to it. It was inspired by artists like Gillian Welch and the Handsome Family. Jeremy and I did the guitars, bass, and drums ourselves, but we enlisted others to play auxiliary instruments. Matt Gardner played some banjo, and I got a pedal steel and dobro player, a cellist, and a violinist. I only made twenty copies, and honestly, the only person who would still have a copy is my mother.

The track listing is hazy, but I remember one song in particular, "Country Song," which was a straight-up classic-country-style tune about the problems of the United States, with a dark political slant. I started it one day when I was sitting at a restaurant called Charlie Bob's, drowning my sorrows with decaf coffee and a slice of apple pie. Jeremy liked it so much that he begged to help finish it. The lyrics are hard to read, but comedic in a way.

People talk through mechanical waves, eat chemical pancakes and
*   hormone steaks*
We rent out houses but buy our graves, while the trash keeps
*   piling up*
People eat anything that's thrown on their plate while their
*   braindead kids play video games*
Three hundred million people in fifty states who never judge
*   themselves*

Pharmaceutical companies charge out the ass, while the sick get
*   jailed for smokin' grass*
The doctor gets kickbacks for pushing smack with side effects
*   unknown*

CHAPTER 18

Ezra and Judah

Time moved slower than molasses, and I grew increasingly isolated. So many doctors' appointments and checkups. We saw lots of specialists at Vanderbilt, and they tried their best to prepare us for the uncertain future.

Despite the looming darkness, I nested, made the nursery cozy, and decorated it the best I could on our shoestring budget. My mother handed us down a rocking chair, and my sisters threw me the most thoughtful baby shower. When all was said and done, we had two of everything: two car seats, two cribs, two mobiles, a double stroller, and onesies that said Thing 1 and Thing 2.

Jeremy and I spent a lot of nights curled up on the couch, watching movies and eating pizza, but he was also restless and went out to the bar regularly. As the months rolled on, I had dark mood swings, angry outbursts, increased anxiety, and intense feelings of hopelessness.

On the night of June 26, Jeremy wanted to go out to see a Beatles tribute at the 5 Spot. I wasn't having it. Although I wasn't due for another few weeks, I had a feeling that the babies were on their way at any minute.

"If you leave me here alone tonight, I'll drive to my parents' house and you'll never see me again!" I threatened, making a big, dramatic scene.

"Okay, okay, you're right. I'll stay home."

We ordered in some Chinese food and watched a movie. Still feeling emotional, I elected to sleep in the basement. I took a guitar and my notebook downstairs with me and penned a song entitled "Cure Me." I finished around one or two A.M., set aside my guitar, and curled up to sleep for a while. At around five, I woke up having to pee and decided to walk up to our bedroom, where Jeremy was fast asleep. As soon as I entered, I felt a warm sensation rushing down my legs and heard a sound like a faucet. My water had broken.

"Jeremy! Wake up! The babies are coming!"

He got out of bed quicker than I'd ever seen and began running around frantically. "Oh my God! Seriously?! Where's your bag? Where are the keys? Let's go!" He struggled to put his pants on.

He drove to the hospital at eighty miles an hour, taking all sorts of wrong turns. The two of us laughed about it nervously. When we arrived, a nurse unceremoniously handed us a clipboard.

"My wife needs to see a doctor right away!" Jeremy cried. "She's pregnant with twins and in labor."

I was pretty calm. Another nurse brought me a wheelchair. "How far apart are your contractions?" she asked.

"I don't know. I'm not sure if I'm having any."

"Well, you'll have to wait here, then. We have a lot of people to deal with," she snapped.

"Our son has a heart defect. This is urgent," Jeremy said.

The woman rolled her eyes and pulled up our chart. After ten minutes or so, a nurse finally approached and wheeled me to the elevator. "I hear you're getting sectioned," he said with a thick southern drawl.

"Excuse me?" I asked.

"You're getting sectioned. I hate doin' C-sections. I hope I'm off by the time you go in." Jeremy and I exchanged a worried look.

I leaned over to Jeremy and said, "Please don't let this man deliver our babies."

They wheeled me to a sterile, white room. They did a sonogram to measure the amniotic fluid and to gauge the position of the boys. One twin was transverse and the other was breech. There was no getting them out without cutting me open. Jeremy put on scrubs and I put on a gown. It was seven in the morning by this time. They prepared me like a piece of meat: cleaned me, shaved me, and finally administered the epidural.

"Lean forward more," a doctor I'd never seen before instructed. "I can't get the needle in the right spot."

"I can't lean forward more, my stomach is in the way," I complained.

He fished around with the giant needle, inserting it several times before reaching the right spot in my spine. The blue sheet went up, separating my top half from my bottom half. There must have been twenty or more people in the room. Doctors and nurses whom I'd never met until now were busily walking around. I was dizzy on morphine and completely disoriented. I realized I hadn't seen Jeremy in a while.

"Where's my husband? I need my husband. His name is Jeremy Ivey. Can someone please get him?"

"We'll bring him in when we can," a stranger behind a paper mask said.

They wheeled me under a giant lightbulb that burned brighter than the sun. I started to fade in and out of consciousness, confused yet relaxed, listening to the murmurs of the nurses and doctors as they began to work.

"Is my husband here yet?" I quietly asked again.

"Yes, he's here," a woman said. I saw Jeremy's blue eyes peering out between his hairnet and paper face mask. There was love in his eyes, but they were clouded with worry. Even in my medicated state, I could see that he was nervous.

"Hi, baby," he said. "How are you?"

"I'm great! I can't feel anything." I smiled.

"You have morphine eyes." Jeremy laughed.

"Yeah? I can't see them. What do they look like?" My voice trailed off.

"They look beautiful," he assured me.

The doctors and nurses began to speak frantically. I saw them moving behind the veil of blue. One of them approached the sink holding something that looked like a baby. I couldn't make out what any of them were saying. They seemed worried.

"Are my babies here? Is he okay?!"

No one answered me.

"Is he here? Where is my baby?! I want to hold him," I said.

"Hang on, dear." A nurse patted my head.

"Why isn't he crying? What's wrong?!" I pleaded.

Suddenly, a sound rose from the corner of the room that resembled the noise a baby lamb might make. The most fragile cry I'd ever heard filled the air and everyone clapped.

"He's here! He's okay. He wasn't making noise at first, but he is now!" the nurse explained. "What's his name?"

"Ezra. His name is Ezra," I told her.

"Beautiful," she said.

"Can I hold him?" I begged.

"Not just yet. He needs to be put in an oxygen chamber to help him breathe. We need to hook him up to a machine."

"What about Judah? Is he out yet?"

"Yes! He's here too." A strong, loud cry emerged in the room. They brought Judah over to me and I saw his face. He was absolutely perfect.

Jeremy reached down and held on to my hand as we peered at our baby. He was a miracle, but I was still so worried about Ezra, I couldn't think straight. "Jeremy, go look at him. Tell me what he looks like. I want to know that he's okay."

"All right, Margo, I will. Try not to worry." Jeremy knew that was nearly impossible.

They sewed me up and wheeled me into the recovery room. It was just Jeremy and me in there—no sign of my babies anywhere.

After an hour or so, I was taken to a room and they brought Judah to me. He was so tiny, so sweet. They brought in a lactation specialist and I began nursing him. I held him in my arms, and it was such a surreal experience, but my mind was constantly split. "What about Ezra?" I asked. "When can I see him?"

"Just focus on this baby for now. Ezra is in the NICU, where they're taking good care of him, don't worry. We'll wheel you down there in just a bit," the nurse assured me.

"I want to save some of the colostrum for him," I told them.

"Okay, you can feed Judah on one side and put the pump on the other breast to save some for the other twin," the specialist instructed.

My boobs were larger than ever, and my stomach was still incredibly swollen, but I had already lost twenty-some pounds postdelivery. I was heavily medicated, but my mind would not rest until I saw both of my babies. They finally put me in a wheelchair, a catheter attached to my side, and pushed me down endless, winding hallways to see Ezra.

Jeremy stayed in the room to watch over Judah. My parents accompanied me to the NICU. We arrived in the baby's room, where a dry-erase board on the door said "Ezra Ivey." A horde of nurses and doctors still swarmed around him. A few were observing, holding clipboards, writing things down. Others were examining him, messing with wires attached to him. There were futuristic machines everywhere with blinking lights and screens. In the middle of it all was my sweet son in a glass incubator, hooked up to several tubes. Little red lights taped to his foot tracked his pulse. Ezra was naked except for a diaper and some oversized socks.

"Can I hold him?" My chin quivered as I tried not to cry.

"No, I'm afraid not right now," a nameless nurse replied.

"Can I at least touch his hand?"

"No, you can't. We need to keep the environment sterile," said a man with a clipboard.

"But I've read a lot about skin-to-skin contact and how good it can be for the baby," I pleaded.

"I'm sorry, Ms. Price. Maybe later."

I just stood there, looking at Ezra through the glass. A nurse put her gloved hand inside the incubator and started messing with the wires. Ezra began to cry his same little lamb cry. He looked so scared, so alone. I wanted to lay him on my chest and cuddle him, but I just watched in total silence, feeling completely helpless, as the doctors did their thing.

As soon as I'd learned of the diagnosis, I'd felt I was to blame for the heart condition. Was it the alcohol and cigarettes I'd had before I knew I was pregnant? Was it my environment—growing up on desolate farmland, where planes flew overhead, cloaking the crops in poisonous pesticides? Was it the fast food I ate growing up? Was it karma for all the bad things I'd done? Was it God punishing me? What kind of God would take my child? What kind of God would do this to an innocent baby?

I had prayed and prayed leading up to the birth of the boys that the diagnosis would be incorrect, that Ezra would be healthy and normal. That all of this was a bad dream. But here I was, watching my son need assistance to breathe, watching his heart fail to beat on its own. I thought to myself, *There is no God. We've been betrayed.*

I stood there for a while with my parents, looking on at our little one, but it was obvious we were in the way of the crowd of people trying to work.

"Let's go back to check on Judah. He might need to be fed again," I said. My parents pushed me back down the long hallways.

On the way we passed a middle-aged man in a ratty trucker hat, dirty jeans, and a crooked smile, who looked at me and said, "Well, it sure looks like you're ready to get that baby out of you!"

"Go fuck yourself!" I told him.

My dad placed his hand on my shoulder without saying a word, trying to calm me down. My mother gave the man a cold look and told him to mind his own business.

For the next few days, I barely slept. All I could think about was Ezra in that incubator all alone. When they released us to go home, I didn't want to leave. I sat in the living room for about an hour, nursed Judah, pumped some milk for Ezra, and then drove back to the NICU.

My parents watched Judah while Jeremy and I visited Ezra. We couldn't hold him, but when he was four days old, they finally allowed me to change his diaper through the little glass holes at the bottom of his incubator. He hated having his diaper changed, and his little voice rose up with a strong cry in protest every time we had to do it. We sang through the glass to calm him. Jeremy and I stood there by his bedside, singing hymns, lullabies, and other songs—"Amazing Grace," "Mary, Don't You Weep," "The Blackest Crow." Our presence seemed to soothe him, and when I got him to sleep with my voice, I felt as though I was at least providing some small amount of comfort.

The doctors explained that at around nine days, he would have his first in a series of many surgeries. They were just waiting for him to grow and gain strength.

On July 3, I entered the hospital and saw something that disturbed me. I knew it was necessary, but it made me so upset. Right in the top of his tiny little head, they had installed some sort of IV or feeding tube. It looked so painful, the needles and tape strapped to the top of his skull. I asked them if he had felt any pain when they did it, but they assured me he was all right.

Life went on at home. Judah nursed every two or more hours and woke up constantly with soiled diapers, crying and begging to be held and hushed back to sleep. I was healing from a C-section and in a haze from pain pills. I was sleep deprived in a way I had never experienced in my life, and I was worried sick about my other baby boy, still in the Vanderbilt Children's Hospital.

The Fourth of July came, and I sat at home that evening listening to the fireworks exploding in the distance. They were coming from downtown and they sounded like bombs, even miles away at our home in Inglewood. I thought of Ezra hearing them in the hospital, frightened and alone, and I started to panic. I called the nurse's station and asked how he was. "Is he crying? Is he scared? Should I come up there?"

"No, Ms. Price, he's fine," the nurse said, trying to set my mind at ease. "Don't worry about coming down here. The traffic is chaos. Just get some rest and we'll see you tomorrow."

I asked the nurse to put the phone up to him. I sang Joni Mitchell's "River" to him through the receiver. It was July, not the Christmastime of the song, but it felt appropriate.

The following day, we had another meeting with the doctor. He explained that Ezra was strong enough for his surgery. I sat there with Judah in my arms and listened as best I could to his words, but I was drifting in and out of consciousness.

"Any questions?" he asked us.

"Before his surgery, could we get a photo of the boys side by side? We don't even have one photo of them together," Jeremy said quietly.

"I'm sure we could arrange that," the doctor said sympathetically. "Stick around and I'll make a call down to the nurse."

We took Judah into his brother's room, a place he had previously been forbidden to go. He was fussy and tired. The nurse removed Ezra's protective plastic bubble. Hearing Judah cry, Ezra joined in. Their two voices became one.

"Lay him down right here," a nurse instructed as they moved Ezra over and motioned me toward the tiny crib. The two babies lay there fussing for a brief moment before leaning in to each other and falling asleep, both completely silent and completely content. It was the most amazing thing I'd ever seen. We watched quietly and took some photos of the two of them. Their heads tilted together, looking so similar, they could have been mistaken for identical twins—except, of course, for Ezra's body wrapped in cords and wires.

"They look so calm. Can we just let them sleep there together for a while?" I asked.

"No, I'm afraid not," the nurse said. "We need to put the cover back on."

"Can we hold him?" Jeremy asked.

The nurse paused and thought about it. "You can, but it will be difficult."

"We've never held him. Not once," I said.

The nurse picked Judah up. Both boys immediately started crying at the separation. My mom took Judah out into the waiting room, and the nurse handed Ezra to me. I held him close to my chest and began to sing. Tubes came out of him everywhere, flowing down like vines onto my lap. I held him until he was calm and then very carefully handed him to Jeremy.

We stood there for about five minutes, staring down at him, cherishing the moment, until the nurse interrupted. "I'm afraid we can't have him out much longer, we must get him back in his safe space."

I kissed his head, and she took him from our arms. He cried loudly, more than when we first entered the room. There was no soothing him with a song this time. Nurses buzzed around him like busy little worker bees, checking his vitals and getting all the tubes and wires back in place. Hearing his tiny lamb cry ring out as they poked and prodded him ripped out my heart. A tear rolled down my cheek and Jeremy wiped it away. Without a word to each other, we exited the room.

I remained hopeful those next two days, praying for Ezra like I had never prayed before. Jeremy and I prayed together, we held hands, we bowed our heads, we prayed in silence, we prayed aloud, we kept faith that I hadn't even known we had. We decided we would temporarily move in to a hotel next to the hospital so we could be close for Ezra's surgery.

On July 6, we sat in the waiting room with both sets of parents and waited for the doctor to come out and give us good news. Hours passed by, and time seemed unreal. The sound of the clock ticking drove me mad, and my mind played tricks on me. Had we always been here in this little room? Would we ever leave? I felt like the whole thing was a nightmare, just some sort of cruel charade. Jeremy's parents, Tom and Sandy, sensed this and prayed with me. My mother sat with pursed lips, rocking back and forth with her legs crossed, just as worried as I. My father left the waiting room intermittently to smoke in the parking garage. At times I wished I could join him.

Finally, the doctor emerged. He still wore his scrubs, mask, and crepe-paper hat. Over time, I have forgotten his name—it doesn't matter. I can still see the look on his face as he entered the room. It was not good; I knew it as soon as his eyes met mine.

He sat down next to us, placed his elbows on his knees, and folded his hands. He took a deep breath and began to talk.

"Things did not go exactly as planned," he started slowly. "We put the stent in his heart, but it was the wrong size. It was hard to gauge how big a stent we would need because of—"

"Is he okay? Did he make it?!" I interjected.

"He is technically still alive," the doctor said, still looking down. He could not look at me. "We replaced it with a smaller stent, but there was a long period of time when his brain was without oxygen. We have him stable now, but we're not sure of his brain activity."

I sat in silence, in total shock, not knowing what to say. Everyone else started asking questions as the room whirled around me. I stared blankly up at the rectangular sections of the drop ceiling. I looked down at Judah in my arms and began to tremble.

"We did the best we could," the doctor said. "Go home and get some sleep. We'll know more tomorrow."

"How am I supposed to sleep not knowing if my son is okay? I want to see him. Can we see him?" I was starting to get angry. Jeremy grabbed my hand and held it so tightly I thought he might break it.

"I agree, it would be nice to see our son," he said.

"It's not a good time," the doctor said. "We're still stabilizing him. Come back tomorrow and we can figure this all out."

We left the hospital in the dark of night, concerned and confused. I was exhausted but not sure I would ever be able to settle my mind enough to actually sleep. Our parents hugged us and returned home. Jeremy and I went back to the hotel. I briefly turned on the TV and tried to distract myself, but it was no use. Judah was extra fussy that night, as if he knew something was wrong. I lay awake all night, and finally at five thirty I went down to the hotel lobby for coffee.

At eight we returned to Vanderbilt. They took us to a small room with a circular table made of fake wood. The doctor who had performed the surgery was there, as well as two other men I'd never seen before.

"Mr. Ivey, Ms. Price, how are you two doing today?" one of the mystery doctors asked.

"Fine," Jeremy answered curtly.

I sat in complete silence, staring off into space, knowing that if I opened my mouth, something rude would come out.

"We need to talk to you about your son," the other mystery doctor began.

"How is he this morning? When can we see him?" Jeremy said everything I was thinking.

"That's a difficult question to answer," the first doctor said. "As you know, we replaced the larger stent with the smaller stent last night and he is stabilized. His heart *is* beating."

"That's great news," I said hopefully.

"The thing is, during the surgery, his heart stopped, and he was deprived of oxygen to his brain for a very long time. It's very unlikely he will come back from this. The machines are breathing for him, they are making his heart beat, but he won't be able to do that without them."

"So you're saying our son is brain-dead?" Jeremy asked point-blank.

"Essentially, yes. That is what I am saying," the doctor answered.

"How do you know that for sure?" I asked.

"Once brain tissue dies, there is nothing that can be done to heal it. We could try to take him off life support and see how he does on his own . . . but it's unlikely he will survive."

The surgeon who'd performed the operation sat silent, his legs crossed, and did not offer any further explanation. He stared down at his hands like he had the night before.

"I don't understand. There was a ninety percent success rate on this surgery. What happened?" I stared a hole in the surgeon's head.

"This is unfortunately the ten percent. It happens sometimes. These babies are so small and it's hard to operate on them. They don't always make it," the second doctor said.

The surgeon finally caught my gaze and broke his silence. "I'm sorry. I did the best I could, and it wasn't good enough."

"Damn right it wasn't good enough!" I yelled.

"Ma'am, stay calm. We have to talk about this calmly and clearly," one of the other doctors interjected. "You and your husband have a very difficult decision to make."

"So you're saying we need to make the decision to take our son off of life support?" Jeremy asked.

"Yes, that is what I am saying," the doctor replied.

"We can't do that. Maybe he'll bounce back. He's just not strong enough right now," I said, crying openly.

"I wish that was the case, Ms. Price, but I'm afraid it's not," one of the doctors explained.

I couldn't believe the words they were saying. They exited the room, leaving Jeremy and me alone to talk.

"Margo, you know what we have to do. It's not right to keep him in a vegetative state like this."

"But what if he is still there? We can't do this immediately. We need to ask another doctor's opinion."

We sat and talked it over and over. I called the doctors back in. I interrogated them as if I were a police detective trying to get to the bottom of a murder case. We went over it and over it. Finally, they convinced me that there was no saving him, and together, Jeremy and I made the hardest decision of our lives. We would turn off the machines and say goodbye.

"We'll let you know when it's over," one of the doctors said, placing his hand on my shoulder. "Would you like to hold him one last time before he passes on?"

"Yes, I would like to," I said quietly. Jeremy agreed.

We waited in the tiny room. I put my head in my hands and wept for a while. It was so much to process, and I couldn't be sure of what exactly was going on. *It's just a bad dream, it's all a bad dream,* I told myself. I dried my eyes and nursed Judah for a few moments until he fell asleep in my arms. After about thirty minutes, a nurse opened the door and asked us to follow her. I handed Judah to my mother, and Jeremy and I followed the nurse down the hall and into a room.

Two nurses were waiting when we entered. They walked over quickly to me, handing me a baby wrapped in a white blanket. It was Ezra, but he was already gone. His face was white and his lips were bluish. I looked down at him in complete and total shock.

"I'm so sorry," one nurse said.

I began to break down. Tears flowed down my face and anger welled up inside of me. My cries turned to screams. "No, no, no! Why would you do this? My baby is dead! Why would you hand me a dead baby?" I screamed. "I wanted to see him before they took him off life support. I don't want to remember him like this . . ." My voice trailed off.

Jeremy cried with me as we stood there in shock. He looked down at Ezra and wiped his eyes, trying to be strong for me. He took him from my arms, and it was like I didn't know how to let go. It was the strongest feeling. I didn't want to hold him, but I knew it would be the last time I ever did. It was the first time I'd ever held him without all the machines and tubes and wires. Finally, Jeremy pried him from my arms and passed him to one of the nurses, and she placed him back in the tiny bed. I rushed to Ezra and stared down, unable to look away from his sweet little face. Jeremy pulled me from the room as I wailed at the top of my lungs. I was having a complete and total meltdown, and everyone was staring at me through the glass.

As we left, I saw the surgeon who had operated on Ezra in another room with about ten other doctors, looking down at another infant. Our eyes met. I was still hysterical, screaming incoherently. I stared at him, trying to communicate hatred and disgust with a look in a way I had never done in my life. His eyes were full of apology and sadness, but somehow that made me hate him even more. If looks could kill, I would have murdered him right there on the spot.

I went back out into the hallway, where our parents and my sisters were waiting for us.

"He's gone! He's gone! I can't believe he's gone!" I cried. Everyone broke down. My mother and my sisters grabbed me as I collapsed to the cold hospital floor. They threw their arms around me and wailed. We all sat there sobbing for several minutes in utter disbelief. They picked me up and took me home, where I spent the next few hours in bed.

But Judah needed me. We gave him his first bath that night in the kitchen sink, and I tried my best to be present and in the moment. I couldn't help feeling like Judah was being deprived of a normal upbringing already. My sadness was overwhelming, and the pain pills left my mind in a desperate fog. I flushed the rest of the OxyContin and Hydrocodone down the toilet that night. I knew I needed to be able to process my emotions, even if that meant enduring more physical pain. In a cold sweat, already withdrawing from the drugs, I woke up five hours later. The baby did too.

CHAPTER 19

Drowning

We had heavy decisions to make. Cremation or burial. When and where to hold the funeral. It all seemed impossible to sort out. My family stayed and helped me through it. Several days later, we laid Ezra to rest. Our friends came with offerings of songs and poems. My busking street sister, Kate, arrived with her husband, Bryan. They had just had twin boys. The four of us embraced and spilled our tears at the funeral home. Steven Knudson sang "Tears of Rage" by the Band, "Strangers" by the Kinks, and "Peace in the Valley." We picked selections from Kahlil Gibran's *The Prophet*. Jeremy and I were in no condition to speak the words ourselves, so Matt read them solemnly aloud.

> *Your children are not your children*
> *They are the sons and daughters of Life's longing for itself.*
> *They come through you but not from you,*
> *And though they are with you yet they belong not to you.*
>
> *You may give them your love but not your thoughts*

For they have their own thoughts.
You may house their bodies but not their souls,
For their souls dwell in the house of tomorrow,
Which you cannot visit, not even in your dreams.

My heart felt cold and black. When people said things like "God has another angel in heaven today," I wanted to spit in their faces. No one could understand my grief, our grief. It was ours and ours alone, just Jeremy's and Judah's and mine.

When we returned to the house, I felt like I was coming out of a haze. The pain pills had finally left my system. I could feel everything, and it was terrible. The mental anguish, the pain from my incision. A sour reality loomed over me. Our friends followed us to the house, and we all sat around in silence. The only thing that brought a glimpse of relief was our darling Jude. I nursed him and pumped some milk for later. I had stockpiled a bunch of colostrum and breast milk for Ezra, but it dawned on me that he would never need it now. I wanted to numb the pain and wished I hadn't flushed the pills. At least I could feed Judah the breast milk from a bottle while I got drunk.

Some family members brought home two giant cases of cheap beer. We all started drinking. I remember being in the basement, where we kept all of our instruments, and eventually Jeremy picked up a guitar and started singing. Everyone joined in. I temporarily sang my grief away. Everyone passed the guitars, took turns on piano, drums, and bass. We smoked inside and drank every single beer. We went to the liquor store to get a bottle of booze. We finished every drop. My mother and my sisters tended to Judah while I drowned my sorrows.

Around midnight, my breasts started to ache. I pumped the milk and dumped it down the drain. I had managed to keep my mind off of everything for a few hours, but soon my thoughts returned to Ezra and I broke down. The booze had temporarily distracted me, but now it just intensified my sadness. I fell asleep that night sobbing uncontrollably into my pillow. I was awakened several hours later by Judah's cries.

People brought by food for us, casseroles and pot roasts. We received cards, sentiments of both congratulations and sympathy, in the mail for months. Eventually I dreaded going to the mailbox because there was always another reminder of our loss. Handwritten checks arrived to help with the medical bills. The house was full of beautiful flower arrangements and potted plants, but they were only cruel reminders of the pain. To this day, I can't look at or smell a white lily without feeling some pangs of grief.

For several weeks, nothing soothed me except for Judah's sweet face. I wept for him too, knowing he would feel the loss of his brother forever. Twins have a strong connection, and I had a feeling he was already missing being side by side with his other half. I did my best to give Judah enough love and attention for two babies. I imagined that, like Elvis, who lost a twin at birth, he would live a life big enough for the two souls. I tended to him like a garden and found happiness in his smile. Jeremy and I made it through the sleepless nights, taking turns spending mornings with him in the sunny front room of our house while the other napped. I nursed him and then let him sleep in my arms or on my chest. We fed each other and bonded deeply.

The fog of grief lifted but I continued to mourn intensely, though I hid it from people. I was haunted by recurring nightmares of the nurses in the brightly lit room handing me my dead baby. Other nights, I was standing in my nightgown at the edge of a pond, and then I waded into the murky, brown water up to my knees. In the distance, I could see the outline of a tiny body splashing and sinking in the water. I frantically swam out to the middle of the pond, diving down and searching for what had to be my child, but the water was too cloudy. Then I could see the outline of a baby at the bottom of the pond, but I couldn't reach it. I kept coming up and gasping for air until finally I pulled up the lifeless body of a child I could not resuscitate. I had this nightmare over and over and over for the next three years.

In hindsight, I should have gone to therapy immediately, but I had convinced myself that I was strong enough to handle it on my own.

The hospital offered support groups for mothers dealing with the loss of their babies, but I didn't want to publicly grieve with people I didn't know. And I didn't want pity. I wanted to be strong, and for a while I did a great job of faking it. I didn't want to cry in front of my husband or my friends, and I especially didn't want to cry in front of my son. When I found myself slipping into sadness or anger, I sought out privacy and let out a primal scream. I cried in the shower, where the water muffled the noise.

My doctors offered me pills and counseling. They urged me to take antidepressants, but I told them to piss off. I grew to mistrust hospitals, and my hatred for doctors intensified.

Fortunately, I didn't dive back into drinking or smoking during the first nine to ten months, because I was nursing Judah. It kept me safe from myself. Around nine months, Judah developed a mouthful of tiny baby teeth, and I quit nursing him. I continued to pump for a month or so until my milk supply ran out and I switched him to formula. That was when I dove back in headfirst and began self-medicating. I was desperate for a way to stop the nightmares, and when I was drunk, I didn't have any dreams at all.

CHAPTER 20

Uppers, Downers, Out-of-Towners

Predictably, I started drinking again. Nothing major at first—just two or three drinks were a good distraction at the end of the day after we put the kid to bed. It took my mind off things. It was a well-known parental coping mechanism, and I wasn't alone—mommy wine culture was everywhere.

I felt isolated and alone, and I slowly started to spiral. I wasn't working much at the time, because childcare was expensive. Jeremy eventually left his job at the deli and got hired at an organic grocery store in the Gulch called the Turnip Truck. It was there that he met a well-kept secret who should have been a legend, Sturgill Simpson, and Kevin Black. Both had just recently moved to town and started to pursue music. Sturgill had a band named Sunday Valley, and Kevin had joined as his bass player. They all bonded over their mutual love of dope smoking in the alley behind the store and their mutual distaste for the job in general. The position only lasted about half a year, when Jeremy was accused of stealing. They fired him in late 2010, a week before Christmas, and it came as a total shock because he never stole a red cent.

Jeremy and I began going out again to bars, booking shows in town, touring a bit around the southeastern states. One night we met a group of musicians called the Lonely H playing at the 5 Spot. They played rowdy rock and roll and had just moved to town from Port Angeles, Washington. They were fronted by a tall, blond, blue-eyed singer and keys player named Mark Fredson. Eric Whitman was on guitar and harmonies, his brother Johnny Whitman played bass, and Ben Eyestone held it down on drums. One of the 5 Spot's drink slingers, Zach Setchfield, also joined them on guitar. We gravitated to them immediately; no one else in town was really playing classic rock and roll besides us. The Lonely H boys were all long haired and skinny, dressed in vintage clothes and looking like they had time traveled from 1975.

We took them under our wing, as they were all much younger than us, and Jeremy and I slipped into the role of the mom and dad of these lost boys. They lived just up the street from us, within walking distance, and we hosted them many nights for family dinners and picking parties. Everyone passed the guitars and sang songs, originals and covers. We frequently had jams in the basement, with everyone switching off between electric guitars, bass, drums, and piano, drunk singing and harmonizing together like one big, happy, dysfunctional family. Buffalo Clover and the Lonely H shared a lot of bills back in those days. We played small- to mid-sized venues like Mercy Lounge, the Basement, or the High Watt, and we were nearly permanent fixtures at the 5 Spot.

We often pooled our money to buy a bottle of cheap bourbon. Benchmark was only $8.99 for a fifth. We began doing picklebacks, a trick I had picked up in Raleigh, North Carolina, on tour, which allow for drinking a lot of bourbon without actually tasting it. You do the shot and then immediately chase it with a swig of pickle juice, which kills the after bite. We put down fifth after fifth this way.

There was also a lot of Adderall and cocaine circulating around. The quality of the coke definitely wasn't very good, but it was everywhere, and partaking seemed like an obligation. It was a cycle: get too drunk, have a line or a bump, sober up, and then get messed up again. I wasn't

proud of either the drinking or the drugging, but that's what was happening back in those days. Our career was still in the toilet, but we were
partying like we were rock stars.

We spent endless nights occupying the barstools at the 5 Spot. We ran
up tabs we couldn't pay for, ordering rounds of shots and beers like we
had money to burn. Sometimes we would just add things on to our tab
and pay a large bill at the end of several weeks of drinking. Occasionally,
one of the bartenders or one of the three owners wiped the tab clean for
us, ripping up the unpaid receipts and erasing our long-running debts.
But many times, we were forced to pay our IOU notes, or hanger tabs,
before we could come in and order more.

Bartenders poured free shots for us for the hell of it. The signature
5 Spot shot known as the orange crush, consisting of orange vodka,
cranberry juice, and Red Bull, tasted just like the soda. They kept you
going, but they got you blind drunk and erased your memory, which
could be incredibly dangerous. We popped little blue pills and snuck
into the bathroom to do bumps of coke, and occasionally, when times
were rough, we crushed up Adderall and snorted it off of the back of the
toilet seat.

Jeremy and I made a bad habit of staying out long past last call, trading
off so that one of us could stay home to care for our young son while the
other raged. It was no way for new parents to act and it was a complete
miracle that we made it out of that era alive. We were high-functioning
in those days. I grew increasingly skilled at managing and hiding my
drinking from the world. I was also protected by many of those around
me, because they were all high-functioning drinkers as well.

We sometimes partied with the bartenders until five or six in the
morning. Being out constantly on opposing nights was hell on our
marriage and our livers. Our bank statement was a sad sight. We were
spending a small fortune on drinks we really couldn't afford. But we
always found a way.

We plowed through our days with a vicious hangover like it was nothing. But we always made sure that Judah was looked after. We kept him

well fed, clean, safe, and deeply loved, but we weren't taking good care of ourselves.

From 2010 to 2015, a constant stream of people crashed in the basement guest room at our house. We had a rotating door open to transients and train-hoppers, and our home on Fernwood was like a hostel for wandering musicians and vagabonds, with our spare bed and couches open to almost anyone in need of a place to stay. We believed in paying it forward and giving shelter to those with little money who came to the city to play a show or pursue a dream. It always came back to us when we found ourselves playing a gig in a strange new town, unable to afford a hotel.

Among the bands and solo artists that we hosted were Brittany Howard and Alabama Shakes, Clear Plastic Masks, Promised Land Sound, Benjamin Booker, Willy McGee, Sam Doores and the Tumbleweeds (later known as the Deslondes), and Hurray for the Riff Raff, who came with an entire entourage of bohemians, dropouts, train-hopping gutter punks, and stray dogs.

One hot summer night, there must have been twenty-five or more people staying at our house. The lot of us carried on until two or three, singing songs, smoking rollies, and taking turns pulling from a bottle of George Dickel. As the night wore on, people began searching for places to sleep all around the house. We eventually ran out of beds and couches, so we made pallets all over the floor as makeshift mattresses. When we ran out of space inside, the rest of the crew crashed outside in the tall grass of the backyard. I felt bad they had no beds, but it was summer and they seemed to enjoy it. There were random hippies and freeloaders passed out all over our property.

The next morning, Judah woke around seven. I picked him up from his crib and carried him into the kitchen. My mission was to put on the coffee, feed Jude some cereal, and clean up the vile mess of beer cans and wine bottles strewn about the kitchen and the back porch. While I was putting the water on to boil, Judah crawled into the living room, where Riley Downing, one of the Tumbleweeds, was sleeping on the couch. Jude took his toy train and began to run it along Riley's arm and head, waking him up with a "Choo choo." Even as a two-year-old, he was pretty used to there always being strangers around and was shy with almost no one. Riley opened his eyes and laughed at the sight.

"Judah, honey, let him sleep!" I said as I noticed the comedic interaction.

"Aw, that's all right!" Riley said with a laugh. "I love little kids." He sat up and grabbed a toy car on the floor next to him and began making an engine sound: "Vroooooooom, vroom!"

Judah toddled back over and started to play with him. He was so adorable at that age, with a cherub face; blond, curly hair; and long eyelashes that framed his big blue eyes.

"I can play with him while you get a shower or do whatever you need to do," Riley offered.

"You are an angel," I said. "I'll just finish makin' some coffee. That's really all I need right now."

While Riley played with Judah, I made a strong brew in the percolator. Then I brought Judah some cereal and sat down on the floor beside them.

"You hungry?" Riley asked. "I can cook up some breakfast for everyone."

"Starving. There's a lot of people here though. I don't think I have enough eggs and bacon to feed everyone."

"I'll run up to the store. I know just what I can make that's cheap and tasty," he said with a grin.

Riley was quite the character; he hailed from Missouri by way of Louisiana and had a real down-home charm about him. He lived an untethered life and had hopped trains with Alynda Lee before joining up with the Tumbleweeds. He talked slow and low but had a great sense of humor, and both his wit and his songs were sharp as a knife.

Twenty minutes later, Riley returned from the Piggly Wiggly up the street.

"Gonna cook up some pork brains!" he announced, holding up several tin cans.

"Yum," I said, not knowing if he was serious or not—but he most certainly was. He cooked up eggs and pork brains that morning, and most everybody ate them, because they were hungry and it was free—and because they didn't know what it was.

That's how it was in those days: a communal effort to inspire each other and take care of each other. We were all loser poets struggling to keep our heads above the water and the booze. Looking back, there was a romanticism in knowing that we might be failures but that we were talented failures in a business that championed mediocrity. Even in the lonely shadows of the burning spotlight, beyond the endless roads to the sprawling cities and trash towns, between the empty gas tank and the underattended gigs, we were spreading the true gospel of meaningful music and the lost art of poetry and songs. We would not sell out.

CHAPTER 21

Burn Whatever's Left

Buffalo Clover continued to flounder in the mid-level cesspool that was the East Nashville music scene. We were naive and disorganized. In two years, Palaver Records had advised us on some less than helpful business decisions that drove us into debt. They did help us release one EP, *Strong Medicine*, and one full-length album, *Pick Your Poison*. In 2011, we put out another full-length album, called *Low Down Time*. It didn't move mountains, but it reached further than our past endeavors, getting some small reviews and write-ups in both the United States and the UK.

We followed through with our plans to finally tour England, opening up for Matt Gardner's friend Mike Badger. We went in the summer, when Judah was just a year old. It was hard to leave him, but I so badly wanted to go to the UK and play music. I rationalized that I spent every waking moment with him, and so leaving for a couple of weeks was reasonable. Still, it hurt to be away.

We traveled by motorway and also by Eurail. Matt had driven in the UK before, so we rented a minivan and he drove us everywhere. The band consisted of me, Jeremy, Matt, Jason White, and Jared Braucht.

We didn't have a proper drummer, so Jason played a small kit part of the time, and we played like a bluegrass band, with an acoustic setup of six strings and banjos, for the rest of the set. The shows were less than spectacular and attendance was nothing to write home about, but those who did come to listen were gracious.

Our band returned to England again just two years later, in search of our humble crowd. We sang in pubs, in cathedrals, and at street festivals. It was small potatoes and we knew it, but we were sustained by the crumbs of the Brits' kindness. Over the month abroad, we chased the spirit of the Beatles down Abbey Road to Strawberry Fields. We made pilgrimages to the Cavern Club and left some poppies on the grave site of Eleanor Rigby.

Houston Matthews was behind the skins now, and we had picked up a brilliant young pianist named Amaia Aguirre by way of Spain. I met Amaia and fell in love instantly, as did most of the band. I was so grateful to have another girl with me onstage and on the road to share clothes and secrets with. Over the next few years, we grew very close.

Buffalo Clover was growing and changing. Our spirits would be temporarily lifted and then quickly trampled down again, only to spring back up, stronger than before—like a lizard that can grow a new tail, or a weed you can't seem to kill. During this time abroad I wrote a poem called "The Transients." I read it aloud to the band one evening after several bottles of wine had been consumed. Mike had graciously let us stay in his garage house behind his cottage in Liverpool, and everyone was half asleep, passing joints, sprawled out in our incestuous way on a pallet on the floor.

THE TRANSIENTS

What happened to the Transients?
The unplanned painters
The sorrow eyed musicians living like ghosts on the road
Peeking through alleys, slipping through cracks

Hunting with heavy hearts on the highway
For a chance to cheat mortality
For a ticket out of the mindless day and into the whipping wild
Erratic lunatics crawling their way out of ridicule and misfortune
Thieving demons smoking out on the platforms
Crossing paths with the well-to-do for a brief moment
Before walking back into the wilderness

The pale green hills covered in paper thin English cows
The stony streets with dim lit lampposts leaning crooked on the
*   ground*
The seedy pubs and damp opium dens
Where painted women dance with silver bells and colorful scarves
Scared straight people shudder to think of these places
But we know
We live
We truly live out on the road
We are at home in her unbridled reins
Where the runaway mare tramples the fresh grass
And tears up the dirt on the covered path
Until she is far away again
And we can no longer hear the pounding of her hooves

We are in a new city with porcelain chimneys and quaint churches
As soon as one place is passed
Another one is adopted and scavenged for memories of life on
*   the run*
Placed in that pocket of my brain where I store inspiration for
*   slower days*
Days where routine becomes the only option
Days without dough
When the sun is down and the moon goes waning high above me
And I dream about all the other cities

Places full of stone buildings and ancient pillars
Places where handsome men walk the streets with shined shoes
*   and good tobaccos*
Places where the cafes are open til dawn
Broken fences lead us out to the prairie fields and open countrysides
We keep walking out of town to set up our tents on a newer hill
*   farther away*
Somewhere where we feel like visitors again

The trip came to an end and we returned home. We continued to play shows around Nashville, same as before, but nothing much changed. Somewhere along the line, after a bad show, I started to take my frustrations out in the form of vandalism. I began sneaking beer bottles or pint glasses outside of the venues and smashing them on the ground or against walls. At the time, it seemed like a good way to cope with failure, but looking back, it was childish and pointless. Jeremy tried to discourage my careless behavior, but there was no stopping me. Over the next few years, I smashed hundreds of bottles.

Ever since I'd left the Midwest, the ground had been shifting beneath my feet, and I hardly ever felt in control. My flaws were like a million fault lines that might at any moment cause an earthquake.

Smashing bottles wasn't the only stupid thing I was doing. Jeremy and I were having major problems in our marriage. We hid our vices from one another, stayed out late, and argued more and more frequently, sometimes in front of our young son. Our friends started calling us Kurt and Courtney. I despised the reference. I didn't want to have a bad reputation, but the town was small, and I knew I was making one.

I stayed home with Judah, and Jeremy kept kitchen jobs, but they never lasted long. After work, he usually clocked in a few hours at a bar for happy hour, hanging out at Edgefield or 3 Crow and tying one on with his friends. I called him and texted him so many nights, asking him to come home, but he rarely answered my calls. I took to driving through Five Points with Judah in the back seat some afternoons to look for Jeremy's car. I'd occasionally track him down and drag his ass out of the bar. He would be sitting there in broad daylight, drinking a beer and a shot, smoking a cigarette, and hanging with our rowdy friends, usually members of the Lonely H. Some days he'd withdraw money from the bank and throw in on a bag of blow.

I complained constantly about his behavior, but my bitching only pushed him away. Jeremy felt he deserved to go out nearly every night after work. It was his reward for working a shitty job. I understood, but I was also home alone all day parenting. I was doing my best to raise our son without much help from our families, since they all lived in other states.

Jeremy and I continued to keep secrets from each other, and motherhood was increasingly isolating. I began to spend more and more time with our guitar player, Matt. It started off innocently enough. Sometimes he came by on his motorcycle to smoke a joint with me while Jeremy was out. At first, we just had long talks about life and music and our favorite authors. Matt was an English major and incredibly well-read; he wrote songs and could play just about any instrument he picked up. He turned me on to some great writers, and we exchanged books. He gave me a copy of *The Unbearable Lightness of Being* by Milan Kundera, and it touched me deeply. The love triangle in the book expressed what, up until that point, we had only said with our eyes. But late one evening after a show, we crossed the line.

It was a heavy betrayal. Jeremy and Matt were as bonded as brothers, and Matt was married. He and his wife had been together for sixteen years. We both regretted it, but it didn't end there. Love and grief are a package deal, and I had a lot of both.

The band was hardly surviving. I felt that my life's work was an embarrassment, a string of disappointing shows and irresponsible decisions. Even with Matt, I kept my innermost thoughts private, never fully sharing how severely depressed and increasingly suicidal I was. I was living a full-blown lie, and I never reached out to tell anyone I was drowning.

To make things worse, Jeremy and I were handling Ezra's death very

differently. He had moved on, and I just couldn't. I hid my binge drinking, sometimes getting drunk on wine alone at the house. I was haunted
by night terrors and slept infrequently. I woke up in the middle of the
night from the recurring nightmare of Ezra swaddled in his blanket—
his perfect face, his eyes closed, his little blue lips. Sometimes, when I
was driving alone, I thought of running my car off the road. If not for
Judah, who knows where I would be? The only reason I was living in
those days was to care for and love him.

When you lose a child, you join a club that no one wants to be in.
There is an unspoken understanding among parents who have suffered
this tragedy. They say that time won't erase the grief, but that it becomes
more tolerable. I didn't know how I would ever learn to live with it.
I wasn't the same person as before. I never would be again. Jeremy tried
to talk me down from a thousand nights of tears and sorrow. Deep
down, I hated him for not grieving like I was. No one could understand
the loss I was feeling, not even my own husband.

He tried reasoning with me. He said our son was lucky because he
wasn't suffering. He said we should be grateful that Ezra wouldn't have
a life full of doctor's appointments and surgeries. He said Ezra was free,
and we were the ones who were left to do the suffering. He adopted a
Buddhist philosophy that I both admired and resented. I didn't connect to anything he was saying. I wanted Ezra back, and I wanted him
healthy. I wanted to know him.

As Jeremy and I drifted further apart, Matt and I grew closer, even
as I knew everything about our affair was reckless. We met up in the
usual places—crummy hotels, restaurants on the edge of town, and
dimly lit dive bars where we drank, played our favorite country songs
for each other on the jukebox, and talked about literature. He bought
me my own slick, black helmet and drove me around on the back of his
motorcycle. We went 120 down the interstate, hoping nobody would
recognize us. Sometimes we drove to the cemetery and lay on the graves
wrapped in each other's arms, chain-smoking American Spirits.

As time passed and our relationship became more and more

complicated, neither of us was very good at hiding our admiration of the other. Matt started coming by the house in broad daylight to pick me up on his bike to go out for a ride. Jeremy never asked questions. The evidence was there, it was happening right in front of him, but at the time I don't think he wanted to know.

CHAPTER 22

Treading Water

They say the definition of insanity is doing the same thing over and over and expecting a different outcome. My marriage and my band were hanging on by a thread, but I wasn't ready to throw in the towel on either. I continued to play shows here and there, mostly tribute nights and random gigs around town with Buffalo Clover. I began working with a woman named Karen, a fast-talking manager who worked with several other bands around town. She initially seemed to be reputable and somewhat well-connected, but she was expensive. She worked on a retainer and wanted $250 a month, no matter what the band earned. It was a lot of money for us, since we were barely making enough to pay the bills as it was. But she promised she could help take us to the "next level," wherever that was.

In 2013, Buffalo Clover released an album called *Test Your Love*, which featured a song with my friend Brittany Howard from Alabama Shakes. Britt and I had met years before, doing background vocal work at the Bomb Shelter. Her voice sent chills up the back of my neck, and just standing next to her was intoxicating. She was younger than me, but I looked up to her instantly. She was a kindred spirit, and she knew how to party. I was happy to have a friend who could keep up with me. Whenever Brittany drove in from Alabama, I knew I was in for a wild night. We spent our evenings together bar hopping and knocking back shots and bottles of beer before soaking it all up with some deliciously greasy food from our favorite all-night diner, the Hermitage Cafe.

When we were first introduced, Brittany was still working as a postal worker, but by the time she sang on my record, Alabama Shakes' album *Boys & Girls* had blown up. They were one of the biggest acts in the country at the time. Jeremy and I assumed that having her on our record would help us attract some buzz. But it was soon apparent it was going to take much more than that to get us any attention. No one can make it for you; you've gotta claw and scratch your way there yourself.

At times it felt like we were a magnet for con artists. For the release of *Test Your Love*, we launched a Kickstarter campaign to raise money for pressing and promotion. To our surprise, fans and friends helped fund the entire goal of $20,000, but the large sum of money attracted sharks. One shark in particular was a publicist named Emily who reached out to offer her services. She promised to help us get the word out, claiming she could help the songs get some great press. I wrote her a check for a cool ten grand, and after months of nothing happening, I heard that she had never even sent the albums anywhere to be reviewed. I was disheartened. We were pouring our hearts and souls into what we were doing, and I felt preyed upon. I had trusted both Karen and Emily because they were women, but I realized they were only after me for a quick payday.

The record was decent but once again flew under the radar and did nothing. We kept going. There was a small label in Muscle Shoals, Alabama, that showed interest in us. We went into the studio yet again and recorded what I would describe as a topical, psychedelic rock and roll record. We had some good songs in the can, but the album never got finished or released. The label merged with a Nashville distributor that, for whatever reason, didn't like me. The label sent their apologies, and we finally took this as a sign from God: it was over. Buffalo Clover was dead.

A band is like a breathing organism. Even when you're not sleeping together, it's like having a marriage with five or six people all at once. The task of keeping everyone's big personalities, unpredictable moods, ids and egos fed is a difficult job in itself. I tried hard to be a leader, but I didn't always succeed. There was no way out of my affair with Matt without the death of the band, and it was time to end them both. We were like Fleetwood Mac without any of the success.

There were many incarnations of Buffalo Clover, but during those last couple of years, the core band was me, Jeremy, Matt Gardner, Houston Matthews, Jason White, and Amaia Aguirre. Amaia had fallen for our bassist, Jason. The two loved and fought passionately and were married and divorced over the span of a few years.

We all fought to keep our musical partnership going. We had traveled the world in an Econoline van. We'd slept on motel floors and slummed it in bunk beds in European hostels. We'd toured the better part of the US, England, and Spain. I was grateful for their allegiance to me, and I felt a great pang of guilt when I finally called it. The drunken soldiers were jaded and wounded by arguments, deceptions, and shifting alliances. I felt like a haggard general giving a speech after losing a long, hard battle. We had lost the war on rock and roll.

We played one last show at our favorite haunt, the 5 Spot. We recorded the show and made an album of the completely new songs we played that night. We called it *Live at the 5*. We sang our hearts out and got drunk together one last time. I was careful whom I locked eyes with.

Afterward we disbanded, and everyone took it hard. We hung out less and less, until it was not at all. I went to Electric Hand Tattoo and got a giant black and red buffalo head tattooed on my upper thigh as an homage to my vanquished troupe.

As Buffalo Clover was deteriorating, I fell under the influence of classic country music. I had always appreciated it, but now I obsessed over it. Jeremy and I scoured local record shops for old albums by the heroes of the Outlaw movement like Waylon, Willie, and Jessi Colter. We wore out the needle playing songs by George and Tammy and Hank

Williams. Every song I learned to cover was like trying on a new suit to see how it fit.

I liked the kinds of artists who didn't shy away from real pain. I related to songs about love and death, drinking and cheating, truth and betrayal, because they were what I was living. Songs that punch you in the gut, like Townes Van Zandt's "Waitin' Around to Die." Townes was dangerous and vulnerable, damaged yet perfect, both crooked and straight, and full of pain though he covered it up with self-deprecating humor. Townes died depressed, drunk, and close to destitute, never knowing how much of an impact his music would have on future generations. I related to all of that.

I started a side project, a country supergroup of misfits and losers called Margo and the Price Tags. I was going to rebuild from the ground up, and I knew I needed a hot band. At least, being in Nashville, I had my choice of the world's best talent. Band members in those days included Kevin Black or Jeremy on bass; Sturgill Simpson, Kenny Vaughan, or Mark Sloan on guitar; Kristin Weber on fiddle and violin; Pete Finney or Alex Munoz on pedal steel and dobro; Eric Whitman on keys; and Moises Pallido or Taylor Powell on drums.

The first Price Tags gig was opening for Shovels and Rope at Derek Hoke's $2 Tuesday showcase at the 5 Spot. I knew it was going to be packed. Cary Ann Hearst and Michael Trent from Shovels and Rope had a strong buzz as the next big thing. They were a rockin' two-piece act that rotated between drums, guitar, and keys, pulling inspiration from the White Stripes.

Sturgill, Eric, and I hit three-part harmony on our opening number, which was the Band's "The Shape I'm In." The crowd lit up, but we didn't wait for it to die down. Moises counted off my cover of Loretta Lynn's "Fist City." The set also included Henson Cargill's dark and political "Skip a Rope," a song about domestic abuse, divorce, and racism that I'd always connected to. Sturgill took the lead on a rendition of "I Never Go Around Mirrors" by Lefty Frizzell, followed by one of Sturgill's originals, "Voices." People were eating it up—they were two-stepping and crying, throwing back shots, and hollering for more after every song. I closed out the set with a couple of originals, "Hurtin' (On the Bottle)" and "Since You Put Me Down."

One morning I had heard Jeremy in our kitchen strumming a new song he was writing. It was called "Since You Put Me Down." He told me it wasn't about me, but deep down I knew it was.

> *Since you put me down,*
> *I've been drinking just to drown*
> *I've been lying through*
> *the cracks of my teeth*
>
> *I've been waltzing with my sin*
> *She's an ugly evil twin*
> *She's a double crossing,*
> *back stabbing thief*
>
> *I killed the angel on my shoulder*
> *with a handle of tequila*
> *So I wouldn't have to hear you bitch and moan*
> *I killed the angel on my shoulder*
> *Since you left me for another*
> *I've been trying to turn my heart into stone*

I felt a sharp pang in my stomach. "That's devastating," I said. "You like it?" he asked.

"I love it." I grabbed the guitar from him. "And I wanna sing it. What about straightening out the tempo?" I began strumming.

"That's pretty. Do that melody again." Jeremy pushed his notebook across the table to me.

I rewrote the melody while he inhaled his breakfast and gave suggestions. I tried different words and chords until they fit my voice. The song poured out of us effortlessly. It happened like lightning. Even though our relationship was in turmoil, we were still musical compatriots; we still finished each other's sentences and spoke almost telepathically. We were writing about cheating on each other for a long time before I ever admitted it out loud.

Jeremy and I were friends with another couple, Caitlin Rose and Mark Fredson; Mark was in the Lonely H. They were both wildly talented artists in their own right, navigating separate careers while simultaneously obsessing over each other. The four of us spent countless nights talking intensely about music, astrology, and on occasion small-town gossip. We were as supportive as we were competitive, and for several years we commiserated frequently, gathering in the evenings at one of our homes or at a bar. The nights often ended the next morning as the sun reared its ugly head and we reconvened, hungover, for chicken-fried steak and Maxwell House coffee at the Pied Piper diner just up the street.

Weekdays and time meant nothing in our world, so on a random Tuesday evening, while the four of us passed around the guitar and a bottle of Bulleit Rye on our porch, we wrote the song "Hurtin' (On the Bottle)."

I had sung background vocals for the Lonely H's new self-titled album. Mark had paid me for my services by letting me pick out whatever I wanted at the liquor store. "Y'all," I slurred, "we put a hurtin' on that bottle."

Caitlin sprang into action. "That's a song! Grab the guitar, Jeremy."

Caitlin was good at delegating. She grabbed paper and we all began blabbering ideas and talking over one another until we had the bones of a pretty solid song. We scrawled the words "Hurtin' on the Bottle" in chalk on our picnic table, and when I came out the next morning, I saw the empty handle of Bulleit next to the song title. There, in the early morning sun, scattered in the ashes of a hundred cigarette butts, was the evidence of a great country song. I cleaned up the evidence and drove Judah to preschool with a punishing headache.

After we wrote it, no one else in the foursome wanted to sing it, so I took it to my band. We added a heavy Waylon Jennings cut-time beat to it, and I started including it in my set as the closer.

One night I got a gig, backed by some ragtag version of the Price Tags, at the Basement over off Eighth Avenue in Nashville. The Basement was a small but hip place for songwriters to play, something like a rite of passage. I shared the bill with my friend, the guitar-playing carpenter JP Harris.

I had my hair teased up past the heavens like Tammy Wynette and wore black eyeliner and false eyelashes. Doing my hair and makeup before a gig always felt like putting on war paint before going into battle. I pulled a pale-blue polyester dress out of my closet and headed out the door. Jeremy drove and I sat shotgun so I could finish applying makeup in the vanity mirror. As I sang along to some Linda Martell to warm up, Jeremy noted, "Your dress has stains on it, babe."

I looked down at the dress and the yellow stains that washed across my chest and stomach. I had bought the dress several years earlier for twelve dollars at the Goodwill but hadn't worn it yet. "Doesn't matter, my guitar will cover it right up." I laughed it off as I applied some light-pink lipstick and finished belting out "Before the Next Teardrop Falls."

The Basement was a listening room of sorts. It was located in a small brick building just south of downtown Nashville. I'd been cutting my teeth in there for years and had played so many shows inside those windowless walls. There were a lot of up-and-coming artists in the crowd, as with many Nashville shows, so I was playing to fellow writers, singers, critics, posers, hipsters, thinkers, and drinkers. I stared into the lights or sang with my eyes closed most of the night. I didn't want to get distracted by who was out in the room listening, although I had an idea I knew at least two of them a little two well.

My new songs gave me newfound confidence and added swagger to my step. I enunciated every word so that everyone in the back row could hear me. At first people were making small talk and clinking their beers, but by the end of "Since You Put Me Down," you could have heard a pin drop. The warm round of applause caught me off guard. For the first time, I was completely transparent to the audience. It was self-deprecation through commiseration. I told jokes where I was the punch line under my breath in between songs: "You know, they say it's a five-year town but I've been here ten." I was so sick of being a loser and a cheater and a boozer, and it was cathartic to say it out loud. From the rapt silence of the crowd, it seemed that others around me could relate.

After the show, I hung around to hear JP and the other bands. A man named Joe Hudak approached me and introduced himself as a writer from *Rolling Stone Country*, a branch of *Rolling Stone* that had just opened in town. "That was a spectacular performance! Where can I buy your album? I want to write it up."

"Nowhere. I haven't recorded these songs yet," I told him. "But I will."

"How long have you been in Nashville?"

"Ten or eleven years?"

"You mean to tell me you've been here eleven years singing like this in clubs and you still haven't made it? You must be one of Nashville's best-kept secrets. That was an incredible set," he said sincerely.

"Oh, I'm a secret, there's no doubt about that." I laughed.

Little moments like that kept me going in those days. Kenny Vaughan once approached me after a show and told me that I had "it" and that I had to keep singing and doing what I was doing because it would eventually pay off. Both conversations were like little fires lit under me. It had been a decade of waiting around. I needed all the encouragement I could get.

CHAPTER 23

Weekender

I was playing more and more country music at every watering hole in Nashville. We were touring more frequently as the Price Tags, though really the band consisted of whomever would jump in the van that night and take a gamble. We found another greasy manager and an independent booking agency who promised they could help book us more worthwhile paying gigs. They didn't have great connections, but it was better than nothing.

I just wanted to play, and I took almost anything the agency threw at us if it was a short drive on the weekend. My mom came down more frequently to watch Judah, and we'd hop in our van, burnin' rubber all over the southeastern states and the Midwest. Sometimes we were offered a $200 guarantee. If we were lucky, we got $500, but we always had to give ten percent to the agency.

After I paid the band and covered the gas and hotel rooms, it was usually a break-even or in-the-hole situation. Occasionally we were offered a free meal or booze or a place to stay, or all three. Once, in the swamps of Florida, the owner said he had meal and lodging accommodations.

The meal turned out to be a live chicken and the lodging was a floor to sleep on. We were living in a van, so you can guess which one we chose.

On one of these little tours, in the summer of 2014, we made our way out west for a run of shows in Texas for a band called Somebody's Darling. I was on acoustic and vocals, Jeremy was on bass and harmonica, Alex Munoz was on guitar and pedal steel, and Taylor Powell (whom we nicknamed Paper Towel) was on drums. The gigs were shit, but we had a great time and sounded pretty big for just a little four piece. We stopped in Memphis on our way back home and holed up in the Exchange Building downtown to take in the sights. I had driven through Memphis many times, but we wanted to explore the city, relax for a couple of days, and eat some soul food.

The four of us went to Earnestine & Hazel's for their world-famous soul burger and the jukebox, Central BBQ for a slab of ribs, and Paula & Raiford's Disco nightclub for dancing. The highlight for me was our visit to Sam Phillips's Legendary Sun Studio. We took the tour and saw where Johnny Cash, Howlin' Wolf, Jerry Lee Lewis, and Roy Orbison recorded. We saw the X marks of tape on the floor where Elvis once stood. Apparently, when Bob Dylan visited, he got down on the ground and kissed Elvis's X. When everyone left the room at the end of the tour, I stayed behind, and when I got a second alone, I too bent down and kissed the mark on the floor.

As we exited through the gift shop, I stopped to buy a Sun Studio coffee mug and saw a flashing neon sign that said, "Make Your Own Recording." In that moment, I knew I would come back and make my album there. I asked the girl behind the counter for the phone number I could call if I wanted to book the studio. That night, back at our place at the Exchange Building, I called and left a message on the Sun Studio answering machine.

A few days later, I spoke on the phone with a young man named Matt Ross-Spang. He had been working at the Legendary Sun Studio since he was sixteen years old. He started as an intern and worked his way up to chief engineer. Matt had an old-school, slow-talkin', southern way about him, and I felt an immediate kinship. He was always cracking jokes and in a great mood. He had slicked-back hair like Don Draper and a beard, and he was a sharp dresser. Sometimes he wore vintage polyester suits that had belonged to Sam Phillips himself. We started talking money and he was sympathetic to our plight. Matt knew we were just young parents struggling to get by. He also knew we had no label and were paying for the studio time out of pocket. He promised to give me a fair rate. Now all we had to do was figure out where to get the money.

For some time, I'd had it in my head that I was going to make an old-school country album, but now that I had Sun Studio in the back of my mind, the idea started to evolve. Memphis was like the missing piece where I could bring together country, funk, and blues. Jeremy and I got into these albums called *Country Funk*, volumes one and two, on Light in the Attic Records. Those compilations influenced us immensely. I knew that my next move would be to continue to write more sad-ass songs with heavy grooves.

One I penned, called "Four Years of Chances," was based on a conversation I had with one of Kevin Black's ex-girlfriends, Chloe Killwell. We were getting loaded together one night and she said, "I gave that motherfucker four years of chances! And now he wants me back? No way." I made a mental note and the next day flushed out the song. I had been listening to Jessi Colter's rendition of "Why You Been Gone So Long" so much and wanted to draw from that vibe. It was my most Memphis song yet, and it solidified the plan to record there.

But we were still financially unstable. Sometimes we cashed checks at the liquor store because we had overdrawn our bank account. We even donated plasma for extra cash, but it never seemed like we could get ahead enough to save up any sort of reserve fund. We were wasting our money at the bar as well, but so was most everyone else. Shows were in bars, and bars sold booze to depressed musicians like we lived off of it. The cycle was never-ending: collect your pay, pay your tab, and walk out with a little bit of dough if you're lucky.

I was still having a hard time grieving Ezra. I numbed the pain with whiskey sours alongside my musical compatriots at the back table of the 5 Spot. I had built little more than a strong repertoire of drunken misdemeanors, and the list wasn't ending anytime soon.

One rainy evening I went over to hang out on the porch of a new friend, Leisa. She was a phenomenal singer with stunning features and dark hair. Leisa sang harmonies on many of the Black Keys' records. She was also a mother. We met singing harmonies together at the 5 Spot, of course, on a Ray Charles tribute night with our mutual friend Ashley Wilcoxson. Ashley reminded me of a young Linda Ronstadt, as she was also a virtuoso singer with brunette hair, shaggy '70s bangs, and big blue eyes. I didn't know either of them that well, but I desperately needed more friends, especially ones who were moms and musicians.

I was in a dark mood that day, though I tried to be upbeat around my new girlfriends. When Leisa asked me how many children I had, the conversation turned to Ezra. I broke down crying in the kitchen. Leisa and Ashley were kind and listened to me, and I eventually dried my eyes. Then I tried to turn the night around with glass after glass of a nice pinot that Leisa had opened. The wine numbed my troubles for a brief moment, and I was grateful. After a couple of hours, Ashley left, but Leisa pulled out her husband's guitar and we took it onto the porch, singing some inspired harmonies for all of Inglewood to hear.

By the end of the night, I knew I had imbibed too much to chauffeur myself home. I called a cab dispatcher. There was no other kind of ride service in town in those days, just Yellow Cab.

"Fifteen minutes," the dispatcher promised.

I started chugging water and eating some of the cheese and crackers Leisa had put out. Fifteen minutes went by, then thirty. I called again and was promised a cab was on the way. Soon, ninety minutes had passed with no sign of a cab. It was late and I was less than a mile from my place. I told myself all I had to do was take two turns and I'd be home. I foolishly got behind the wheel and began to drive. It's a moment that makes me wish I could turn back time and make different mistakes.

I took a left turn onto Riverside Drive, where the beloved record store Fond Object used to sit, and *boom*, I hit a telephone pole with the front right corner of my Ford Explorer. Then I saw two cop cars parked in the lot. Their headlights came on, and for a brief moment I panicked, not yet ready to pull over and face the music. I kept going up the road, contemplating whether or not I could turn into a dark driveway and hide. The cops drove right up on my ass, and I surrendered in front of the Dalewood Baptist Church.

The rain poured down as they put me through a series of sobriety tests. I walked a crooked line, and they cuffed me and put me in the back of a police car.

I spent the night in jail and knew there would be more serious consequences ahead. I decided to quit drinking yet again. I hated who I had become. I felt my chest tightening with anxiety as I sat in the drunk tank looking down at the paper bag with a bologna sandwich inside. I had to do better for my son, for Jeremy, for me. I prayed for mercy.

I had no extra money for a lawyer, so I called my dad. He listened more than he talked as I explained my mess. He agreed to help me with the cost of hiring a lawyer. I promised I'd pay him back some day. When all was said and done, I was charged with a misdemeanor and reckless endangerment. I lost my license for a year, paid some hefty fines, and took a few courses on substance abuse. I also had to do a weekend in the Davidson County Jail.

As I waited in a mint-and-tan room to be checked in, I noticed the other women waiting with me. Most were staring down at the floor. No one seemed to want to make eye contact, and who could blame us? In groups of five, we were taken into the back, made to bend over, spread our legs, and cough. Then we were given tan shirts and pants and told to dress. They handed me an ID with a photo of my mug shot from the night I was arrested. I was struck by how broken-down I looked in the photo. It was something of a suggestion, like *Maybe you should think about what you've done.* And believe me, I did.

Breakfast was powdered eggs, dry toast, and a congealed brownish liquid that one guard referred to as red-eye gravy. I never tried it, because I didn't trust the way it moved. After breakfast, the pill line formed next to the cafeteria tables. Lots of the inmates were on one sort of medication or another, and women lined up to get their little paper cups. My roommate was heavily sedated and she slept most of the day and night away. When she woke up, she introduced herself. "My name is Christina, but my mama always called me Tina 'cause she loved Tina Turner."

"So do I." I smiled. "Tina it is."

"Sorry I been sleeping all day," she went on. "I took some methadone . . . told 'em I was coming off of heroin. They'll give you whatever if you tell them straight up, 'cause they don't want anyone to be having withdrawals in here." She walked over to the mirror and turned on the faucet. "I'm not addicted to anything anymore. I just wanted some extra help sleeping at night." I watched her splash some water on her face in the reflection of the dirty glass.

"You're only gonna be here for the weekend, huh?" she asked.

"How'd you know?"

"Your shoes. All you weekenders wear Keds shoes. We can't have shoelaces on ours." We both glanced at her Velcro shoes by the cell door. Tina went on, "Say, do you think you could snail mail some letters to my boyfriend for me? His name is Cash. I just know he wants to hear from me. We can't stay mad at each other for too long."

She told me she was in there because she had hit him in the face while they were both high on crack and fighting. She had been in there for months and was awaiting trial. He had stopped answering her calls from jail. She had written him a handful of letters and wanted to know if I could mail them when I got out. She reached under her pillow and pulled out a stack of letters bound with a little white ribbon. I could see the name CASH tattooed on the front in bold capital letters and decorated with Cupid's hearts. I promised her I would.

We could have no books, no belongings, and the mattress was so thin, I barely slept at all. I smuggled a pen up to my room at one point from the commons area, along with some blank paper and a couple of crossword puzzles. I lay awake that night staring out the tiny window, covered by a thin, itchy blanket, and started humming a tune.

> *I went down to the county jail*
> *And turned myself in*
> *Spending all my weekends here*
> *Far from my good-timing friends*
> *Things just went from bad to worse*
> *But I don't know when*
> *The only thing I know for sure*
> *Is I ain't going back again*
>
> *They took me down to cellblock B*
> *After stripping off my clothes*
> *Put me in a monkey suit*
> *And threw me in the throes*
> *Like a rat in a maze*
> *A cow in the herd*
> *Or a sparrow with a broken wing*
> *Now I know the reason why*
> *The caged bird has to sing*

I wrote the song that came to be "Weekender." For the first time in a very long time, I thanked God for my hands and my lungs and my ability to sing.

Later that night, the fire alarm went off and the sprinklers began pouring water down on the entire cellblock. Immediately, everything—our sheets, pillows, and mattresses—was soaked. Everyone was evacuated from their rooms and brought down to the entryway on the first floor. Rumors flew that a couple of inmates had been smoking weed up in their room. I was impressed by their failed attempt.

When Jeremy picked me up, he treated me to a meal at Hermitage Cafe, the same spot where Brittany Howard and I had often finished our evenings of drunken achievements. It was like a locally owned Waffle House, with greasy eggs, hash browns, and one of the best jukeboxes in Nashville. I couldn't wait to put on some Patsy Cline and drink a stiff black coffee.

Before we went there, I told Jeremy we had to go get a carton of Newports for one of my new friends. "Margo, you've been in jail for just three days and you're buying someone you met cigarettes? Guess you've already formed some alliances then." He laughed. He took me to the gas station and we returned to the prison to drop off the cigarettes.

The next day, I mailed those letters from Tina to Cash. I still wonder if he ever got them and if she ever got out, or if she's still stuck inside that cold, broken system.

CHAPTER 24

A Band of My Own

After my long weekend away, I made a promise to myself to keep my life on track, and felt more excited for my record. *At least I got a song out of the whole shitty experience*, I thought. I had been slowly writing traditional country songs, and now I realized I nearly had an album's worth. I *had* to make the record immediately. And to do that, I needed the right band.

I said it before: Nashville is home to the best musicians in the world. I knew I could put together a solid band for the studio and the road from people I had been playing with around town. Dillon Napier was the obvious choice for the drums; he had played for me for years in Buffalo Clover and in lots of other projects in town. Born in Los Angeles, raised in North Carolina and Nashville, Dillon grew up surrounded by the music industry. But beyond that, I wanted Dillon because he was the best drummer I'd ever played with and a well-rounded musician in general. He also played guitar and wrote, and he had a deep intuition for how to serve a song.

Jeremy had killed it on bass when he came out on the road with me.

He knew all the chords because he helped write a lot of the songs. For the past few years he had been getting more and more into playing bass, but he'd always had such a good Paul McCartney–type ear for melodic bass parts. Plus, he was free, and we could share a hotel room on tour.

I needed a guitar player too, because Kenny Vaughan was full-time with Marty Stuart, and Sturgill was off being Sturgill. When I was up at the 5 Spot one hazy night, I heard about this cat Jamie Davis who was new to town from Pennsylvania. I was skeptical, but I liked the idea of picking up somebody who wasn't playing in a million projects and who was still more green than jaded. I invited him over to audition. When a dark-haired hippie showed up at my door in a Canadian tux with a tattered guitar case in his hand, I had a good feeling about him.

We sat down in the basement and picked through some songs. Jamie was good. He had amazing tone and a natural feel, and he didn't hit a bad note through the eight or nine songs we played together. He had a background in bluegrass but had played in a country band out in Colorado for a few years that was real into Gram Parsons. After we jammed that night, Jamie, Jeremy, and I hung out on the porch getting tight for a couple of hours. Jamie was a huge stoner and maybe one of the only people who could outsmoke me. I knew he was the guy.

I had seen a stellar violinist named Kristin Weber one night at Cannery Row, and I approached her about playing for me. Kristin was younger than me but organized and always impeccably put together. She had dark-brown hair cut into a sharp, chin-length bob. There was something about her that said she was tough and could hold her own in a town where most session players are men. She had mastered both fiddle and violin and had technique and accuracy and a down-home feel that I liked. She could also sing perfect harmonies along with me that felt natural.

I recruited the brilliant Micah Hulscher on keys. When I say brilliant, I mean it. He had perfect pitch and was a prodigy—he'd started studying piano when he was three. I met Micah outside of 3 Crow Bar, a local haunt in the Five Points area that I've mentioned before. He had just moved from Seattle, where he had worked as a professional keyboardist, backing artists such as Emmylou Harris, Wanda Jackson, Rufus Wainright, Buddy Miller, and Daniel Romano. He could play any style. He had an extensive collection of vintage and analog instruments, and played anything with keys, including a B3 organ, accordion, Farfisa, and synths. Micah was already basically an honorary member of Buffalo Clover, but he played in many projects around town. I was just happy to get him down to Memphis to play on my debut album.

All of my favorite country records were dripping in pedal steel, and I knew I wanted it to be a big part of my sound. I needed something to answer the mournful cry of my powerful voice. There were lots of pedal steel players to choose from in Nashville, and I had played with some greats. One of my favorites was Luke Schneider, who played through weird guitar pedals and made sounds on the steel that were more rock than country. He didn't sound like a traditionalist, but he could if he needed to, and I liked that. Neil Young was one of his greatest influences, and we bonded through conversations we had around town and seeing some shows together. I approached Luke one night at the Basement and asked if he might want to join the band and tour. He was wary about going back out on the road because of the lifestyle. Luke had been fighting off his own demons. About nine months earlier, he'd landed in the ER during a tour with his rock band. I assured him that we were all growing up and this project wasn't going to be a drunken spree. I was, after all, fresh out of jail myself and riding safely on the back of the wagon. I would fall off again and again, but in that moment, I was putting my distractions aside to focus.

That's not to say that everyone in the band was sober, because they definitely weren't, but we were collectively, for the most part, being good to ourselves. The cocaine that was so prevalent in our Buffalo Clover years took a back seat to some cold beers, a joint, and maybe a few vape pens, give or take. I wasn't completely sober because I was still smoking weed. But when I woke up the morning after smoking a little grass, I was much more productive than when I was sipping on Kentucky's best, Maker's Mark.

I spent almost all of my spare time scheming—obsessing, really—about how to make my dreams a reality. I could finally see the pieces, and now I just needed to put them together. In my dreams I was wearing a rhinestone Nudie suit, sharing a joint and cowriting with Willie Nelson, singing on the Grand Ole Opry stage. But I woke up in a dirty house, with overdue bills and a marriage that was in desperate trouble.

There was a looming sense of desperation in what and how I was writing, and a similar desperation in figuring out how to do it. To make a good record, we needed money.

One afternoon I started looking around for things of value to pawn. I had that nice 1956 Gibson from my uncle, but I was gonna need that. We had a few tube microphones that we hawked. We sold a tape recorder and a mixing board to our friend Willy up the street. One day I looked down at my hands, and my diamond ring caught the light. *Why the hell not?* I thought. *I can always buy another if my record does well.* So I took it, as well as a couple of other pieces of jewelry I had inherited from my great-grandmother Grace Price, and I went to the Cash America Pawn on Gallatin Road in East Nashville. When I walked in, an older woman behind the counter eyed me. "What you lookin' for, sugar?"

"I'm lookin' to pawn this engagement ring, actually." I slid my silver band from my left hand across the counter.

"You gettin' divorced or what?" She got out her loupe and began looking it over.

"No, not yet. Just need some cash." I looked around, noticed a few guitars, and wondered whose dreams had died.

"Oh, honey, this ring has a nasty crack in it. I can only give you like $200 or something for it." She handed me back my ring along with the loupe so I could look for myself.

"Wow, just two hundred bucks, huh? I guess I'll take the money if that's all you can give me." I left with the cash in my hand. As soon as I got in the car, I started to cry. When I got home and told Jeremy, he wasn't mad.

"Can you get it back if you pay them for it?" he asked tenderly.

"I don't know! I guess I'll have to pay more or something. Isn't that how it works? It's a temporary loan, I think." I looked down at my naked finger and felt sentimental already.

The next morning, Jeremy walked into the kitchen and announced, "I'm selling the car."

I was scrambling to get Judah ready for school.

"What are you talking about?" I asked, rolling my eyes.

"Yeah, why, Dadda?" Judah laughed, spilling cereal and milk onto the table. "Why" was his new favorite word.

"I'm selling the car. We need money to make your country record if we want to do it right. We'll never make enough on our own to fund it properly."

I sat down and listened, agreeing with what he said, but I still tried to talk him out of it. It was no use. Jeremy went down to CarMax on Gallatin that afternoon, and then the car was gone. It was the most romantic thing he'd ever done for me. Then he marched into the pawnshop and got my ring back. He came home with a big pile of cash, and we went to Holland House in East Nashville to celebrate our plan with a fancy meal. We talked the entire night about the track listing and the players, down to the details of where we would stay and what we would eat while we were in Memphis making the record.

I could finally see myself clearly in the room at Sun Studio. There was a little glimmer of hope creeping back into my psyche. Maybe this would be the album that could change it all.

CHAPTER 25

Midwest Farmer's Daughter

About a week or two before we left for Memphis, I sat alone in our basement with a couple of lines bouncing around in my head.

> *When I rolled out of town, on the unpaved road,*
> *I was fifty-seven dollars from being broke,*
> *Kissed my mama and my sisters and I said goodbye,*
> *And with my suitcase packed, I wiped the tears from my eyes*

When I first sat down with pen and paper, I was writing in another song frame. I had just recently heard Emmylou Harris's version of Steve Earle's "Guitar Town," and the line about the Japanese guitar struck a chord with me. *I could write a song like this*, I thought. The words came flowing out, and the frame changed and rearranged. I felt I had been trying to write this song my whole life. I scribbled down the words to what would become "Hands of Time." As I wrote, I let go of a lot of anger, a lot of pain. Being able to put into words what I had been through helped me close the door on my darkest chapter.

When I hit the city, I joined the band
Started singing in the bars and running with the men
But the men they brought me problems
And the drinking brought me grief,
I thought I found a friend, but I only found a thief

Soon I settled down with a married man
We had a couple babies, started living off the land
But my firstborn died and I cried out to God,
"Is there anybody out there looking down on me at all?"

Tears poured down my face. It felt like such a relief to say it all and to get the weight off of my chest. I stopped and looked down at the words on the page. "Now there's a fucking song," I said aloud.

I picked up the guitar and started strumming. The chords moved too fast for my words, and it wasn't flowing. I got frustrated but just kept trying different chord progressions and keys. E major, A minor—nothing worked. Finally, I put the guitar down and sat at the out-of-tune piano in the corner of the room that had hosted many drunken jams. I struck an A major chord and crudely hammered out a steady heartbeat. I did a normal 1-4-5 melody because that's all I really know how to do on the piano, and then, when it came to the chorus, I modulated down to the key of G.

All I wanna do is make something last
But I can't see the future, I can't change the past
I wanna buy back the farm
Bring my mama home some wine
And turn back the clock on the cruel hands of time

That was the song I needed. The album finally felt complete. When I looked at all the songs I had penned and the ones Jeremy cowrote, we had a cohesive theme. It was a concept album about my life, a thread of my stories, my family's stories, and who I was, for better or worse. I had been hiding so much of my failure and struggles from a lot of the people who knew me best, and I almost couldn't wait for my friends and family to hear the songs so I could be honest about who I was. Many of my relatives did not know about the recent drinking, drugging, depression, and run-ins with the law. Not even my own sisters.

We made plans to head to Memphis with the band. I booked time at Sun Studio with Matt Ross-Spang as the engineer. I reserved several rooms at the Exchange Building, where we had stayed the last time we came through, and everyone was excited. There was a warm feeling as we drove west, even though it was February and the air still had a cold bite to it. Alex Munoz had talked us into having him coproduce the record. He was aware that we didn't have much money, but he had faith and said we could pay him on the back end.

The sessions started every evening around six, six-thirty, when the tours ended. We had all day to rehearse, finish up loose ends of songs, eat killer barbecue, and explore places like the Stax Museum of American Soul Music for inspiration. We loaded in the first day and started cutting live. The room had perfect acoustics, and I liked that we weren't all in isolation booths; we were there together in the room playing, just like onstage at our live shows, as one organism.

Everything was relaxed. Matt Ross-Spang got the best sounds, and he worked so effortlessly. He told jokes and cut up the whole time, and we all laughed so hard we cried. Halfway through a session, we would stop for a late dinner or snack. Half of the band cracked beers, the other half smoked weed, and we all reconvened with bellies full of ribs. The groove lay back in the pocket nicely after that.

The second night we were recording, the band went out back for a smoke. Up in the sky a light flashed, and we all looked up. The mysterious light zigzagged unnaturally and took off into the night sky. Of course none of us can be sure, but at the time, we swore we saw a UFO. It seemed like the strange sign we needed to know this record would take us to worlds unknown.

The *Midwest Farmer's Daughter* sessions were completed in just three days in early 2015. I was impressed that we flew through them so quickly and was so satisfied with the outcome. We had ten solid songs. No fat to trim, no fucking around. It was a great record. The icing on the cake was that I hired an all-female string section for "Hands of Time" and "How the Mighty Have Fallen." I couldn't wait to release the album. Driving back to Nashville, I had faith in my pocket and a shit-eating grin on my face. Someone would want to release it, I just knew it.

I wasted no time in sending my songs to every label and distribution company in town. Jeremy and I wrote up a convincing argument as to why this was an earth-shattering album, and we did our best to hype up exactly why the world needed to hear it. I knew beyond a shadow of a doubt that even the story of how we had pawned everything to make it would be a talking point. But weeks went by, and we heard nothing. I was discouraged. I had fired my no-good manager by that point, so a couple of well-connected friends sent the album out for me, including my lawyer, Kent Marcus, who had a Rolodex of managers, labels, and publishers. Months passed. Radio silence. I grew more frustrated.

Finally, I got a few emails back, but they were all rejections. One morning I woke up and picked up my phone before I even got out of bed. I opened an email, forwarded from my friend Jenny, from a midlevel-distribution-type label based in Nashville. The message read, "We are aware of who Margo is and we are not interested."

They didn't even say whether they'd listened to it or not, but the message was loud and clear: they didn't like me. I was heartbroken. If this small-time record label didn't want me, who would? I got out of bed, tears streaming down my face. I hadn't been drinking since I was charged with reckless endangerment, but this was too much to process unmedicated.

Around noon, I went down to 3 Crow Bar, met up with some friends, and asked the bartender for a double bourbon. I drank for almost twelve hours that day. When I started fading around nine o'clock that night, somebody offered me a key and a bag of blow. I cried in my friend Alex's kitchen and bitched about the music business. I was doing lines until around two. Then I called myself a cab, went home, and crawled into bed.

When I woke up the next day, I had a good, long look in the mirror. I hated who I had become, but I didn't know how to change. I had fallen off the wagon again, and I had no real plan for how to jump back on it. I gave myself a pep talk: "You can't do this every time things don't go your way, Price. Get yourself together! This shit ain't over yet." I dusted myself off and vowed not to go off the rails again, even though it was probably wishful thinking. I picked up the shattered pieces and started again.

This cycle of rejection and heavy boozing went on for most of 2015. I often had panic attacks when I woke up after a long night of drinking. One morning, it was so bad, I began searching for rehabilitation centers and mental wards on the internet. I was worried for myself and for my family.

I called an older friend named Royann who used to be a writer, singer, and close friend of Townes. She had been through all sorts of terrible things and was now sober in her midfifties, and working at the 5 Spot as the resident cleaning woman. Royann actually convinced me not to check in to rehab or a psychiatric hospital. She warned that, if I did, my name would be on a list forever, and it would be hard to get a decent job with that in my history. Instead, she suggested Alcoholics Anonymous, but attaching that word to myself seemed more terrifying than being diagnosed with bipolar. I pushed down my worries and carried on.

Throughout all of this, I was touring and being booked by the small agency out of Knoxville. The entire year after recording *Midwest Farmer's Daughter* was like a short little purgatory for me. I had that ace in the hole but nowhere to play it.

There were glimmers of hope. An indie label in Chicago wrote a semi-interested response and said they would come out to our show at City Winery when we played there. I was excited because they were from Illinois and I was too. I took it as a good sign. We played the show, and afterward I went to the bar area to meet up with the man who ran the label.

I sat down at a little round table with a white tablecloth and a candle. He was drinking a beer and had a smug look on his face. I ordered a glass of wine and began listening to him and his opinions on my work.

"Well, I've got to say, you put on a pretty decent live show, especially for a place where people are sitting down and eating dinner," he began. "Now, this 'Hurtin' on the Bottle' song, it's okay, but it's pretty sad. Don't you have any happy, upbeat drinking songs? That's what people want to hear when they're out having a good time."

I looked him dead in the eyes. "Interesting. Can I ask you, does anyone in your family abuse alcohol?"

He squirmed in his seat and adjusted the collar of his shirt. "Well, that's a pretty personal question. I'm not really sure how to answer that." He laughed uncomfortably. "Look, I'm not telling you how to write your songs."

"Would you have said that to George Jones? Write a happy drinking song? You either like my songs or you don't." I searched for Jeremy and shot him a look that said, *Get over here and help me,* but he just looked confused and went back to yukking it up with the band.

"Well, I don't mean to offend you, but I don't think my label is going to be able to put out this album. It's just not what we're looking for right now. But we are going to do a compilation of drinking songs, so maybe we could talk about you doing a song on there with some of our other artists." He was offering it as some sort of consolation prize. "Can I buy your drink?"

"No, I'm good. Listen, I have some family here, so I'm gonna go talk to them now, but I don't want my song on your C-list compilation record, and I don't need you to buy my drink either." I stood up. "I still have free drink tickets."

I walked away and went to a table where a couple of my cousins were. "What was that about?" my cousin Haley asked.

"Oh, nothing. Just another pigheaded man wasting my time."
I laughed. I used my last drink ticket on a glass of malbec.

The nonacceptance got slightly easier to swallow with time. I kept
telling myself, *Be patient, have faith, and in the meantime, sing your heart
out onstage.* I got booked for festivals like Rhythm N' Blooms in Knoxville and Bristol's Rhythm and Roots. Summer and fall weren't looking
too bad. I had some shows on the horizon that I was actually excited
about. There was a proper tour on the books. We'd be out for several
weeks. The band was Jeremy on bass, Jamie Davis on guitar, Kristin
Weber on fiddle, and my friend Aaron Shafer-Haiss on drums.

Dillon Napier couldn't come because he actually got a gig with a pop
country act. I was sad, but I couldn't blame him; he had a wife and a kid
to feed. He couldn't live off of fifty dollars a day plus a small per diem.
None of us could! But that's all I had to offer back in those days. I saw
Dillon at the 5 Spot one night and we got to talking. He felt bad he
couldn't be out playing with me. I said, "One day, I'm gonna get you
back." (And dammit, I did.)

The five of us crammed in a Ford Explorer with a U-Haul trailer
hitched on the back for the gear. The tour took us down south through
Sarasota, Lakeland, and Fort Myers in Florida and then back up to
Georgia for the Savannah Stopover Festival. Then for no good reason,
we had to zigzag like alligators back down to Florida, then on to Knoxville, Chapel Hill, Rochester, Wrightsville, and Millheim. Then home.

The tour lives in infamy as one of the worst of my life. The crowds
were spare, the venues were small, the money was shit, and many times,
even when we played a festival, we were relegated to the worst stage possible with a thin crowd. I hadn't planned ahead to get hotels and ended
up on the internet at the last minute to get one or two shitty rooms I
couldn't really afford. Most nights we just tried to find other bands to
crash with. Sometimes we were so desperate, we stayed with fans, and let
me tell you, that's never a good idea.

The gigs were an absolute embarrassment, and I felt bad that I had
invited Kristin, Jamie, and Aaron out on the road to play with us. In one

room we played, in the back side of a bar, there were only four people. Four. And in the back of the room was a cardboard cutout of Kenny Chesney. It stared at me, almost mocking me. *Fuck Kenny Chesney*, I thought. I wanted to rip his cardboard head off, but I didn't.

Another especially low point was at a bar called Tony B's down in Florida. When we got there, we realized it was just a restaurant with a tiny raised stage positioned awkwardly in the middle of the room. It was definitely more of a jazz vibe than honky-tonk, but we set up our shit anyway. Of course we had to do our own sound, and we all kept getting shocked from the microphones, which were not grounded. But the gig had promised a free hot meal, and at least we had that to look forward to. I was starving. Most days we lived off of granola bars and peanut butter and jelly sandwiches until dinnertime.

"Could I see your menu?" Kristin asked the waitress.

"Sure, but our cook just went home," the waitress said in her sticky Florida drawl.

"Oh, that's okay. Just let us know when the cook is back and I'll order then." Kristin continued looking at the menu. My stomach growled.

"I don't think she's comin' back tonight at all. She got in a fight with Tony and just left all mad. She said she's done with this place." The waitress told us this while cleaning the glassware.

"We were promised a meal, though. Can't y'all whip something up back there? Pizza? Anything?" I pleaded. There was just a little time before the show, and I knew everyone was on the verge of a blood sugar crash. Especially Jeremy, who was always struggling with his hypoglycemia.

"Let me ask Tony, but I don't even know how to turn the oven on, y'all. I'm sorry."

When Jeremy heard the news, he got on the phone with our booking agent. "You don't even understand. These shows are so bad, we're hemorrhaging money." He paused to listen and then started talking again, angrily. "How about you come out here and see if you like being punched in the dick, because that's what this is like. We're all getting real sick of being punched in the dick."

The waitress brought us some carrots, celery, and hummus. "Sorry, it's all we can do right now, but the cook is coming back, she says."

We got up on the tiny stage and began to play. Over the course of the three-hour set, we played to about twelve or so people. We made fun of ourselves and used all the drink tickets we could to take the edge off. I began to have fun, just goofing off and playing covers, songs we had never played together before. What did it matter? We just had to fill the time, get the measly check, and tie one on after.

When we stopped halfway through for a break, the cook had returned. She introduced herself as Misty. It turned out that the "free place to stay" that was included in the advance was just an offer to crash at her house. She seemed harmless enough, but we'd been hoping for a hotel voucher. Still, Jeremy and I were close to overdrawing our account. We took our chances.

Misty offered to make food for us while we finished the last hour of the set. When it was all over, we packed up our gear, ate our mediocre pizzas, and made our way to Misty's. We stopped at a liquor store along the way to pick up a bottle of Four Roses to kill the sting of yet another underattended show.

When we showed up, there were several dudes hanging out around a campfire outside, and they were excited to see that a band had showed up with lots of weed and a bottle of brown party liquor. Misty took me inside, and I knew right away we had made a grave mistake. Now, I'm no clean freak by any means, but this place was on the verge of being unlivable. There were lots of animals inside, loads of animal hair, dust, and an overwhelming stench of cigarettes. An algae-ridden fish tank in the corner of the room looked like it hadn't been cleaned maybe ever, and the saddest turtle you ever saw sat stranded on a rock. Several disheveled hippies sat in the living room smoking a dirty-looking bong.

"Wanna pull?" one of them offered, smoke pouring out of the corners of his mouth.

"I'm good, thanks!" I smiled. Misty led me through the house. Each room seemed more trashed than the last.

"You and your husband can sleep in my bed," Misty said when we got to a dimly lit room at the end of the hall.

"Oh, no, that's fine. I can just grab a couch or whatever." I was uncomfortable and began to wonder if it was too late to look for a hotel.

"Seriously, I don't mind!"

"I mean, okay. I think my fiddle player, Kristin, will sleep in here too. She has her own little mattress she can put on the floor." I set my stuff down.

We went outside to the fire. Right away, Misty started hitting on every guy in the band. We all squirmed and did our best to stay away from her. Meanwhile, on a dare, the bong-smoking burnout drank the entire bottle of Four Roses we'd brought in just a couple of gulps.

We were out of booze, being bothered by a drunk lady, and sleeping on cat-hair-carpeted couches and dirty sheets. Jeremy and I got into bed with Kristin beside us on an inflatable mattress. The other two dudes held down the living room. We closed our eyes and tried to sleep. Just a few short hours later, Kristin woke me up, looking upset.

"Misty just tried to get into bed with me," she whispered.

"What?!" I said, waking up. "Like, to sleep next to you?"

"No, like, she tried to come on to me!" Kristin sounded scared.

"Dear Lord, what next?" I woke up Jeremy and told him the situation. The bed was big, so Jeremy just moved over and Kristin lay down next to me. We were both annoyed, but we had to laugh a little bit as we heard Misty stumbling drunkenly around in the hallway, confused.

We woke up early and left before anyone else in the house got up.

Later on down the line, we had a day off. I went to a liquor store and picked up a bottle of tequila and a bunch of soda waters. Then I got online and found a four-star hotel with a hot tub, right on the beach. Our rooms were at a different, more modest hotel in the city, but I knew from being on the beach earlier that there were plenty of cooler places where we could hang out.

"I found this really cool bar area with an infinity pool right on the ocean. They have bocce ball and a hot tub. Wanna go?" I didn't wait for their answer. I started to shove a swimsuit, the bottle of tequila, and a bunch of soda waters into my backpack.

Jamie and Aaron were skeptical.

"What do you mean, we're gonna go hang at this fancy hotel pool and hot tub? We don't have a room there," Aaron said. "What if they kick us out?

"Yeah, I don't know," Jamie said. "Don't you need a room key or something like that to get into the back?"

Kristin looked at them and said, "Don't y'all get it? Margo is going to do what Margo wants, and that's just that. I don't think she's concerned with something being legal or not."

The guys shrugged and we made our way to the five-star hotel by the water. I found a way around to the back entrance, flipped up the latch on the inside of the gate, and walked in like we owned the place. I asked the bartender for a glass of ice water and explained that I was the designated driver that night. I drank the water, kept the ice, and poured tequila and soda over it. The band and I played bocce, relaxed in the heated pool, and chatted it up with the tourists.

We were having a lovely time until the guys accidentally locked our keys in the back of the U-Haul trailer. We had to call a locksmith to come saw off the lock, and he charged us an unforgiving $500 that we most definitely didn't have.

They say bad luck comes in threes, but we were on an endless trail of misfortune during what we began to refer to as the "Desperate and Depressed" tour. Jeremy left his phone on top of the vehicle at one point and drove off. When we went back for it, it had been run over multiple times by cars on the freeway. I dropped my debit card in a swamp and had to jump off the dock at a fancy restaurant to try to retrieve it. Nothing good came our way. As I watched the card sink to the bottom, all I could do was laugh.

When Jeremy and I arrived back home, we were so happy to see our little boy. When we pulled in to our driveway, he ran up and gave us the world's best hug. Jeremy and I agreed that the tour had been a waste of time and that it was not a wise decision for our family to take gigs that lost money and took us away from our son.

The year dragged on. Looking back on 2015, it feels like one of the longest years of my life. Another "manager" had come and gone. He was a bro from Knoxville who drove a Camaro and promised things he could never deliver. I was disappointed but not surprised when he completely ghosted us, failing to follow through on any of his empty words.

One day I got an email from a label in Georgia. They were actually going to listen to the record. They said they thought I had potential, and they also wanted to come see a show. This company had several different labels under one umbrella, and I thought I had a fighting chance to be signed by them.

We had another tour booked that would be less than glamourous. We were playing haunted taverns, half-filled honky-tonks, and the occasional restaurant gig.

I felt like I was on the verge of a mental breakdown, and my clothes reflected it. I bought a tacky two-piece number that was a mix between a Gram Parsons Nudie suit and a tracksuit covered with emojis of pot leaves, hearts, smiley faces, and dollar signs. I paired it with a Stetson cowboy hat and a fake-fur coat. I wore it to sleep in and onstage and when we went to eat breakfast all hungover in some small-town diner on a Sunday. Boy, did I catch some looks from the church crowd.

We kept chasing the illusion of good news. We were added last minute to a new festival called Wildwood Revival that my friend Libby Rose curated. The lineup was hip, and although we had to drive through the night from Pennsylvania to be there to play at two in the afternoon, we were thrilled at the prospect of a proper show. Most important of all, the festival was in Georgia, and the president of the label that had contacted us was going to come see us play.

The band and I squeezed into the Explorer and hightailed it from Pennsylvania down to Arnoldsville, Georgia, through the night. Jeremy and I took turns behind the wheel for the twelve-hour drive. It was brutal. We burned rubber to get there, and when we arrived, everyone was exhausted, sore, and cracked out. I was worried about whether I would be able to remember the words to my songs, but I was determined to stay focused and give a memorable performance. After all, it could be our big break.

We loaded in, changed into our show clothes, and tuned up. There wasn't much time before we took the stage, but somehow we pulled it together and put on a great show. The crowd was deeply engaged, and we were given a round of applause to play an encore. When we got off that stage everyone was on cloud nine. I set out to find the mysterious president of the label, who was no doubt watching out there, and I hoped he was blown away.

But no one had seen him. It wasn't that big a place and there was only one stage, so there was no way he missed us. I went out to a field and stood next to a fire by Jamie.

"I don't even know if he came, man." I lit up a joint and passed it to him. "Can't believe we drove through the night to get here and he probably didn't even show up . . . what a bummer."

"Aw, shucks, don't worry about it. It's not your fault," Jamie said between inhales. "I have a feeling it's all gonna work out."

I found out a few hours later that the president never showed. When I asked if he was still interested and wanted to come see us at another show, a representative from the label replied, "Actually, we're sad to say that we have to pass on Margo. We like the album, but we already have two girls on our label and we just can't sign any more."

The news hit me like a ton of bricks. I had no idea what my being a "girl" had to do with it. That specific rejection stuck with me for a long time because it wasn't personal, it was sexist. I wondered how many other talented women out there weren't being signed simply because they were women. I carry that moment with me today, knowing that I've always had to work twice as hard as the men to get what I want. But the way I figure, twice the work means twice the practice, and maybe that just makes me stronger in the end.

CHAPTER 26

One Dark Horse

My lawyer, Kent, met up with me every so often to help me come up with my next plan and so he could buy me breakfast. He believed in me long before many others did.

"I've got a manager who might be interested in working with you. She's great but she doesn't take on a lot of clients," he said over a fancy omelet at Pinewood Social. I loved meeting with him, even if he only had bad news, because the food was always amazing.

"Oh! Awesome! I can't wait to meet her." I sipped my latte. "I have some good news too. I have a meeting with Sony next week! My friend Jenny sent them my album several months ago, and they're actually interested in hearing more. They want me to come in and play some songs."

"Wow. Well, that's great news, but I heard their CEO just resigned and there's not anyone there really steering the ship, so to speak." Kent always had the inside scoop.

"It's always somethin'," I said. "I also heard from a couple friends that Third Man Records is interested to hear what I'm doing. I feel like they could be a great fit."

"They only put out singles, though. They don't really do full album deals. But you should definitely talk to them." Kent was always real with me.

The next week I went down to the Sony Nashville office dressed in all black, channeling Johnny Cash, my guitar case in my hand. I had brought along my fiddle player, Kristin, and my steel player, Luke, to add some dobro. At the front desk, a man handed me a pen and a sign-in sheet. He looked at my guitar and said, "Are you the next Taylor Swift?"

"Taylor who?" I retorted. He looked at me like I had an extra head. I signed my name in bold, confident cursive.

We got in the elevator and went up to one of the top floors. "It's all downhill from here," I said, nervously making jokes.

A couple of middle-aged ladies greeted us.

"So, Margo, our friend Jenny says you're gonna be the next big thing," a brunette wearing a lot of gold jewelry said. She sounded skeptical.

"Well, I think there's a chance this album I made could be big. Did you listen to it? Jenny said she sent it to you last week." I began tuning my guitar.

"Yes, we did listen!" the other woman said. "There's definitely some potential there. I like that Tennessee song."

"Thank you! I was planning on playing that one for y'all."

I tapped my toe for the tempo, strummed a D major chord, and began doing the hammer-ons as Kristin put some Scarlet Rivera *Desire*-era violin on there. I sang it like I meant it, because I did. I kept my eyes closed most of the time because the vibe in the room felt kind of stiff—the woman sitting cross-legged and dripping in gold, the leather couches, the fake plant in the corner of the room. I just tried to focus on the music.

When I got done playing, one of them looked at me and said, "It's so cute because you're like really country but you're not a hillbilly, you know?"

"No, I actually don't know." I laughed and stared down at my hands.

"So, Margo. How many other songs do you have besides the ten we heard?"

"I've got endless songs. My husband, Jeremy, and I write together all the time. But this album is done. It's a fully realized idea and I don't want to add any more songs to it."

"Well, how would you feel about maybe toning down some of the overtly traditional elements? Like maybe less fiddle or walking bass lines?" the lady prodded.

"That's what makes it cool, in my humble opinion. And I wouldn't be comfortable with that. Like I said, the album is done. That's the record." I stared back at her, my expression unwavering.

"We just think it would be more commercially successful if it was a little more modern, you know?"

"I don't like modern. I like vintage." I went on, "You know what y'all need? You need the female counterpart of Sturgill Simpson or Chris Stapleton. And that's me. I'm your girl. This is the record. You can take it or leave it."

"Well, that is actually some very good advice. Unfortunately we don't have the power to say whether or not Sony will put this out. There's a ladder here, and lots of people will have to sign off on this before we can say if we want to release the album or not."

"Alright. Sounds like my work is done here." I got up, put away my guitar, and shook their weak hands. And with that we walked out the door.

Sony reached out a few more times to inquire if I had any different songs or if I would change the arrangements and instrumentation. I wouldn't budge. A couple of months later, they signed Maren Morris.

As we walked out that day, Luke reminded me that Ben Swank from Third Man was very interested in coming out to see the band play our next hometown show at the Basement East and that Swank also wanted to hear the album. "Don't get discouraged with these assholes, Margo. They would want to own your art and control your music."

"They'd probably just shelve you or something. Major labels have a tendency to do that," Kristin offered.

I was excited about the idea of working with Third Man. They were my dark horse and the only label in town that hadn't rejected me yet. I was so nervous when the Basement show finally came around. I kept thinking that Swank wasn't gonna come, or that if he did, he would hate it. When the band hit the stage though, my worries melted away. We were sounding so sharp, it seemed like we had cut to the core of those usually hard-to-win-over Nashville crowds.

Afterward, my friend Manda, whom I had worked with at the Belcourt, wanted to grab a drink with me. The place was clearing out, and as we approached the bar, I saw Swank talking to the bartender. We only spoke briefly, but he came off as kind and trustworthy. I was nervous to meet him—as Jack White's right-hand man, Swank was a legend in Nashville—but he was the nicest guy ever. He was very complimentary about the show and said I should come in to the office and check it out. We exchanged contact details and I left that night with a good feeling.

The crazy thing about the music business is how long everything takes. Over the next couple of months, Ben, who was laid back but was always busy with a show or an art installation, and I exchanged many emails and had many meetings. Third Man put me through an unspoken screening process. I think they wanted to make sure I wasn't a diva, that I could play the guitar and actually sing.

At one point, I arrived at the Third Man office for a meeting. I had been inside the record store, but this was the first time I was invited into the back. It was the most creative space I'd ever been in. Everything was black and white and yellow and red. There were plush velvet couches, rhino skulls, all sorts of taxidermy, a retro kitchen, and a big shared open work space. There was a Blind Willie McTell record on the turntable when I walked in, and everyone was so nice to me. I grabbed a cup of black coffee, and Ben and I went into his office to talk. He told me they were cutting some live-to-acetate recordings in the Blue Room for a couple of bands.

"Would you like to record a song direct to acetate? You can walk out of here with a record," Ben offered.

"Sure, I'd love to, but I didn't bring my guitar." I was suddenly nervous.

"Oh, we've got guitars in here. Take your pick!" We walked into the storage area, and he began rummaging through dozens of old guitar cases.

I grabbed a little black-and-white parlor guitar with bad action and slightly rusty strings. "This one has character," I said, choosing my fighter. I walked onto the stage in the Blue Room, where a vintage-looking mic stood. I did a little walk up the neck. I started to sing "Desperate and Depressed."

I'm pissed off at the number of people that I meet
Who go to shake my hand with a viper up their sleeve
They freeze me out in the winter and burn me up in the summer
Try to take my money when I'm desperate and depressed
Ain't it a mess?

I've played for free and paid for the miles on my truck
Got no sleep in the motel 'cause the worry keeps me up
It almost drives me crazy, thinking about my baby
And how he's gonna love me if I'm desperate and depressed
Can't get no rest

Mama never told me that things would be this way
Daddy tried to warn me that there'd be hell to pay
And if I can't find the money then I can't buy the time
I'm stuck here making someone else's dime

We busked in Sarasota, made twenty-seven bucks
I wept for Richard Manuel thinking I might have his luck
You talk behind my back, why don't you stab me in the front?
But don't think you can hurt me 'cause I'm desperate and depressed
Ain't it a mess?
Oh please, somebody tell me how to make it stop
This world feels like a roller coaster I just can't get off

Tried rehab and probation, tried self-medication
But none of that can cure you when you're desperate and depressed
Ain't it a mess?

Mama never told me that things would be this way
Daddy tried to warn me that there'd be hell to pay
And if I can't find the money then I can't buy the time
I'm stuck here making someone else's dime
I'll be desperate and depressed until I die

When I finished playing the song, Ben came back into the Blue Room smiling ear to ear. "That was outstanding! Did you write that song?"

"Jeremy and I wrote it after our last terrible tour in Florida," I said.

"I know all about terrible tours," Ben commiserated.

There was something so genuine about him that I hadn't ever felt from a guy at a record label. Ben used to play drums in a garage rock band called the Soledad Brothers. He was hired by Jack White to run Third Man when they first moved to Nashville in 2009. You could tell he was passionate about his work.

We went back to his office and began talking about the album. I told him about my idea for the title, *Midwest Farmer's Daughter*, and I showed him the lomographic photo my friend Danielle Holbert had taken of me in a field. I was thinking about using it for the cover. Ben loved it. As far as he was concerned, they were gonna release this record. But Jack and another guy, Ben Blackwell, also had to vote.

I left that day with a little manila envelope with a brand-new 45 inside it. I wrote on the front "Desperate & Depressed" and went out to the car where Jeremy was waiting. I was so excited to share the news with him. I found out later that Jack was there watching me cut that record behind a two-way mirror. There would be more tests, but this was a big one, and I had passed with flying colors.

In the fall of 2015, I finally signed a contract with Third Man for a two-album deal, and we made our big announcement. Let me tell you,

I was shittin' in tall cotton when that check hit the bank. I walked into Carter Guitars and bought the prettiest 1965 Gibson J-45 money could buy.

After that, everything happened very fast. Suddenly all sorts of managers were interested in taking me out to fancy brunches and dinners, and booking agents were trying to sign me. I had my choice of publicists. Everything just clicked.

I signed with Monotone for management. They were based in Los Angeles, and they flew me out to stay at the Chateau Marmont. I could drink fancy wine and champagne and order room service and whatever else I could think of up to my room. They have a list of records they can bring up for you to play, so I ordered Bob Dylan's *Blonde on Blonde* and a pack of American Spirits. When I was celebrating instead of commiserating, the drinking didn't feel so bad. I dropped the needle down on "Rainy Day Women #12 & 35," lit up a cigarette on the plush velvet couch, and smoked right there in the room.

In December, I released the first single, "Hurtin' (On the Bottle)," and got an immediate offer to play *The Late Show with Stephen Colbert*. I called my mama and daddy to tell them the news.

"I'm going to New York! I'm going to be on TV! Can you believe it?!" For the first time in my life, I felt like my family was actually proud of me. The 5 Spot threw a viewing party, and all of our friends showed up to watch the show on the TVs behind the bar, raising a glass to the misfits who had somehow made it onscreen.

From there, we hit the ground running. We played shows leading up to SXSW 2016 in Austin, where we played an NPR party on the big stage at Stubb's Bar-B-Q with Mitski, Anderson .Paak & The Free Nationals, Charles Bradley, and others. I had a friend rat my hair into a beehive for that show. It was sweaty and we were the only country band on the bill, but I knew we would win over the skeptics. Little did we know, the run of shows during SXSW was about to send us into the stratosphere. There were scouts from *Saturday Night Live* there, but I didn't think too much of it.

Several weeks later, I was back home, in the bathroom brushing my teeth, when I got a call from my manager, Ian.

"Listen, listen—what are you doing? You might want to sit down for this. Margo, are you ready to play *SNL* on April 9?"

"*What?* Are you shitting me?!" I screamed so loud Judah, who was six at the time, ran into the room.

"Mama, what's going on? Are you okay?" he asked.

I was jumping up and down, crying and laughing simultaneously. I could not believe the news. My mom ran into the room. She had started living with us part-time to help out with Judah.

I told her the news and we started hugging and screaming. Jeremy ran into the room and I told him too. Then he joined in on the celebration. Judah was still confused.

"Your music is gonna do good, Mama? That makes me happy." He hugged my legs, and I bent down to kiss his sweet little head.

"Yes, baby, my music is doing good. It makes me happy too."

CHAPTER 27

The Recent Future

About a week before *SNL*, Jeremy dislocated a tendon in his left hand and was unable to play bass. It put us in a tough situation, but the universe was sorting everything out. Kevin Black had recently parted ways with Sturgill's band, and since he already knew our songs and was a good friend, he reclaimed his place. He's been the bass player ever since. Jeremy would play harmonica; it was something he did really well and could still do without the use of his finger.

The band and I packed up the Mercedes Sprinter van that Third Man let us tour in for free. It wasn't a bus, but it was a far cry better than the minivans, Astros, SUVs, and U-Haul trailers we were used to. We had a tour manager, sound engineer, and jack-of-all-trades on the crew, Evan Donahue, an acquaintance from Nashville and a musician in his own right. He had curly blond hair and glasses, and although he was in his midtwenties, his baby face made him look like he could have been seventeen. Evan has a great sense of humor and is incredible at live sound. It was a game changer when I was out front to know he had my back. More than the sound, Evan did all the advance work for the shows, drove the

Sprinter, booked hotels, dealt with the promoters, helped set up the stage, and did his best to keep everyone under control when things got tough.

At Studio 8H, my dressing room door had a printed plaque that said "Margo Price/SNL." I ran my hands over it as I walked in to make sure it was real. The room was decorated with photos of musicians who had played there before: Paul Simon, Bill Withers, Elton John, Bonnie Raitt, Tom Petty, Stevie Nicks, Tina Turner, John Prine, Linda Ronstadt, and my current mentor, Jack White. The faces of my heroes were all around me, and in front of the makeup mirror were two dozen pink roses and a personal note from Lorne Michaels.

I had never really worked with hair or makeup artists before; I always just threw on a little mascara and wore my hair down in long, messy waves. I felt pressure to look good, so I had ordered a bunch of fancy dresses. Later, I would sit back while a couple of pros teased my hair and contoured my cheekbones.

The band felt really energetic and in the pocket during the run-throughs, and there was a magnetism in the room when we played. My voice was strong and I felt completely comfortable on that stage. I had dreamed about being on *SNL* since I was a little girl, and I did not want to blow this opportunity. Everyone was trying to behave themselves. For the entire week leading up to the show, I was stone-cold sober. I was eating healthy, working out, getting great sleep, living like a nun, and praying like a monk. I wanted to actually sing and play my song instead of lip-syncing or relying on tracks, like I had seen so many pop stars and bands do on television.

Everything was going great until Friday night. The *SNL* social media team asked me to post on their Twitter and Instagram accounts. It seemed like a fine idea, especially since I didn't have much of a social media following at that time. I agreed to do it, and we took a few pictures in the dressing room. I didn't log in to their account to post anything personally—they made the captions and posted them periodically throughout the day. By the time they put up the last photo on Friday at ten P.M., I was in tears. It was the first time I had experienced so much exposure and the bullying that can go along with it.

"Ugly bitch."

"She should get a nose job."

"Who the hell is Margo Price?"

All of my feelings of insecurity came flooding back. I wanted people to focus on my art, my lyrics, and my singing, but they were already writing me off because I didn't live up to their standard of beauty.

"Don't read the comments, honey," Jeremy said. "You need to get a good night's sleep and be well rested for tomorrow." He took a sleeping pill and turned on the TV. But I just sat there reading all the things people were saying about the way I looked. I couldn't take it.

"I'm going outside to get some air. I'll be back." I left the hotel room with swollen eyes and ran in to Kevin in the lobby.

"What's the matter?" he asked. "You okay?"

"Man, just these people talking trash. It's stupid, it doesn't matter." We walked out the front doors of the hotel, and I lit up a joint.

"You want to go on a walk?" Kevin offered. "I was just heading out to meet up with Swank over at his hotel."

I took off and didn't get back home until four the next morning. We destroyed ourselves. I wanted to be a rock star, but when I crawled into bed with Jeremy that night as he slept like a baby, I felt more like an idiot. We were due at 8H at ten A.M.

I woke up around eight not feeling well. I was too excited to try to sleep more, so I called Matt Pollack, who worked at Monotone with Ian and was based in New York. "Matt, I have a situation. I'm feeling rundown. I need a B12 shot. You know a rock doc?"

"Not off the top of my head, but we'll get it done."

It seemed like the natural thing to do. I had never had a vitamin B12 shot before, but I had read so many stories about musicians being hung-over and tired and getting shots in their hip to bring them back to life.

Matt Pollack sent me an address, and I set out on a good brisk walk to a little clinic. I felt my lungs open up. When I finally arrived, I was led back into a small room, and a doctor in a white coat came in and started asking questions.

"Why do you want a B12 shot, dear?" she asked.

"I'm feeling tired. A little exhausted, that's all."

She took my temperature, listened to my heart, looked inside my mouth—all the usual stuff. "Does your throat hurt?" she asked.

"Maybe a little bit." I started thinking about the night before.

"I'm going to do a strep test on you, okay?" She reached into the drawer and pulled out a Q-tip in a sealed bag.

"I don't really think I have strep throat," I said, but I let her swab my throat.

About ten minutes later she came back in. "I was right, you do indeed have strep. I'm going to put you on some antibiotics, and you know what? I'm going to give you that B12 shot too. You are rundown! I hope you do well on *Saturday Night Live* tonight. That is so exciting!"

I thanked her, and she jabbed a needle in my butt cheek and sent me on my way. Matt Pollack put me in a cab to the studio while he went to the pharmacy for me. I didn't want to tell anyone in the band I was sick and make them worry. I grabbed two bottles of water, poured myself a giant cup of coffee, grabbed a croissant, and went into my dressing room.

I picked up my guitar and began to sing "Blue Yodel (T for Texas)" by Jimmie Rodgers. My voice was still there, and I knew after a few warm-ups that I would sound clear as a bell. I was gonna raise some hell tonight—sick, tired, depressed, it didn't matter.

The energy on the day of the show was upbeat and contagious. It seemed the whole studio was vibrating and everyone was happy. All that evening, folks popped in and out of the dressing room, including my publicist, Matt Hanks, and my lawyer, Kent. The band buzzed about, asking me if I liked what they were wearing. They all cleaned up nice. I could sense that they were feeling nervous as they paced around backstage tuning their instruments and playing scales.

I wasn't thinking about the fact that I had strep throat. I wasn't even thinking about all the haters on Instagram who had broken my heart the night before. I told myself, if I was gonna be in the spotlight, I had to accept that it made me a good target. Jack sent me a dozen white roses and called me before the show, telling me to give 'em hell. His words of encouragement helped renew my confidence.

That I was so calm seemed to make everyone around me a little on edge.

"Are you sure you're okay?" asked Matt Pollack.

"Never been better!" I strummed my guitar and sang a few more notes before I stepped up onto that classic stage, looked out into the camera, and gave America a little smile.

Dillon counted off four hard beats on his drum sticks, and the band and I clung to our instruments like weapons, yielding a big, loud G chord together that rang out into the live audience. I had been waiting my whole life for this, and nothing was going to knock me down. We dedicated our performance to Merle Haggard, who had just passed away. We nailed it. When I walked off the stage I was accompanied by a euphoria. I felt like I was walking on air.

About two weeks later, after playing a mediocre show in Middle America, we all crammed into two small motel rooms in a La Quinta Inn in Helotes, Texas. Half the band slept on the floor.

As we drifted off to sleep, Dillon mused, "Y'all, we played *Saturday Night Live* last week."

We all broke out in roaring laughter, well aware of the irony of the situation.

Blurred visions played on the back of my heavy eyelids as I lay on that hard motel mattress. A decade had passed and faded away, but as I drifted off to sleep, ruminating on that moment in time when there was an electrical current pulsating through East Nashville, I wished I could have preserved that feeling in an empty bourbon bottle forever.

Although some of the memories are hazy, I can still recall knowing that time was special and that it meant something to be there. No matter how high or how low or how drunk you got, it was gonna be okay, because there was always someone there to help you lift your head out of the toilet so you could aim and shoot again, or loan you twenty bucks for one more round. Or, at the very least, commiserate. It was an era that belonged to us and us alone. It can't be embodied by just one band or one song or one bar or one specific moment. It both took forever and was gone in a flash, and I didn't ever want it to end.

Epilogue

The band and I hit the road harder than we ever had. I worked the album, doing all the shows, meeting all the press, kissing ass at all the radio stations. I always made it a point to go out to the merch table after our set, grateful to sign autographs, shake hands, or hug any fan who had paid to see me perform.

Navigating my new and unpredictable schedule was wild. My mother had retired, and she often graciously helped out with Judah so Jeremy could join me on the road. Other times, Jeremy stayed behind and took care of our growing boy, who desperately needed to have at least one parent around. From the outside, everything looked perfect. Jeremy had been an instrumental part of my success, and I thanked him often and publicly for always believing in me and for selling our car to fund the record that changed my life.

But I missed holidays, Mother's Day, Jeremy's and Judah's birthdays, anniversaries, and even funerals. My absence wore a hole in our already unstable marriage. And although Jeremy and I had always had fights and disagreements, it was reaching the boiling point. One afternoon, he called right before I was to go onstage in Northern California to tell me he was divorcing me. I was devastated but not totally surprised. Six months prior to that, he'd asked me casually over dinner one night if I had ever been unfaithful. Without hesitation I told him I had. It might sound strange, but I had been waiting for him to ask me for so long, it actually came as a relief. My affair was long over, but I'd carried so much regret, remorse, and guilt; the burden had grown too heavy to bear.

Jeremy was angry, of course, and I couldn't blame him. The truth backed him into a corner. While I was out touring all over the world, he was back home, searching in a bar for comfort and revenge. He ran around on me as best he could, but by that point people in town were aware of who we both were, so it wasn't as easy to take an eye for an eye.

During the cold winter of 2016, we temporarily separated. For a time, Jeremy lived out of a motel up on Gallatin Road. He thought it would be good for him to sort out his feelings away from me. He brought his guitar and hoped to write songs, but he was so downhearted, he couldn't focus. He could only muster the energy to chain-smoke cigarettes and watch reruns of *Cops* on the crummy hotel television. Most nights, he'd turn to Jack Daniel's and drunk-dial me, and I always answered. After about a week, he showed up on our doorstep with a look of acceptance in his eyes. Forgiveness isn't easy, but somehow he found it.

I started writing this book a few years later, at the end of 2018, when Jeremy and I found out we were pregnant with our daughter, Ramona. The news took us both by surprise, and I worried I wouldn't be physically or mentally strong enough to go through another pregnancy, especially with the demands of touring.

When I was only a couple of months along, I had plans to travel for my first-ever tour of Australia and New Zealand. I spent the majority of the twenty-three-hour plane ride throwing up in the tiny bathroom and crying under a blanket in my window seat. My hormones and emotions were all over the place, but I tried hard to keep it together; I hadn't even told the band yet that I was expecting.

But everything happens the way it's supposed to. The pregnancy was a breeze, and Ramona's presence in our lives has been a blessing beyond measure. Judah got the sibling he always wanted, and the two of them are incredibly close despite their nearly ten-year age gap. Being able to care for a newborn again without the immense grief I'd experienced after Ezra's death was a lovely experience. I felt so much more prepared to give life.

During the beginning of my pregnancy with Ramona, I felt so creative, so invincible. I was playing great shows to massive crowds, and both my music and my family were flourishing. But as the term carried on, I had fears that the pregnancy would damage my career. At times, I think it did. My momentum came to a sudden halt, and I worried my shelf life was up. When I was nominated for a Grammy for Best New Artist in 2019, I was the only nominee who didn't get to perform or speak on stage. Everyone else was invited to sing or introduce an award or another nominee. I also was turned away when I tried to go into the backstage area to use the restroom.

"Please let me in, I have to pee. My name is Margo Price and I'm up for Best New Artist," I said to a man in a security uniform with a bluetooth headset. He looked me up and down, pausing for a moment on my round, pregnant stomach, then looked at his clipboard list to search for my name. I could see waiters walking around with tiny hors d'oeuvres on fancy silver trays, and all I'd eaten that day was a single hard-boiled egg.

"I'm sorry, Ms. Price, but you'll have to go up to the third floor of the arena to use the other bathroom."

I felt foolish and awkward, walking up three flights of stairs with the train of my dress balled up in my hands, very pregnant, and wearing high heels. People gawked; I could feel their eyes on me.

In spring 2020, as the world shut down in response to the pandemic, Jeremy contracted COVID-19. His preexisting conditions, cerebral palsy and hypoglycemia, made him more vulnerable than most people. After a couple of weeks of increasingly losing lung capacity, he struggled to breathe. At night he dreamed there was a demon sitting on his chest, watching him sleep. Around the same time, Ramona had endless ear infections and unexplained fevers. I took her to the pediatrician, looking for answers, but the doctors had none. I worried that my entire family would die in their sleep. In the middle of the night, I checked to make sure they were still breathing. The house was trashed and the kids watched too much TV, but I didn't care. I just prayed that the love of my life and our precious new baby wouldn't be taken from me. Finally, Jeremy and Ramona both made a full recovery, and for that, I am so grateful every single day.

Near the end of 2020, I quit breastfeeding Ramona. The pandemic dragged on, and so did my drinking. I missed playing music something fierce, and without touring and festivals, I felt purposeless. I didn't wake up and start boozing, nor did I drink every day. No one around me ever said, "You're at rock bottom, you should take a break." Of course, by that time I had taken many long, self-mandated breaks, and I enjoyed them. But they also gave me the illusion of control.

I was sleep deprived, stagnant, and still dealing with postpartum depression. I knew my drinking was only fueling my unhappiness, but I didn't stop. After I put the kids to bed, I would sit down outside, planning to have "one or two," but it usually ended up being a lot more. I was the steward of my endless emotions, and I was drowning them once again.

I lost weight. I gained weight. I yo-yoed up and down, relapsing into the same unhealthy eating patterns that I thought I had shaken years earlier. The truth was, they were never far away; they waited to resurface at the first sign of weakness. I felt like the whole world had watched me go through childbirth and judged me for the weight I had gained. I starved myself and meticulously tracked my calories, trying to account for the beverages I would undoubtedly consume later in the evening.

One morning I woke up with my head in the shower and my feet by the toilet. The children were with their grandparents for the weekend, and I had used that as an excuse to binge. My knuckles were bleeding, my face was red, my body was bloated, and my mind was on edge. It scared me. All the rules I had set years before when I reentered the drinking world had gone out the window by the end of that first year of the pandemic. I was drinking away my crippling fears about the end of the world and how the children I'd brought into it would navigate it. Meanwhile, I couldn't navigate it myself.

What happened next truly feels like an unexplainable supernatural phenomenon: an answer to a question that I had asked myself a million times finally came to me. It was the next evening and I was sitting by the fire in my backyard. The children were still gone, and I was stuck in that familiar loop of pouring another drink to combat the deadly hangover. When a dear and trusted friend arrived and offered me some psilocybin mushrooms, I took them, once again looking for my way out of what had become a dark and twisted path. Sure enough, they answered back. I *could* quit if I wanted. All I had to do was *not* drink.

On the night of January 8, 2021, I started listening to myself, to what I had known all along. I needed to give up drinking for good. I looked at the aluminum can in my hand and poured it out. I didn't reach for another drink for the rest of that evening, and no one even noticed. I put out my cigarette too. I don't blame alcohol for all my bad decisions, just some of them. All the years I spent pouring poison down my throat and throwing my money away, only to end up with heartaches and hangovers, were finally over.

That's not to say I suddenly have all the answers, and I don't pretend to. I still struggle immensely with issues of body dysmorphia and negative self-image. I'm no longer angry at myself for these thoughts; I'm angry at a culture that bullies us into feeling that we are not good enough. We are marketed countless products, diets, creams, serums, Botox, even surgeries, because God forbid we look or age like our natural selves. I work in an industry that objectifies women, that judges us and holds us to impossible beauty standards. I have dealt with critics who have picked apart my appearance and tried to tear me down because I threaten their patriarchy and intimidate them with my opinions and politics.

The longer I'm inside the music business, the more cracks I see within the system. At times, I feel helpless to change any of it, but still, I can't help but try. I'm proud to stand for equality, diversity, and fair pay. Musicians and writers are fighting for the right to be paid for our intellectual property. I've been called radical and controversial for repeatedly speaking my mind, but I'm not going to stop.

This life has tested me. Call it God, call it whatever, but I believe in a greater power, and a common thread that connects us all. I believe our souls live on in some other dimension after we leave this earth. Judah, Jeremy, and I have a tradition of releasing a Chinese paper lantern into the air each year in July, on the anniversary of Ezra Alan Ivey's departure. We hold hands and say a few words for our lost twin as we watch the tiny flame dance upward until it escapes into the hot summer sky. I pray he hears my song and knows how grateful I am for what he gave me with the terrible absence of his life: a long, hard glimpse at who I am and who I one day hope to be. May God give me the strength to one day carry his soul to the Yavapai Point of the Grand Canyon and spread his ashes in the Verde River.

I'm standing barefoot in the kitchen of our Tennessee country home, washing dishes in our copper sink. It gets dark early out here in the holler, and the winter months always make me feel restless. As I watch the sun sink through our kitchen window, I see my children playing together in the thick woods surrounding our home, their shadows dancing like Peter Pan and Tinker Bell. Judah is now eleven and Mona is two and a half. Since we fled East Nashville and the city life, we spend most of our time outdoors, scouring the creek beds for crawdads and hunting the hills for treasures. These acres of woods are more precious to me than anything else I've ever bought. I cut a switchback up the mountain on our property, and I hike up there often when I need a place to escape. I let my mind wander like a wild horse, galloping toward the future while keeping one eye on the past.

Acknowledgments

There are so many folks I have to thank for bringing this story to life, including my brilliant editor, Naomi Huffman; Jessica Hopper; Casey Kittrell; Charles L. Hughes; Abby Webber; Gianna LaMorte; Lynne Ferguson; and the entire staff at the University of Texas Press. I could not have shaped this into what it became without their guidance and encouragement. Thank you to Third Man Records for being my dark horse. To Jack White and Ben Swank, I will always be grateful for your support.

To my bandmates of all eras, including Dillon Napier, Kevin Black, Jamie Davis, Micah Hulscher, Alex Munoz, Luke Schneider, Jared Braucht, Matt Gardner, Jason White, Amaia Aguirre, Kristen Weber, Houston Mathews, Aaron Shaifer Haiss, Taylor Powell, Ashley Wilcoxson, Larissa Maestro, Eleonore Denig, Paul Thacker, Diego Vasquez, and Kirk Donovan, thank you for rolling down the road with me. Here's to making more music and touring 'til the wheels come off.

Thanks, Amy Schmalz and Ian Montone, for managing what my parents and many bosses claimed to be "unmanageable." Thank you,

Matt Pollack, for walking with me through the rain in NYC to get that vitamin B12 shot. Thank you, Jonathan Levine, for your indomitable spirit, your inspirational speeches, and your never-ending drive. To Kent Marcus, thanks for having my back and believing in me before anyone else did. Thanks also to Matt Hanks at Shorefire who has been as instrumental as the hand of God in getting me press and recognition I never thought possible. I'm grateful for your impeccable taste in music.

To extended family, friends, and heroes—Patti Smith, Willie and Annie Nelson, Lucinda Williams, Loretta Lynn, Jessi Colter, John and Fiona Prine, Emmylou Harris, Kris Kristofferson, Joan Baez, Joni Mitchell, Bob Dylan, Bobby Fischer, Matt Ross-Spang, Andrija Tokic, Brittany Howard, Alynda Lee Segura Riley, the Deslondes, Riley Downing, Sam Doores, John James Tourville, Dan Cutler, John Baldwin, Lorne Michaels, Stephen Colbert, Sturgill Simpson, Chris and Morgan Stapleton, Kate Cunningham, Steven Knudson, Caitlin Rose, Mark Fredson, Danielle Holbert, Chris Phelps, Nadine Braucht, Adia Victoria, Katie Studley, David Ferguson, Lester Snell, the McCrary Sisters, Mike Badger, Tom Whalley, Ryan Walley, Maddie Case, Jazz Atkin, Andrea Ambrosia, Kylie Almedio, Mallory Mason, Marissa Moss, Dave Paulson, and Joe Hudak—thank you all for inspiring me and lifting me up.

To my family, blood and otherwise; to my grandparents, Paul Price, Mary Price, Duane Maule, and Patricia Louise Maule; and to my parents, Duane and Candace Price, thank you for raising me with compassion, empathy, and unconditional love. Thank you to my sisters, my best friends: Britni and Kylie, whom I still adore. To Tom and Sandy Ivey, thank you for adopting and raising such a good man in Jeremy.

To my children, Judah, Ezra, and Ramona, who made my heart explode into a million tiny pieces and then glued it back together: you've enriched my life in ways I never knew were possible. I wish you could learn from my mistakes, but you will have to make your own.

And last but certainly not least, thank you to Jeremy Blain Ivey, my twin, my partner, my best friend, my soulmate, my hero, my orphan, my rock, and my one true love: maybe we'll make it.